AF557834

INDIA TODAY
INDIA TOMORROW

Also by the author

Lutyens' Maverick:
Ground Realities, Hard Choices and Tomorrow's India

INDIA TODAY INDIA TOMORROW

WHERE WE ARE HEADED AND
HOW WE WILL GET THERE

Edited by

Baijayant 'Jay' Panda

RUPA

Published by
Rupa Publications India Pvt. Ltd 2021
7/16, Ansari Road, Daryaganj
New Delhi 110002

Sales Centres:
Allahabad Bengaluru Chennai
Hyderabad Jaipur Kathmandu
Kolkata Mumbai

ISBN: 978-93-90356-65-2

First impression 2021

10 9 8 7 6 5 4 3 2 1

Printed at Parksons Graphics Pvt. Ltd, Mumbai

CONTENTS

PREFACE

With the 75th anniversary of India's Independence less than two years away, many are beginning to take stock of the nation's progress—those already achieved as well as those in the offing. For instance, the government has been making plans to celebrate this upcoming milestone, and also to highlight the goals being set for the coming years. These include the country's gross domestic product (GDP) gearing up to cross the landmark US$5-trillion target not long after the 75th anniversary, as well as social goals, such as housing for all.

This discussion will undoubtedly get more animated in the coming months. Even as that is worth engaging in, it is also vitally important to look beyond this short horizon, examine the landscape, analyse the opportunities and pitfalls, and yes, set goals. Thus, this book. What might India look like a generation from now? What should it look like when we complete 100 years of Independence? The chapters in this book are by active politicians, cutting across parties, whose actions will impact what the India of the next generation will look like.

At the outset, I must clarify that the opinions expressed in these chapters do not necessarily reflect my own, let alone my party's. In fact, as my own body of work will clearly demonstrate, while I may agree with some of these chapters, I quite clearly do not agree with some others. However, that is as it ought to be. No collection of essays from such a number of people can or should be expected to conform to a particular worldview, least of all among public figures representing parties with different stands, and that too in the largest, loudest and most boisterous democracy in human history.

The coronavirus pandemic happened when the writing for this book was already underway. The effects of the lockdown as well as the impact of the pandemic on both public health and the economy have been enormous, not just for India but throughout the world. Spread over the next quarter century, the lingering effects of these may be somewhat less pronounced than may be perceived today. Nevertheless, this year has been unprecedented in living memory, and at least some of the changes it has brought about in the way we live and work will likely continue to prevail. The contributors did take all this into consideration, with many rewriting their initial submissions.

The book covers a range of topics—from the economy, education, defence and energy, culture, sports, health and the nation's demographics, to terrorism, urbanization, water management, and much more. Not all aspects of the future envisioned by these politicians will come about, but some will, and it will matter whether and how soon those ideas acquire broad support. Futurology is a risky affair, as any review of past predictions can demonstrate. In this case, too, while no one can foresee the future, an essential element is that all these contributors are not just theoreticians but practitioners, engaging not just in policy prescriptions, but ground realities of trying to implement them. This is where ideology and planning meet the challenge of getting buy-in from millions of stakeholders, and where practical realities and politics contribute just as much.

If this is truly the Asian century, as many pundits have been hailing for decades, then surely it is just as much an Indian century.

The other Asian and global giant, China, saw epoch-making growth in its economy, military capability and clout, spread over the past four decades. Yet, many see its trajectory plateauing as its income and debt levels, labour costs and investment efficiency struggle to maintain that earlier breakneck speed.

By contrast, India is just knocking at the door of middle-income-country status. It has a lot more headroom to grow before it faces those challenges on the same scale. Of course, we have our own challenges, not least of which is our track record of anaemic policymaking, especially implementation. But India is now witnessing a historic inflection point. Under Prime Minister Narendra Modi, there has been a determined push to implement long-stalled policy changes. Whether a national goods and services tax (GST), a transition from a cash-based to formal economy, a massive thrust on infrastructure, or the more recent deep-seated reforms in labour laws and the agriculture sector.

Beyond crucial economic policymaking, India has shown that it can muster political will to bring about social and political rights legislation, which have long been given lip service but had acquired the aura of being unachievable. The Triple Talaq law, for instance, is something that even many Islamic nations had reformed long ago; it had no place in a modern democracy and was a crying need for exploited Muslim women. Similarly, the abrogation of Article 370, the only one in the constitution which had the word 'temporary' attached to it, and had long permitted discrimination against Dalits, women and the LGBTQ[1] community in Jammu and Kashmir (J&K).

India is seeing not just a fillip in policymaking, but also its implementation. The Jan Dhan-Aadhaar-Mobile (JAM) trilogy demonstrated its potential during the lockdown earlier this year, with transparent and swift cash transfer to millions of needy

[1]An acronym for lesbian, gay, bisexual, transgender and queer or questioning.

citizens. Similarly, the stepping up of border infrastructure construction, including tunnels, roads and bridges, and the ability to push back and impose costs on aggressors at the Line of Actual Control (LAC), has shown the world a New India.

This is an India that *can*. It can build and implement, it can fight and fend off attackers, and it can pass and implement policies that set the stage for a long-awaited renaissance, including achieving the status of the world's third-largest economy. As the catalyst of this transformation, Prime Minister Modi has emerged as one of the most respected global leaders, with immense clout. He is welcomed worldwide with not just affection, but something more akin to rockstar-like adulation. His engagement with the large, influential Indian diaspora amplifies that presence. And his helping hands, such as with medicines and aid to many countries during the pandemic, has added immensely to India's goodwill.

From this time of change and transformation will emerge the contours of India's destiny over the next quarter century. This book is about the road ahead to modern India at 100, and the look and feel of it.

PART I

THE MANY FACETS OF INDIA

1

REVITALIZATION OF THE AGRICULTURE SECTOR

SUJAY VIKHE PATIL

In his book *India 2020: A Vision for the New Millennium* (2014), former president of India, Dr A.P.J. Abdul Kalam, mentioned that enhancing agriculture productivity is the key to the growth of agro-food processing and related industrial, manufacturing and service sectors. The agriculture sector has the potential to be the single largest contributor towards achieving the dream of a US$5-trillion economy. While this sector employs close to 47 per cent of the country's workforce, it contributes only 15 per cent to India's gross domestic product (GDP). As per Census 2011, 54.6 per cent of India's population was engaged in agriculture and allied activities and the estimates of national income released by the Central Statistics Office (CSO), Ministry of Statistics and Programme Implementation state that agriculture and allied sectors contributed approximately 16 per cent of India's gross value added (GVA) at current prices during 2018–19.

The issue of farmer welfare and agrarian crisis is the focal point of the government under the able leadership of Prime Minister

Shri Narendra Modi. We saw the importance and sensitivity of the agriculture sector, for which a discussion under Rule 193 was initiated during the Winter Session of parliament and recently the Union Budget also had several announcements regarding the agriculture sector and rural economy. The Economic Survey 2020 also spoke about the importance of sustainable agricultural practices through a combination of resource-efficient methods, including dynamic cropping patterns, the judicious use of chemical fertilizers and efficient irrigation systems.

Under the current dispensation, there have been several notable achievements in the agriculture sector, for example, the production of horticulture crops is estimated at a record 313.9 million metric tonne (MMT) in 2018–19 as per third advance estimates. The total agricultural exports from India have grown at a compound annual growth rate (CAGR) of 16.45 per cent and in financial year (FY) 2019, was US$38.54 billion. The introduction of the electronic National Agriculture Market (eNAM), with the aim of creating a unified national market for agricultural commodities, has resulted in the registration of 9.87 million farmers and 1,09,725 traders along with 585 mandis in 2018–19. The agriculture storage capacity in India has also witnessed an increase at 4 per cent CAGR and is estimated to be 131.8 MMT.

As per estimates from NITI Aayog, marketable surplus (per cent of her total production that she offers for sale in the market) has been rising every year since 2001 by more than 3 per cent. The data provided by the Agricultural and Processed Food Products Export Development Authority (APEDA) states that the agricultural trade surplus has been rising every year at an average of 11.6 per cent. The Indian farmer has aided economic development by producing and exporting large quantities of agri-products which has helped the country achieve food security at the national level. The government's policies have always been pro-agriculture and a number of programmes have been initiated in the last five years with a single and concerted aim of increasing the area under irrigation, improving soil health, promoting agro-processing and providing insurance for crop loss.

Challenges Faced by the Agriculture Sector

The farmer of our country has established his credentials not only as an 'annadaata' but also an entrepreneur through his consistent efforts, which have led to an increase in the production of foodgrains. The problems plaguing the agriculture sector range from loss due to floods and unseasonal rainfall to growing incidents of loss due to stray animals, pests and rodents. A growing area of concern which has been witnessed in my parliamentary constituency and across the state of Maharashtra in the month of October 2019 was crop loss due to unseasonal rains, which point towards global warming and climate change. The farming practices in our country have witnessed a change in the climatic pattern, which has been attributed as the biggest reason for crop failure due to the high degree of dependency of Indian farmers on rainfall for better productivity. The effects of climate change can be felt daily, especially by farmers, but very few solutions have been discussed to address this catastrophic threat.

The challenges faced by the farmers of our country are manifold, beginning from lack of research and development (R&D) in agriculture to lack of necessary infrastructure to augment higher production. Analysis of the impact of climate change under the National Innovations in Climate Resilient Agriculture (NICRA) project has found that climate change is expected to affect yields, particularly in crops such as rice, wheat and maize. The need of the hour is that the government has to take new and flexible adaptive measures to cope with the changing agricultural patterns, which would include using alternative crops to changing irrigation techniques. The lack of availability of a database is a drawback in India's agricultural research landscape. There is an imminent need to invest more in preparing a database on the impact of climate change while segregating areas into the land type and water availability in the region.

Another problem faced by farmers in India is the availability of proper research inputs and advanced technology that is suited for the type of land and the crops they sow. The establishment of the Krishi Vigyan Kendra was a welcome move, but it needs to be spread across the country at block levels to ensure a higher level of interaction with farmers, who can draw benefits out of it. In addition to these issues, the Economic Survey 2019–20 also points to an increase in soil fatigue due to the overuse of chemical fertilizers, which has been substantiated by the fertilizer response ratio, which showed a declining trend. Concerns have also been raised over awareness amongst the farmers regarding the right product, dosage, time and method of application of fertilizers. A major cause of the low income of Indian farmers is the small size and scattered nature of agricultural landholdings, which result in low productivity per acre. This a major challenge faced by our famers while selling their crops.

Union Budget 2020 and Agriculture Reforms

The Union Budget 2020 presented by Finance Minister Nirmala Sitharaman can be easily described as a revolutionary budget, focusing on revitalizing the agriculture sector through policy initiatives. The Budget was premised on the themes of aspirational India, economic development for all and building a caring society, and the common factor integrating these three themes was agriculture. The announcement made during the Budget will usher in a new era for farmers and is a right step towards achieving the goal of doubling farmers' income by 2022.

The announcement of the 16-point action plan for farmers will boost the agriculture sector by increasing the demand for crops and helping the rural economy. The Krishi Udan scheme is an innovative concept that will help increase agricultural exports both at international and domestic levels, as farmers will be able to transport their produce and earn remunerative prices for the same. Agricultural credit has been a pressing issue and the government has increased the agricultural credit target from ₹12 lakh crore to ₹15 lakh crore for fiscal 2020–21. This increase in agricultural credit will assist farmers to avail loans at subsidized rates and use it for carrying out agricultural activities. The priority of the government towards boosting the agriculture system and promoting the welfare of farmers is vindicated by the allocation of ₹2.83 lakh crore for agriculture and irrigation for FY21 along with the allotment of ₹1.23 lakh crore for rural development and the panchayati raj.

The allied sector is going to play a crucial role in achieving the goal of doubling farmers' income by 2022. The government has made a few remarkable announcements in this direction, including raising fish production to 200 lakh tonnes by 2022–23 and doubling the milk-processing capacity to 108 MT by 2025. The lack of irrigation facilities and recurrence of drought have been major challenges for our farmers, who are pushed into poverty due to crop failure and lack of remuneration for their produce. The government's announcement to improve the situation in 100 water-stressed districts will help address the issue of unavailability of water for irrigation in drought-prone areas. Horticulture crops have immense potential to generate revenue through exports, which has been promoted through the One District One Product plan.

The announcement to expand the Pradhan Mantri Kisan Urja Suraksha evam Utthaan Mahabhiyan (PM-KUSUM) scheme will provide 20 lakh farmers with standalone solar pumps along with helping an additional 15 lakh farmers to solarize their grid-connected pump sets, which will enable them to set up solar power-generation capacity on their fallow/barren lands and sell it to the grid. This step will not only generate additional income for farmers, but also promote the use of renewable energy (RE) in the agriculture sector, which will be a huge support in implementing our commitments under the Paris Convention. The introduction of the village storage scheme to be run by self-help groups (SHGs) will not only offer farmers a good holding capacity and reduce their logistics cost, but will be a good step towards promoting entrepreneurship amongst the rural women.

Measures for Revitalizing the Agri Sector

Modernization of Agriculture

There is going to be a significant shift in agricultural practices in the next decade, as the focus will shift towards the use of machines and drones. The increased use of capital-intensive techniques in agriculture will require that Indian agriculture keep pace with the changing scenario. The agriculture sector will require modern technologies to be more efficient, competitive, sustainable, resilient and environment-friendly. Modernization of agriculture can only be achieved by increasing the investment in agricultural research, and working towards developing linkages between research and industry and service centres for disseminating modern technologies.

Providing Solutions to the Lack of Storage Facilities

A 2019 report by the Federation of Indian Chambers of Commerce & Industry (FICCI) has stated that for the first time, the Government of India is incurring a buffer stock loss of 57,000 tonnes due to the lack of warehouse facilities. As most of the crops are of perishable nature, the primary concern of the farmer is their produce being wasted due to the lack of storage facilities. To revitalize the farming sector, the government needs to upgrade and establish better cold storage facilities in rural areas, particularly those which can be modelled on the lines of Brazil and Israel, which have low-cost, modern technology models to store agricultural commodities. Additionally, the food-processing sector should also be developed right at the agriculture cultivation centres to enhance the rural economy and boost consumer demand.

Export Ban and the Amendment of the Essential Commodities Act

My parliamentary constituency of Ahmednagar is one of the major onion-producing districts in Maharashtra. The farmers of the region were adversely affected firstly due to the unseasonal rainfall, which led to crop loss and subsequent increase in the price of onions, and later due to the ban on export of onions to cool down domestic prices.

An ad hoc approach to export bans had serious repercussions and the government should remove onions from the purview of the Essential Commodities Act and undertake agricultural marketing reforms to facilitate direct purchase from the farmer in a transparent way. Inclusion of onions in the essential commodities list would mean that the storage of onions by farmers, will be considered hoarding and hence, illegal.

Reforms in Minimum Support Price Method

The concept of minimum support price (MSP) was meant to provide remunerative prices to farmers and protect them from a drop in prices due to various factors. However, it led to excessive focus on the cultivation of wheat, rice and sugarcane in the procurement states, which fetch higher prices, and the neglect of other crops such as pulses, oilseeds and coarse grains, thereby distorting the cropping patterns.

Reforms are required towards how MSP is determined, and this has also been proposed by the NITI Aayog in its 'Strategy for New India@75' document in December 2018, whereby it suggested replacing the Commission for Agricultural Costs and Prices (CACP) by an agriculture tribunal in line with the provisions of Article 323B of the Constitution. The report also advocates the introduction of the concept of maximum retail price (MRP), which can be the starting point for auctions at mandis and will help in fetching better price for farmers.

The Pradhan Mantri Fasal Bima Yojana

The Pradhan Mantri Fasal Bima Yojana (PMFBY) was introduced in 2016 to protect farmers from crop loss for a small premium amount for rabi, kharif and horticulture crops. The intent of the scheme was the welfare of farmers and it has managed to benefit a large section of them. However, there are a few core issues that are hampering the implementation of the PMFBY, which include the absence of necessary infrastructure in banks to pay the premium.

Rural areas have poor internet connectivity and, at times, farmers have been forced to pay a premium online; additionally, there is a lack of awareness amongst the farmers. There have been instances where agents mandated under this scheme by insurance companies do not cooperate with the farmers. In case of horticulture products, it has been my personal experience that there is no agent to contact. Therefore, the government should take strict action against such defaulting companies to ensure that farmers do not go through the problems while claiming compensation for crop loss, and that the actual vision behind this scheme, which is to benefit the farmer, is achieved.

Water Conservation Techniques

With the advent of technology and the visible effects of climate change, there is a need to introduce new metric in farming, which should be based not only on yield per acre, but also on productivity per litre of water. The government should focus on moving from flood irrigation to micro-irrigation methods such as drip or hose reel. These methods can save up to 60 per cent of water and also help in preventing pest incidence.

Credit for Farmers

The Union Budget has spelled out an ambitious target for agricultural credit, but there is still a need to promote major initiatives in the areas of public–private partnership (PPP) in new seed research for the development of seed technology and industry. Farm credit is a major concern because farmers fail to secure the required funds in time due to hesitation from banks on account of the high cost of reaching farmers, high rate of non-performing assets (NPAs) and threat of loan write-offs. The government has been making efforts to enhance the flow of credit to the agriculture sector and they are bearing fruits. However, the demands for agricultural credit are still unmet from the formal sources and, therefore, farmers resort to informal sources to meet their borrowing needs.

Promote Farming as a Profession

The most important step towards bringing about reform in the agriculture sector is to promote farming as a profitable activity. The average age of a farmer in India today is 40 years. This reflects the biggest challenge for this sector in India and also for all of us who are surviving on the food that they produce—Indian farmers are ageing. In 2016, the average age of an Indian farmer was 50.1 years. In 2011, 70 per cent of Indian youths were living in rural areas, where agriculture was still the main source of livelihood. According to the 2011 Census, every day 2,000 farmers give up farming as an occupation. The income of a farmer is around one-fifth of a non-farmer. Like in India, farmers are quitting farming worldwide. In Japan, for instance, in the next six to eight years, 40 per cent of the farmers are expected to quit farming. In fact, the Japanese government has embarked on a massive plan to encourage people below 45 years to become farmers.

The PM-KISAN Scheme

The ambit and purpose of social sector schemes such as PM-KISAN and the Mahatma Gandhi National Rural Employment Guarantee Act (MGNREGA), which impact the rural economy, should be expanded. The allocation for MGNREGA needs to be increased to provide 100 days of work and the government should also formulate an employment guarantee scheme for the urban poor. The government should increase the amount given under the PM-KISAN scheme from the current ₹6,000 per annum (in three equal instalments) and also include landless agriculture labours, who constitute 55 per cent of the agricultural workforce, under the ambit of the scheme.

Conclusion

The revitalization and success of agricultural reforms require a strong political will, which has been exhibited by the Bharatiya Janata Party (BJP) government under the leadership of Prime Minister Modi. The huge mandate given to our government is a vindication of how the success of schemes relating to the agriculture sector has benefited farmers. The government has also taken various steps such as the Pradhan Mantri Kisan Samman Nidhi Yojana, which guarantees minimum income for farmers; the Kisan Credit Card Loan scheme, which provides short-term, interest-free loans of up to ₹1 lakh for a period of one to five years on the condition of prompt repayment of the principal amount; and the Pradhan Mantri Kisan SAMPADA (Scheme for Agro-Marine Processing and Development of Agro-Processing Clusters) Yojana, which aims to expand warehousing facilities along the national highways to ensure logistical linkages. Other initiatives include dairy processing, an infrastructure development fund, a micro-irrigation fund, a blue revolution scheme, market reforms such as eNAM, the Rashtriya Gokul Mission, the PM-Kisan Yojana, the PM-Kisan Maandhan Yojana pension scheme, a Farmer Producer Organization promotion, the Fisheries and Aquaculture Infrastructure Development Fund, etc. with the vision of doubling farmers' income by 2022 and ensuring that agriculture has a crucial role to play in making India a US$5 trillion-dollar economy by 2025.

The agriculture sector can be further promoted by harnessing our resources through the cultivation of high-value horticulture products such as almonds, pistachios, exotic fruits, oilseed products, medicinal plants, etc., which can benefit farmers while enhancing their income and also provide solutions to the import of such products. With the renewed focus of the government on the cultivation of agricultural produce, the contribution of the agriculture and allied sector to the GVA is bound to increase in the times to come.

With the welfare of our farmers as our topmost priority, the government should prepare a focused and time-bound programme to support and encourage farmers to take up agriculture as a profession, which in turn, will help them contribute to the nation's development through food production. The government should also focus on drafting a new agricultural policy, keeping in mind the medium- and long-term road map for various reforms in the agriculture sector.

◆

Dr Sujay Vikhe Patil, a member of the Bharatiya Janata Party (BJP), represents Maharashtra's Ahmednagar constituency in the 17th Lok Sabha. He is a qualified neurosurgeon and is also the chairman of Pravara Sugar Factory, Pravaranagar, in the Ahmednagar district of Maharashtra.

2

TRANSFORMING RURAL INDIA

SACHIN PILOT

As per the last Census data and subsequent figures released by the World Bank in 2018, India is rapidly urbanizing but yet remains a predominantly rural country, with two-thirds of its population living in villages. Rural India must, therefore, lead India's transition to a high-performing economy. There, too, must begin realization of the Sustainable Development Goals (SDGs). Against this obvious truth, the reality is troubling. There are wide differences between urban and rural access to education, healthcare, clean drinking water, sanitation, safe public areas, communication and logistics infrastructure including roads, warehouses, internet and entrepreneurship. Inadequate response to these challenges is hastening rural to urban migration, stretching municipal systems, displacing people from their communities and worsening urban sprawl and its attendant challenges of basic amenities as well as governance.

The situation demands long-range thinking and action backed by adequate nonpartisan political commitment, financial knowledge and management resources. There must be a long-term policy aimed at making rural areas rewarding to live and work in.

Presently, rural policies have a strong central or regional bias. There is too little contribution to policymaking from gram panchayats or ownership of implementation at that level. We must begin by greater empowerment of gram panchayats to fulfill the constitutional mandate of responsible and representative government at national, state and village levels. Their charter must include meaningful participation in development works that happen in panchayats, power to raise revenues and authority to enforce decisions. Rural economy is inextricably tied to agriculture, which is not performing well. The Green Revolution, aimed at eliminating famine and making India self-sufficient in the production of cereals, has fulfilled its mandate, and is now in need of strategic reorientation.

Our agriculture sector suffers from structural constraints such as age-old methods of farming, small size of farms, low value addition, unscientific use of fertilizers and other inputs, poor logistics, rudimentary risk mitigation and unregulated intermediation. These have combined to highly leverage even small farmers, placing them in debt to moneylenders as well as banks. At the same time, macroeconomic mismanagement of the kind we have been witnessing lately reduces the competitiveness of our products, creates wide fluctuations in the selling price of agricultural goods and worsens socio-economic stresses, leading to farmer protests and suicides. Empowerment of rural governance would be an essential beginning.

All other factors being equal, people living in villages do not migrate to cities simply in pursuit of higher incomes, sacrificing their family and social networks. If healthcare, education and other public services, as are available in urban areas, can be provided in and around villages, it will increase opportunities available to the rural population so that they too can realize their economic and intellectual potential without pains and risks of migration, and the rural landscape can be transformed within a generation. Accordingly, development budgets of the ministries concerned must flow preferentially and in bulk to rural areas.

As I have stressed earlier, there must be greater local control over implementation. Today, thanks to the digital revolution that has delivered broadband to most rural areas, it is possible to better monitor the utilization of funds, respond faster to local rural needs and leverage entrepreneurship. Greater investments and commitment in this space are necessary. Over the last 25 years, self-help groups (SHGs) have stabilized in several states. Present schemes of providing revolving funds and interest subventions to SHGs do not go far enough. They need hand-holding to help them access urban and international markets. Rural incubators need to be well funded. Capital investments in SHG- and cooperative-run projects need to be heavily subsidized. Technology should be used to enable farmers to sell their produce at the most competitive rates. Inadequate government support resulted in decrease in agricultural exports from ₹2,62,778 crore in 2013–14 to ₹2,13,555 crore in 2015–16.[1] Policy and infrastructure for promoting niche value-added agricultural products must proceed hand in hand with efforts to improve the quality of identified agricultural products.

Since agricultural revival is crucial to rural prosperity, this must be approached holistically. Massive public works to improve soil and water conservation must be undertaken without compromising on profitability of farmers, especially the ones with small landholdings. Rural agricultural service providers can play an important role in this. By providing knowledge and technical support and making available supply of agricultural equipment to small farmers, they

[1]'Overview of Trade Division for Website,' D/o Agriculture, Coop & FW, Trade Division, http://agricoop.nic.in/sites/default/files/overviewTrade7082015.pdf, last accessed on 1 September 2020.

can bridge the gaps in productivity, quality and market access. This may require tariff concessions. Such rural entrepreneurs may bring agriculture benefits of satellite imagery, artificial intelligence (AI), agricultural robotics, automated processing, sterile packaging, and efficiencies in nutrient and pesticide delivery (for example, through the use of drones). Much thought has recently been paid to adequately capitalize scheduled commercial banks. Regional rural banks, cooperative banks and other rural credit institutions need a distinct focus to improve their governance, product offerings and capital adequacy. It is equally important to recapitalize our agriculture universities with strong extension programmes. They should be established on par with the All India Institute of Medical Sciences (AIIMS) and Indian Institutes of Technology (IITs) in all states, with more than one in larger states. They should be placed under professional governance and scientific leadership. Specialization should be encouraged, permitting niche expertise to become available to farmers across the country.

Dependence on international markets, climate change, breakthroughs in genetic manipulation, resurgence of old threats—massive locust attacks in Africa and parts of South Asia this year come to mind—runaway crop diseases and other geopolitical and natural factors must induce us to devote energy and resources to prepare for adverse scenarios and make plans on how to deal with them. Prevention and risk-mitigation infrastructure must be set up in rural areas. Technologies to mitigate unforeseen events such as flooding and frost must be made widely available. Urban and coastal focus of our disaster preparedness must be extended to the hinterland. Availability and diversity of insurance products for rural residents in general and for farmers in particular must be increased by an order of magnitude. Rural components of capital markets must be developed consciously to give people a wider choice of investments.

I have been able to indicate only the broad directions in which rural transformation in India ought to proceed, according to me. This transformation is not the job of any one tier of government, or of any one sector. It does not depend on a magic bullet, but on simultaneous interwoven efforts across sectors and segments guided by a unifying political vision across parties and intellectual persuasions.

◆

Sachin Pilot formerly served as the deputy chief minister of Rajasthan and the president of the Rajasthan Pradesh Congress Committee.

3

SMART CITIES: THE NEED OF THE HOUR

SHRIKANT EKNATH SHINDE

The concept of smart cities started gaining attention in India since the launch of the Smart Cities Mission in 2015. It has sparked a debate about the imminent need to conceptualize and build cities in such a manner that they cater to the core needs of the people, thereby facilitating the concept of Ease of Living. Development of smart cities has become a global phenomenon and its market is projected to exceed US$1 trillion by 2020 and US$2.5 trillion by 2025. As we move towards achieving the dream of a US$5-trillion economy, our country and its current leadership need to address the contemporary challenge of developing good infrastructure, efficient solid waste disposal management, flood control, storm water and sewerage system, etc., which lead to urban decay and traffic gridlock, thus resulting in a deteriorating quality of life for many of its citizens.

India's history is replete with evidence of urban planning and the concept of well-planned cities, which trace their origins to the Indus Valley Civilization of 2500 B.C. The planned towns of Mohenjo-daro and Harappa, which had a drainage system, water supply in brick-lined wells, houses of different sizes and sites such as the granary and public bath, bear testimony to this fact. One of the prime examples of city planning during the Mughal rule was Shahjahanabad. It had a central avenue leading to the main gate of the Red Fort along with Chandni Chowk, which housed the market. There were political and strategic reasons behind the building of prominent towns and cities such as Fatehpur Sikri in Uttar Pradesh, Sindhudurg in Maharashtra, Chittorgarh in Rajasthan and Gwalior in Madhya Pradesh during the precolonial era. Subsequent to the arrival of the British, the cities were planned to establish military and political dominance. The concept of town planning during the British rule was modelled around public health and sanitation and led to the establishment of agencies such as civil works departments in addition to the use of census. The evolution of various civilizations in India had a common notion of cities being important centres of economic productivity.

One of the prominent policies in the post-Independence era which actually realized the importance of urban planning and how to tackle the challenge of rising urbanization was the Eighth Five-year Plan (1992–97). The plan identified key issues concerning urban planning, which included bridging the gap between the demand and supply of infrastructural services; the need for access to basic services such as clean drinking water, sanitation, education and basic healthcare; and dealing with the unabated growth of urban population and aggravation of housing shortages, which have led to the proliferation of slums. The advent of globalization, Industrial Revolution and growth in employment opportunities have spurred large-scale migration from rural to urban areas, leading to a strain on the existing resources and hence, making it imperative for our policymakers to ensure urbanization and planning are carried out in a sustainable and inclusive manner. Rapid urbanization across India is an opportunity as well as one of its most serious challenges.

Need for Smart Cities

Urbanization is a direct result of the process of migration from rural to urban areas in India. According to Census 2011, about 450 million of 1.2 billion Indians migrated within the country, out of which 78 million, or 15.6 per cent of all domestic migrants, moved from rural to urban areas. India's urban population is expected to grow from 410 million in 2014 to 814 million by 2050. As India moves towards becoming a global superpower and one of the world's fastest-growing economies, we need to also focus on controlling the dispersed pattern of urbanization by enacting a new urban vision. The case studies of Argentina, Brazil, Mexico and Venezuela—countries which have been unsuccessful in managing the rapid growth of illegal, unserviced settlements, and failed to provide adequate services—are ample evidence of what can happen if urbanization and city planning are not done in a comprehensive manner. With the intent of providing a solution to the combined challenge of rapid urbanization and migration coupled with the need to provide core infrastructure and basic facilities to the people, the government came up with the idea of the Smart Cities Mission, which was launched on 25 June 2015.

The Smart Cities Mission is in continuation of India's evolving policy on urban development in the post-Independence era, which has its beginnings in the First Five-year Plan (1951–56). In 1992, the Seventy-fourth Constitutional Amendment Act allowed for decentralization, which vested greater powers and autonomy to urban local bodies (ULBs). This was followed by the launch of the Jawaharlal Nehru National Urban Renewal Mission (JNNURM) in 2005, which is considered as the pioneer scheme in the area of urban reforms.

The document specifying the modalities of the Smart Cities Mission states that the objective of the scheme is to promote sustainable and inclusive cities that provide core infrastructure, a decent quality of life to its citizens, a clean and sustainable environment, and the application of 'smart' solutions. The guidelines do not define 'smart cities', and state that the definition varies from country to country. As part of the mission, emphasis is laid on the concept of core infrastructure, which comprises adequate water supply; assured electricity supply; sanitation, including solid waste management; efficient urban mobility and public transport; affordable housing, especially for the poor; robust information technology (IT) connectivity and digitalization; good governance, especially e-governance and citizen participation; sustainable environment; safety and security of citizens, particularly women, children and the elderly; and health and education.

In order to carry out proper implementation of the scheme, it has been bifurcated into strategic components, which include city improvement (retrofitting), city renewal (redevelopment) and city extension (greenfield development) along with a pan-city initiative in which Smart Solutions are applied, covering larger parts of the city. Under these strategic components, the scheme aims to promote area-based development for transforming the existing areas, including slums, and convert them into planned human settlements which will improve the living conditions in cities. To address the problem of expanding population in urban areas, the scheme also talks about the development of greenfield areas around the cities. A welcome and innovative step has been the inclusion of Smart Solutions, which will enable cities to use technology to improve infrastructure and services. The result that the scheme seeks to achieve is the comprehensive development of a city in such a manner that it improves quality of life, creates employment and results in incomes for all.

Through the Smart Cities Mission, the government has also used the concept of competitive and cooperative federalism and conceptualized a selection process for shortlisting the cities under the Mission. As on date, a total of 100 cities have been shortlisted and a total investment of ₹2,01,981 crore has been proposed by the cities under their smart city plans. The strategic component of area-based projects are estimated to cost ₹1,63,138 crore and pan-city initiatives account for the remaining ₹38,841 crore of investments.[1]

The scheme also proposes a unique funding mechanism for the implementation of the Smart Cities Mission, which will be carried out by a special purpose vehicle (SPV) to be set up at the city level in the form of a limited company under the Companies Act, 2013. The SPV will be promoted by the state/union territory and the ULB jointly, with both having 50:50 equity shareholding. Post the selection process, each smart city will set up SPVs and initiate work on implementing the Smart City Proposal by preparing a detailed project report. The proposal should also include a financial plan with extensive details of itemized costs, resource plans, revenue and payback mechanisms, plans for recovery of operation and maintenance (O&M) costs, financial timelines and plans for mitigating financial risk.

The Smart Cities Mission will also bring about a change in urban governance. Currently, our cities are not well-equipped with any appraisal mechanism that deals with monitoring and evaluating the performance of projects and plans. The use of technology and data to monitor changes and developments in city-level indicators at regular intervals will be a right step towards bringing about a change in the performance of urban-sector programmes.

The Ministry of Housing and Urban Affairs has been made the nodal authority for monitoring the progress of the Smart Cities Mission with an aim to adopt the bottom-up approach to bring about a revolution in the area of urban development. The

[1]'Smart Cities,' Ministry of Housing and Urban Affairs, Government of India, http://mohua.gov.in/cms/smart-cities.php, last accessed on 21 October 2020.

concept of smart cities is also unique because it promotes the involvement of citizens while formulating the city vision and smart city plans as well as furthers the spirit of cooperative federalism by involving the ULBs and state governments. Till November 2019, 5,151 projects worth ₹2,05,018 crore have been proposed by cities participating in the Smart Cities Mission. Of these, 4,178 projects (81 per cent of the total projects) worth ₹1,49,519 crore (73 per cent of total project cost) have been tendered out. Of the tendered projects, work orders for 81 per cent projects have been issued. Cities participating in the Smart Cities Mission have completed 1,296 (25 per cent) of the total planned projects.

Ingredients for a Model Smart City

The concept of a smart city should not be limited to the use of technology and IT. A smart city should also address the core problems of pollution, waste management and transportation. A smart city can achieve its true meaning only if these basic issues are addressed, because in the pursuit of going digital, we often tend to ignore these issues which, if not addressed, can hamper city planning. The improvement of the urban waste collection service and, in general, the achievement of a more efficient waste management system is one of the main challenges that cities face, especially due to population growth. Waste management should be a priority for any smart city and so should be a holistic policy that takes into account the management of urban waste from collection and transport to its treatment.

Our country faces challenges across five key areas in the waste management lifecycle, namely, generation, collection, transportation, treatment and disposal. A key challenge to effective waste management is the shortage of manpower and garbage vans, as municipal bodies often outsource this activity to contractors without having the necessary mechanism to effectively track and monitor these services. Efficient waste processing and treatment can be carried out only if the waste is treated at source and segregated into multiple categories (biodegradable, recyclable, biohazard, etc.). The final step of disposing the waste is the biggest challenge due to the lack of planning of landfill sites. Initially, these sites were designated in places away from the cities to minimize harmful effects to inhabitants, but with growing urbanization, they now fall within city limits.

A long-term solution to this burgeoning problem can be the use of Internet of Things (IoT). IoT-enabled waste collection and transportation have the capacity to bring about significant advantages, which will aid in providing waste-management solutions. This can be used by municipal corporations for the purpose of tracking and monitoring the deployment of smart bins, garbage pickup trucks and sanitation workers; route optimization for trucks; cross-checking of garbage weight; etc., which can help in bringing transparency and penalizing the violators. Apart from this, IoT-enabled sensors can also help in analysing the amount of alternate fuel generated from the processed waste, which can also cater to the fuel needs of the city.

The other issue that needs consideration is the development and integration of multi-model transport. Urban mobility is going to be one of the key determinants of the Smart Cities Mission. The negative effects of reliance on private transport reflects in the pollution levels in Delhi, traffic congestion in Bengaluru and low average speed of mobility in Mumbai. If the issue of urban mobility is not addressed, it will add to the existing issues being faced by Indian cities, such as severe congestion, deteriorating air quality and increasing road rage and road accidents. Urban mobility can be provided not only by creating the necessary infrastructure through the construction of railway stations with modern facilities or bus stops with digital facilities, but also creating a mechanism, such a mobile application, to provide accurate and timely information about public transportation, which is extremely necessary to increase its dependability. If the commuter is aware of the arrival/departure time of trains and buses, it will help them in time management. A smart city has to embrace the use of available technology to develop its transportation system, an example of which can be through smart parking, the construction of ring roads to segregate traffic, the availability of passenger amenities at railway stations and a mechanism to enforce road discipline by use of IT. An important aspect of urban mobility is suburban railways, which cater to a huge population, but unfortunately, lag behind in terms of infrastructure, resulting in increased deaths due to train accidents. The government should consider converging the Mumbai Urban Transport Project (MUTP) Phase 2, 3 and 3-A with smart cities, particularly in areas such as Kalyan, where local trains are the lifeline. The timely completion of projects under MUTP will aid in urban mobility and also provide sustainable transport solutions along with last-mile connectivity.

Recommendations

In her recent Budget Speech, Finance Minister Nirmala Sitharaman announced the government's plan to develop five new smart cities under the Smart Cities initiative with a goal of maximizing the benefits of three separate economic activities: the economic corridors, the revitalization of manufacturing activities and the technological demands of aspirational classes. The government had also announced that to monitor the progress of the Mission since its inception, it would be publishing a report card for the 100 selected smart cities in June 2020.[1]

[1]PTI, 'Centre to Release Report Card of "Smart Cities" in June,' Mint, 27 January

The concept of smart cities is indeed unique. It has the potential to improve Ease of Living through the integration of sustainable solutions, IT, people's participation and the use of renewable energy to address several challenges, such as pollution, lack of affordable housing, the supply of clean drinking water, sanitation and urban planning, which can be the adverse outcomes of rapid urbanization and growing population. India is on the road to becoming the world's youngest nation in terms of demography, and there have been several discussions on how we can channelize our demographic dividend. The concept of smart cities can offer solution by not only creating the required infrastructure, but also generating employment for our country's large labour force. However, every reform and scheme faces several bottlenecks, which need to be addressed for the scheme's success. The same is the case with the Smart Cities Mission. The Mission was launched in June 2015 and since then, 5,151 projects, worth more than ₹2 lakh crore, have been identified which are at various stages of implementation. There are certain issues which are hampering the swift implementation of this scheme, such as the creation of SPVs and tendering process, which have taken a long time and strained its progress. There are certain steps that the government and stakeholders need to implement in order to achieve the intent behind smart cities.

- **Tackling Lack of Coordination**: One of the primary issues plaguing the successful implementation of the Smart Cities Mission is the lack of coordination between various government agencies and project execution which play a critical role in ensuring smooth operation of the scheme. Successful operation of smart city solutions can only be

2020, https://www.livemint.com/news/india/centre-to-release-report-card-of-smart-cities-in-june-11580129218270.html, last accessed 12 November 2020.

achieved with proper horizontal and vertical coordination between various stakeholders, which comprise the central government (the Ministry of Urban Development [MOUD]), state governments and local government agencies. The focus should also be on issues related to the financing and sharing of best practices and service delivery processes.

This issue has also been red-flagged by the Standing Committee on Urban Development in its twenty-third report (July 2018), whereby it had observed numerous instances of one agency undoing the work done by another agency. The committee also highlighted that the lack of coordination between the implementing agencies is a major reason why the intended benefits of the Smart Cities Mission are still not visible to the public.

The absence of proper convergence of and coordination between the Smart Cities Mission and other schemes of the ministry such as the Atal Mission for Rejuvenation and Urban Transformation (AMRUT), the Swachh Bharat Mission, etc., is hampering its progress. Proper integration of these schemes with overlapping goals and objectives will assist in making smaller towns and villages 'smart', which will aid in avoiding the creation of uneven development and digital divide by the new/retrofitted smart cities.

- **Handling Issues Concerning Urban Local Bodies**: ULBs play a crucial role in the successful implementation of the Smart Cities Mission. The current condition of most ULBs is not very good, as they are not financially self-sustainable. The funding process of the Mission requires revenue generation from ULBs as well and most of these, on account of having limited technical capacity, are unable to ensure timely and cost-effective implementation. The decision of the central government to provide internship of up to one year for unemployed engineering graduates with an urban or local body is a welcome step, as it will help in addressing the issue of technical manpower and enable ULBs to attract the best of talent at market-competitive compensation rates.

- **Designing of a Master Plan for Cities**: One of the core challenges to urban development and proper city planning is the absence of a proper master plan, which serves as an essential document and is useful while designing strategies for upgrading infrastructure and devising plans to provide better opportunities to its citizens. The Smart Cities Mission in its guidelines should also incorporate the submission of a detailed master plan and a long-term vision document, which should anticipate the technological and infrastructural interventions needed for developing core infrastructure.

The vision and intent behind the Smart Cities Mission along with the reform measures envisaged under it have a novel outlook towards changing the current framework of urban governance system and public service delivery in India. The primary requirement for effective implementation of the Mission is rigorous monitoring and tracking to assess its overall impact. This scheme has the potential to be a pioneer of reforms, which can have tremendous implications on the functioning of the manner and method of delivery of public services. This, in turn, will benefit every section of the society, especially the poor and marginalized sections including unorganized sector workers in the cities.

◆

Dr Shrikant Shinde is a Member of Parliament from the Kalyan constituency of Maharashtra and is a member of the Shiv Sena.

4

INDIA'S URBAN MOBILITY CRISIS

TEJASVI SURYA

Mobility is one of the most important facets of the evolution of human civilization. From the founding of the wheel to the designing of the most sophisticated aircrafts, man's quest has always been to find ways to travel in the most efficient and comfortable manner. The progress made towards efficient means of travel and communication has resulted in many benefits to the human civilization, primarily in the growth of large urban centres, that is, cities that are the epicentre of science, commerce, culture and innovation.

Ironically, these urban centres, which are a result of the evolution of efficient means of travel and communication, are now staring at a deep mobility crisis. No big city in the world is an exception to this new reality. So is the case with most Indian cities, including Bengaluru, Mumbai, Delhi, Pune, Chennai and Kolkata, all of which are facing mobility and logistical challenges owing to poor infrastructure, erratic urban planning, and sluggish and obsolete regulatory framework. This has become a stumbling block to the further growth and development of these cities and the country in general.

Bengaluru: A Classic Case of Urban Mobility Crisis in Indian Cities

A report by the Boston Consulting Group–Uber estimates that high levels of congestion across India's top four cities cost an economic loss of over US$22 billion every year.[1] The average speed for vehicles in some metros is reported at 17 km/hour.[2] This has been the case despite an eight-fold increase in the demand for public transport in India since 1980. Since the demand for public transport was not addressed in an appropriate manner, the dependence on private vehicles increased manifold. Even then, in India, car ownership is lesser as compared to developed countries of the West—an average 22 out of 1,000 people own a car in India as compared to 980 and 850 in the United States (US) and United Kingdom (UK), respectively.[3]

According to a recent survey conducted by TomTom, the Netherlands-based global provider of navigation, Bengaluru has the worst traffic in the world, while Delhi, Mumbai and Pune feature in the top 10 most congested cities globally.[4] The study claims that

---

[1]'Unlocking Cities: The Impact of Ridesharing across India,' The Boston Consulting Group, http://image-src.bcg.com/Images/BCG-Unlocking-Cities-Ridesharing-India_tcm9-185213.pdf, last accessed on 15 October 2020.

[2]Express Drives Desk, 'Time Spent in Cabs Goes Up as Average Speed of Cars Down by 3km/h: Bengaluru, Hyderabad, Delhi Worst Hit,' Express Drives, 5 January 2018, https://www.financialexpress.com/auto/car-news/time-spent-in-cabs-goes-up-as-average-speed-of-cars-down-by-3kmh-bengaluru-hyderabad-delhi-worst-hit/1001845/, last accessed on 15 October 2020.

[3]Muntazir Abbas, 'India Has 22 Cars per 1,000 Individuals: Amitabh Kant,' ET Auto.Com, 12 December 2018, https://auto.economictimes.indiatimes.com/news/passenger-vehicle/cars/india-has-22-cars-per-1000-individuals-amitabh-kant/67059021, last accessed on 15 October 2020.

[4]'Bengaluru Has World's Worst Traffic, 4 Indian Cities In Top 10: Report,' NDTV, 30 January 2020, https://www.ndtv.com/india-news/bengaluru-has-worlds-worst-traffic-4-indian-cities-in-top-10-report-2171827 and https://niti.gov.in/writereaddata/files/document_publication/BCG.pdf, last accessed on 31 August 2020.

the people of Bengaluru driving during peak hours lose 243 hours a year on traffic. The productivity loss due to the mobility crisis in Bengaluru is pegged at US$4.75 billion per annum. A notorious 17-km stretch on Bengaluru's Outer Ring Road, which accounts for almost 13 per cent of India's information technology (IT) revenue, moves at a dismal speed of 4 km/hour during peak hours. The lack of a seamless, reliable and affordable public transport system has made people in Bengaluru depend heavily on private transport. As of 2017, 5 million two-wheelers and 1.4 million four-wheelers are privately owned in a population of approximately 12 million. The increased usage of private transport over mass transit has given rise to nightmarish traffic jams, urban congestion and pollution, a mess experienced daily on the city's roads.

Response of the City's Parastatals

In case you are wondering how the city's parastatals are responding, given this nightmarish problem, it is a case of too many cooks spoiling the broth. The administrative and functional overlap between the Bengaluru Development Authority (BDA), Bruhat Bengaluru Mahanagara Palike (BBMP, Bengaluru City Corporation), Bengaluru Metropolitan Region Development Authority (BMRDA), Directorate of Urban Land Transport (DULT) and three other such urban planning authorities is a sure-shot recipe for disaster.

Take the example of Bannerghatta Road in my constituency, which people feared travelling on till recently. While one part of the road had been occupied for the contruction of the Metro, a 300-metre stretch of the road from Vega City to Arekere was notorious for its potholes, noisy traffic signal stoppages and waterlogging even when there was no rain. It would take at least 30 minutes to cross the 300-metre stretch, which leads to one of India's premier business schools, the Indian Institute of Management (IIM), Bengaluru. Ambulances heading to and from major hospitals located on this route would often get stuck in the traffic jam, leading to avoidable casualties.

The root cause of the problem was the lack of coordination among the civic parastatals, namely, the Bengaluru Metro Rail Corporation Ltd (BMRCL), the Bengaluru Water Supply and Sewerage Board (BWSSB) and the BBMP, which is accountable for the upkeep of the road. All work was being conducted independently and the authorities of the respective parastatals worked without any coordination between them.

Only after intervention from our office were the repairs carried out by bringing all the concerned civic parastatals and infusing synergy and coordination between them. The office of the Member of Parliament (MP), Member of Legislative Assembly (MLA), senior officers of BMRCL, BWSSB and BBMP, vigilant press and various non-governmental organizations (NGOs) had to come together to fix a simple 300-metre stretch—a clear indication of the seriousness of the administrative rot in the system. What should have ideally been a routine road repair demanded the attention of the MP!

The city's civic and public transport authorities, ranging from the traffic police to the corporation, concentrate on providing band-aid solutions instead of addressing the root of the problem. Constructing more roads, flyovers and underpasses or increasing the number of road lanes is not the solution for an ever-growing problem of traffic congestion. Such myopic arrangements will only further incentivize private transport. Urban transport planning should rest upon the idea of the movement of people, not of vehicles. Nevertheless, our urban planners seem to be thinking and working in the opposite direction.

A case in point is the lack of support to the city's major public transport carrier—the public bus. The Bengaluru Metropolitan Transport Corporation's (BMTC) fleet size has remained stagnant at around 6,500 buses since 2015. The disinterest of the BMTC in adopting novel technology to provide real-time information on its fleet and route options, until recently, has left digitally sound commuters in Bengaluru with a sour taste in their mouth. While the BMTC is also planning to introduce more services on its routes by leasing electric buses, it still leaves a lot to be desired as the service is severely short of providing more last point-to-point routes even among localities situated close by. Even then, the BMTC claims a rigid monopoly over the sector and prohibits private buses from operating on routes where there are no BMTC buses plying.

Nevertheless, the concept of shared mobility took off quite well in Bengaluru. Increased options in point-to-point road movement facilities with app-based services such as Bounce, Vogo, Yulu, Quickride and so on have been catering to need-based transport. The state government, however, continues to show resistance to novel potential mobility solutions by private operators. The services of a tempo and mini-bus aggregator were banned by the state government citing that it may cut into the BMTC's profits. Last year, the state government had also directed Ola and Uber to do away with the ridesharing option in their apps as the transport laws didn't permit for carpooling—unmindful of the fact that the idea of carpooling was non-existent at the time of drafting the archaic law. While the services continue to exist at present, the state government's aggressive raid on bike taxis have forced them to go off the grid.

While this was the treatment meted out to road-based public transport options, the city's authorities haven't been too kind to even rail-based public transport solutions. Bengaluru has a Metro whose functioning length is only 42.3 km as of today. According to the BMRCL, which operates the city's Metro, it will expand the current network by 56 km, all the way to the Outer Ring Road and Airport Lines. This is expected to contribute to a combined daily ridership of 7.5 lakh by 2025. However, even this will not be sufficient to lessen the burden on the roads.

The 2018 BCG–Uber report titled 'Unlocking Cities' notes:

> Bangalore and Kolkata intend to significantly increase rail-based public transport capacity. Despite these plans, we estimate that the added capacity of rail transport alone will not be sufficient to reduce their congestion levels. This is especially true for Bangalore, where we estimated that the added rail transport capacity still falls below the required level to maintain its congestion levels by 2022. According to our estimates, additional rail public transport adoption of close to 21% of total kilometers is essential, in conjunction with public transport, to maintain today's congestion levels.[1]

Therefore, the city's three decades-long pending demand for an efficient suburban rail system, which is now awaiting the Union cabinet's approval, assumes all the more significance.

Policy Solutions

In the light of these challenges, what can be the broad policy solutions that we can offer?

It's essential for any public transport network to be accessible, seamless and inclusive. Citizens have to be incentivized to avoid private transport even for short travel, with sufficient investment on non-motorized transport as well as last-mile connectivity.

---

[1]'Unlocking Cities: The Impact of Ridesharing across India,' The Boston Consulting Group, https://image-src.bcg.com/BCG-Unlocking-Cities-Ridesharing-India_tcm21-185213.pdf, last accessed on 15 October 2020.

A remodelled and integrated regulatory framework for urban mobility should be among the first steps in tackling these challenges. The present framework is sluggish, with a multitude of agencies and inefficient coordination between different modes of transport. All stakeholders, including urban planners, service providers and the state, must arrive at a common ground to encourage an innovative, sustainable and environment-friendly movement of people in our cities.

The urban planning of a city needs to relook at the workplace travel of its citizens. Instead of crowded and densely populated clusters commuting to other clusters for work, the urban design can be thought of as having a central core city linked with independent clusters supporting the system through tech-driven, seamless and affordable public transport networks, thereby reducing the density of population and decentralization of traffic. In particular, a safe public transport system catering to the needs of women and senior travellers has to be prioritized along with infrastructure development.

Ideally, what Bengaluru requires is a unified metropolitan transport authority which integrates the different public transport agencies that are presently competing with each other for space and revenue. All modes of public transport should be integrated with an Intelligent Transport System (ITS) giving real-time data on their location and availability. The commuter should be able to use one smartphone app which enables interaction between various public transport entities so as to plan his/her trips seamlessly between any or all of them. This involves integrated public and private services along with access to information on buses, metros, trains and the feeder services thereof. However, this all-important integration between civic agencies cannot happen unless all of them are brought under one single authority, backed by an exclusive legislation.

There is not one single umbrella authority which is responsible for looking after the various parastatals of urban planning and management. Consequently, accountability in local governance has taken a back seat, with one agency pointing fingers at another when it comes to the most basic of tasks such as digging up of roads for laying underground drainage pipes.

While one section of the civic authorities is governed by the Karnataka Municipal Corporations Act, 1976, the other agencies fall under the state government. As for the act, its legislation dates back to a period when Bengaluru was neither the IT capital of India nor was it a magnetic urban settlement. This archaic legislation has proven to be detrimental in addressing the modern-day issues concerning Bengaluru. And if you feel Bengaluru's governance model is outdated, just ponder over this—India's city planning is based on the 1947 Town and Country Planning Act of the UK!

The mayor, and his power and tenure, further give an insight into a lethargic system. The mayor has no substantial executive powers under the Karnataka Municipal Corporations Act and his term is only for one year.[1] The mayor does not have any executive authority, which instead lies with the state government-appointed commissioner, unlike in the global cities such as New York, Johannesburg, Sydney and London.

A 2008 report drafted by the government-appointed committee headed by Dr Kasturirangan noted that even in cities with a directly elected mayor, the failure to accord executive powers to the mayor made the office dysfunctional anyway. According to the report, 'There seem to be basic institutional design failures in the directly elected mayoral system.' It further notes, 'Most

---

[1]'Dr Kasturirangan Committee Report on BBMP,' https://www.scribd.com/document/96103531/Dr-Kasturirangan-Committee-Report-on-BBMP, last accessed on 16 October 2020.

significantly, the Mayor has not been vested with the necessary political and executive power in order to carry out his mandate... We have to learn from the success of this model in countries like the US or France and adapt the Presidential system of government to the Indian legal framework at this level of government.'

Most big cities in the country require an exclusive legislation for the city's urban governance. There have been several demands, including from my constituency, for the state government to introduce the Greater Bengaluru Governance Bill, 2018, drafted by an expert committee in charge of BBMP.

A directly elected mayor for a five-year term, with adequate executive powers would be a good first step. All the different parastatals, which hitherto have failed to communicate with one another effectively, have to be brought under one single authority—the Greater Bengaluru Authority. Furthermore, citizens' participation in ward and zonal meetings will ensure strengthened and inclusive local governance. The Greater Bengaluru Governance Bill, 2018, which has taken various forms through the years, has always been put in the backburner by successive governments. It is only when the citizens demand these basic structures and facilities from their elected representatives that a cascading effect will be felt. As much as the political will of an elected representative is required, it is also the sentiments of the general public that will decide policies and give them shape.

Building Cities of the Future: PM Modi's Plan

The story of Bengaluru is the story of every other Indian city—only the severity of the challenge differs. Therefore, Prime Minister Narendra Modi has formulated the National Urban Policy Framework (NUPF) 2018, which lays down the essentials for policymaking for all of India's urban spaces. While the road network of cities are planned as 'traffic zones', where movement is generally designed only for motorable vehicles, other general urban spaces need to be redesigned as 'social zones', where a combination of traffic, cycling and pedestrian movement is made possible on a single road line.

The Atal Mission for Rejuvenation and Urban Transformation (AMRUT), launched by the Centre to support and encourage infrastructure building, has been a welcome step. Along with AMRUT, the Smart Cities Mission supports in developing modern, standardized and all-inclusive urban movement mechanisms, including restructuring of roads and footpaths to make them accessible to pedestrians and the differently abled. City plans must mandatorily take into account suitable funds for pedestrian pathways and cycle tracks and also ensure sufficient footpaths and streetlights.

More recent policies exclusively designed to address mobility crisis nationally include the National Urban Transport Policy and the National Electric Mobility Mission Plan 2020. The latter has been particularly aimed at serving green solutions. PM Modi is also making a significant push for green technologies and the state governments have also been incentivized to follow on these lines. Karnataka is the first state to have an exclusive policy for electric vehicles (EVs). The state offers specific incentives to promote the manufacture of EVs and setting up of EV parks to develop batteries. Coupled with the Centre's push for EVs, Karnataka has the potential to take a giant leap and become the hub of EV manufacturing in India and the world.

In summation, this is the appropriate time for revamping India's city planning so that we can build massive cities which will truly be the engines of the country's economic growth and act as the launch pad to make India a truly modern, progressive and prosperous country. For this to happen, we need to change the way we think about our cities. Like they say, if you change your thinking, you change the outcome.

◆

Tejasvi Surya, a member of the Bharatiya Janata Party, represents the Bengaluru (south) constituency in the Lok Sabha. He was elected to the 17th Lok Sabha at the age of just 28. A lawyer by training and profession, Surya has a deep interest in history, philosophy, science and civilizational studies. His lectures and articles on these subjects are widely followed.

PART II

NEW HORIZONS

5

INDIA: A LEADING ASIAN POWER

GAURAV GOGOI

In 1991, India pivoted into the global market economy through its landmark economic reforms under Prime Minister P.V. Narasimha Rao's government. The overwhelming merits of these reforms ushered India towards unparalleled geopolitical and diplomatic achievements. The reform agenda continued well into the 2000s, resulting in an average growth rate of 7.6 per cent in the 15-year period between 2003–04 and 20017–18, which marked a full 2 percentage points increase from the average growth rate of 5.6 per cent in the period 1980–81 to 1991–92. Specifically, between 2005 and 2008, India routinely clocked in an average of 9 per cent growth rate annually. Beyond domestic achievements, India successfully managed to attract steady foreign investment, totalling up to US$10.55 billion in 2016. India's economic reform path coupled with its large market, democratic values and political stability became the foundation of its global strategic weight. This led to the development of strategic relationships with several global superpowers, including the United States (US), with whom the groundbreaking Indo-US Civil Nuclear Treaty was signed in 2008. After 2014, India's foreign policy has also seen a tangible growth in high-level dialogues between India's Prime Minister's Office (PMO) and its equivalent counterparts with countries across the world, including the US, Australia, China, and those in the Middle East and Africa. Parallel to India's growth as a resounding power, there is a wide-ranging consensus that India must transform its identity from that of a rule-taker to that of a rule-shaper in international diplomacy.

However, several observers suggest that India has been unable to tap into its maximum potential. The inability to fruitfully utilize its economic talent has led to a stalled structural reform agenda, rise in non-performing loans, twin balance sheet problems, complex bureaucratic rules and lengthy arbitrations. In the last few years, India's gross domestic product (GDP) has considerably plummeted, while unemployment levels are soaring past the last 45 years' levels. A hastily implemented goods and services tax (GST) has led to a shortfall in government revenues, with states suffering the most, as their GST compensations are either inadequate or delayed. The gradual economic slowdown and its corresponding impact on the declining domestic investment prompted the government to shy away from international trade negotiations. Since 2014, India has refused to sign any free trade agreements, eventually exiting the Regional Comprehensive Economic Partnership (RCEP) in 2019. While countries such as Vietnam and Taiwan have benefited from the US-China trade wars, Indian manufacturing prowess has suffered, as its share of the GDP and exports has slowed down. These trends have been further amplified in the aftermath of the spread of COVID-19. The lockdown in several parts of the world, including India, has led to an economic crisis paralleling the Great Depression.

In a world that that will hence be divided pre- and post-COVID-19, India must actively utilize the opportunities underlying the crisis. Policymakers and institutions must go back to the drawing board in order to position India as a leading Asian power. The only way to respond to the COVID-19 crisis is with boldness and sound policy. The road ahead must focus on attracting global investment, focused diplomatic outreach, building capacity for trade and military, and supporting entrepreneurs in technology and healthcare. None of these goals will be achieved without India sticking to its best democratic traditions, federal principles and constitutional values.

Looking Within to Promote Trade and Investment

In marked contrast to the 2008 Global Financial Crisis, the macroeconomic and financial casualties of the coronavirus pandemic have occurred at a faster, more severe pace. This has only sped up the phenomenon of deglobalization, which began in 2008. This phenomenon has witnessed distinct ramifications. Populist leaders across the world are asking private companies to scale back their investment in emerging markets. Nationalism has been redefined to rely less on imports and focus more on domestic production. Even prior to COVID-19, the US-China trade wars were pushing companies to shift their factories outside of China. Overall, the world was growing increasingly wary of China's overtly aggressive diplomacy, especially in South China Sea. This global distrust multiplied after several questions arose over China's role in spreading COVID-19.

In this global context, attracting and sustaining foreign investments in India must go beyond well-intentioned summits, involving pragmatic reforms based on the experiences of more successful democracies in the world. The existing roadblocks to investment in India, such as the complex compliance requirements, excessive regulation, lack of capacity-building in state and local governance, policy uncertainty and land availability, must be tackled in the COVID-19 context. Indian industry, especially the micro, small and medium enterprises (MSMEs), if given the necessary support and encouragement, will not only benefit from the increased competition but also simultaneously integrate with global supply chains. As mentioned earlier, the federal collaboration between states is important, as domestic supply chains lie across India. The regular interactions we witnessed between chief ministers in the GST council and the COVID-19 response team must be more regular to give a concerted push towards foreign investment. Foreign direct investment (FDI) is necessary, given the fact that domestic investment is yet to pick up, despite corporate taxes being reduced in 2019. Nonetheless, the steps towards attracting foreign investors will also assist our domestic private sector, as the challenges are similar. Underlying these efforts must be a strict vigil on India's benchmark competitors in Asia, namely China in the field of high-skilled manufacturing, and Bangladesh, Vietnam and Taiwan in low-skilled manufacturing.

To ensure a competitive trade surplus with partner nations, India must also increase its exporting capacity. Identifying key products and services as well as target markets, and supporting companies and entrepreneurs as job-creators, will be essential. Based on my research, India should focus on oil, mines, commodities, mobile manufacturing, healthcare technology, generic medicine, textile, electric car technology and automobile components. For instance, textiles and garments have always represented a major growth possibility for India. The textile sector must be approached as an industry where small, medium as well as large producers have an opportunity for growth. Local companies and products such as Kashmiri Pashmina wool and Assamese eri silk must be encouraged to integrate with global brands and supply chains. In the case of mobile manufacturing, following the global scale back from China post COVID-19, India must step up its effort to motivate companies such as Apple and Samsung to expand their Indian manufacturing presence. The push towards electric vehicles is also exciting, provided a road map can be designed for India to be integrated into global supply chains.

Healthcare has received a lot of attention in the last one year. The current situation presents a unique opportunity for India to compete with China in pharmaceutical production. Indian policymakers need to take a series of crucial steps, including identifying essential drug ingredients, incentivizing local drug manufacturers and rescuing ailing state-run drug makers. As experts posit, a growth of US$3.3 billion in income for Indian drug manufacturers is possible if India expands its capacity and global supply. Most of South Asia, Africa, the Middle East, Eastern Europe and Latin America will become an attractive market for India's exports in pharmaceuticals and other products such as generic medicines and Ayurvedic medicines. Critical to this is supporting India's MSMEs and start-ups, with a focus on registration, recognition and funding.

Much of India's ability to be a leading Asian power relies on the governance capacity of central and state governments. The central government must work with state governments to build the capacity of ministry officials and local administration. Going forward, key Indian states must be allowed to open their respective trade and business councils in foreign countries to attract foreign investment. I highlight this because the role of diplomacy in pushing India-centric investments and exports is critical in a post COVID-19 deglobalized world. The competition for global markets and investments will become even harder; therefore, Indian consulates and embassies abroad must be buttressed with state-centric missions, whose aim will be to promote the interests of their respective states. The exact form of this para-diplomacy can be further nuanced, but there are examples from both Australia and China that can be studied.

Public–Private Partnership for New Technology

With our civilizational emphasis on mathematics and science, India has a natural affinity with technology. The role of technology in people's lives and global societies will continue to grow. India must strive to maintain its competitive advantage without tiring. The government must introduce technology as the overarching goal that several ministries in India must work towards. Ministries such as Information Technology (IT), External Affairs, Defence, and Information and Broadcasting must unite their efforts in promoting the advancement of India's technological capacity. The government and Indian tech companies must be motivated by a common vision and build the principles of accountability and transparency in their relationship. Emerging technologies and data protection will require a closer working relationship between regulators, central and state agencies, the academia and the private sector.

The global market for artificial intelligence (AI) applications will touch US$190 billion by 2025. To prevent the unethical use of data, while at the same time fostering innovation and the growth of the data economy, India's data policy must accommodate both big-technology giants and domestic entrepreneurs. India can lean on the experience of countries such as Singapore and the United Kingdom (UK) in building the capacity of Indian institutions and regulators to operationalize the Personal Data Protection Law in a conducive manner. Legislation should also focus on developing a skilled workforce and ensure that the education sector equips the future generations with the right tools.

Redefining Diplomacy in a Deglobalized World

If the 2008 Global Financial Crisis pivoted the world towards deglobalization and spurred the rise of populism and Brexit, then COVID-19 is likely to push countries to become more inward-looking. This is a particularly worrying prospect for India, which has benefitted enormously from the cross-border flow of jobs, capital and ideas. In this new context, India's diplomacy will need to be more sophisticated and nuanced. In order to become a leading Asian power, India will need additional diplomatic assets. In this regard, India must not shy away from looking at its global diaspora and the large student community as its strengths. The scope of bilateral relationships will have to be widened and in many cases, the relationships with existing strategic partners will need to be strengthened.

While India's diplomatic engagement with the US and the UK is well-defined, Europe needs greater attention. Especially after Brexit, India has more flexibility to develop a new road map for strategic partnerships with nations such as Germany, France, the Netherlands, Belgium and Austria in the areas of technology, defence, cybersecurity, maritime security and energy. Germany offers the ability to bring its technological and manufacturing prowess to the Indian market while being an important academic destination for millions of Indian students. France can become a key ally as India's indigenous defence industrial complex grows, as I have envisioned in the later part of this chapter. The Netherlands, with its proximity to central Europe, fast and reliable regulators, accessibility, efficient legal infrastructure and other benefits can be viewed as a major hub for India's investments in the European Union.

In the past few years, India's Neighbourhood First policy has seen a few obstacles. Both Nepal and Bangladesh have communicated their discomfort with India's position on issues involving domestic politics, boundary, human rights and trade. Therefore, repairing and strengthening these relationships is the key to establishing a peaceful and prosperous neighbourhood. India must be more generous in allowing its market to be accessed by businesses based in these countries. This will also have downstream impact on the states in east and northeast India, bringing benefits to the retail, transport and logistics industries. South Asia is also a vital market for India's exports in the field of defence, technology and automobiles. Collectively, the region must aim to triple the volume of mutual trade, which stood at about US$19 billion around 2018.

In the Association of Southeast Asian Nations (ASEAN) region, despite the initial withdrawal from RCEP, India cannot afford to permanently remain on the outside. India must utilize its advantage in the services, pharmaceuticals and technology sectors to have the ASEAN countries converge on common goals and mutual benefit. The ASEAN countries, especially Thailand, Singapore, Vietnam, Malaysia and Indonesia, are critical partners for India in Asia. India must, therefore, ensure that its relationship with these countries goes beyond high-level visits and be more outcome-centric. This will enable India to join RCEP at a later stage.

There is a need to widen the breadth of India's relationship with Japan, South Korea and Australia. While the relationship has seen significant achievements in the government-to-government and business-to-business domains, greater focus must be placed on people-to-people exchange so as to bring the countries together. Greater collaboration in the fields of cinema, sports, music, travel and fashion can be promoted with the support of governments and the private sector. This will eventually result in a more robust strategic and commercial co-operation with these countries and create a stronger Asia-Pacific region.

Managing Conflicts

India's relationship with two neighbouring countries—Pakistan and China—has been particularly contentious since Independence.

China

Over the past few years, tensions between the US and China have engulfed the major as well as the emerging countries across the world. Within this context, there is a larger, growing consensus surrounding the US's retreat from global politics. This is in tandem with the US's previous international diplomatic abstentions, including its withdrawal from the Paris Climate Change treaty, pulling out of Afghanistan, reworking the North American Free Trade Agreement (NAFTA) and issuing statements against the World Health Organization (WHO), the North Atlantic Treaty Organization (NATO) and the United Nations (UN). However, amidst the pandemic, one realization has become widespread—that countries all over the world have become increasingly dependent on China. For instance, in Japan, China is the key source of importing protective equipment, contributing to mostly all of the 70–80 per cent of imports in surgical masks. Similarly, China's share in the US antibiotics market is more than 95 per cent and most of the ingredients cannot be manufactured domestically.

The gradual retreat of the US has hence created a vacuum for global leadership, which China will be happy to step into. While President Donald Trump threatened to cut off funding to the WHO amidst the pandemic, China tactfully responded by granting an additional US$2 billion in funding. The current situation marks a dramatic reversal from the period when the world witnessed the Ebola crisis, which was marked by the US rallying global effort to fight the epidemic and support the cash-starved African nations. Due to this drastic change in global affairs, it is likely that other nations will maintain comfortable relations with both the US and China. This is because, for most nations across the world, partnership in defence and strategic affairs with the US is complementary to a trade and commercial partnership with China. Simultaneously, several nations will attempt to get out of the import trap with China and drive up diversity in trade partnership.

Similarly, when it comes to India's relationship with China, the guiding principle must be preserving national interest and promoting domestic security. It is an unfortunate reality that China is currently three decades ahead of India on most social indicators. The focus has to be on growing the scale and strength of the Indian economy, boosting our infrastructure, modernizing our workforce, investing in health and education, and building the capacity of the Indian state. According to the UN, China and India will become the world's largest and second-largest economies respectively in the next 30 years. In order to achieve this goal, the relationship between these two countries will need to be calibrated carefully. Doklam and Ladakh are reminders that India must counter its strategic deficit with China, by rapidly building the Indian economy, diplomacy and military. This is the only sustainable road map for India to counter Chinese ambitions in the neighbourhood, without depending on the Quad or the US.

At the same time, India must also remain prepared for a Chinese opposition to its swift rise. The trade deficit between the two countries, which currently exists in China's favour, must be fixed. A substantial number of products being imported from China have alternate suppliers in the world. Besides developing these new supply chains to diversify imports, India should also propel manufacturing under Aatmanirbhar Bharat. For instance, pharmaceutical products such as active pharmaceutical ingredients (APIs), which are majorly being imported from China, should be manufactured in India. India should also be mindful of the emerging importance of data markets. As one of the world's largest data markets, India should be cognizant of its leverage and be prudent in employing it to its advantage. While the nations have bolstered trade in agricultural commodities in the aftermath of the Wuhan Summit, the issue of market access for Indian products in the areas of medicines and pharmaceuticals, IT and IT-related services needs to be resolved to better the trade with China.

Pakistan

One of India's most complicated bilateral relationship rests within its proximal neighbourhood. Even amidst a pandemic, terrorists from Pakistan have been attacking innocent civilians in India. State-based terrorist attacks continue to impact Indian territory and civilians, even after Indian armed forces carried out successful surgical operations post the attack in Uri and Pulwama. Realistically, it is unlikely that Pakistan will take any concrete steps towards eliminating the intelligence-military-terrorist complex that exists within its own country. Therefore, it is necessary for India to defend itself from Pakistan's belligerence. Within such a hostile neighbourhood, a limited military confrontation or a limited war cannot be ruled out in the future. On the upside, a military victory for the Indian army will provide a major psychological blow for the supporters of state-based terrorism in Pakistan. To achieve such a victory, the government must invest heartily in overcoming ammunition shortage for artillery guns, air defence, weapons and tanks, particularly the 152 total types of ammunition considered critical by the Indian army to fight a war. The Chief of Defence Services has publicly remarked the role of indigenous defence weapons in the next war. Running alongside the military strategy must be a diplomatic strategy for India to expose the terror complex within Pakistan to global leaders and establish it as the aggressor. India must, therefore, always attempt to fulfil its role as a net-security provider and bring an end to the state-based terrorism policy of Pakistan—a much-needed move that will contribute towards making the world and the South Asian neighbourhood much safer.

Asian Defence Power

India's defence sector has received a lot of attention in public media during the National Democratic Alliance (NDA) government. Modernization and indigenization of defence have to be the next logical steps towards achieving India's goal of being a leading Asian power. However, it would be inaccurate to claim that any tangible progress has been made. Certain procedural and policy changes have been successfully instituted to empower the sector significantly. For instance, in addition to a Defence Planning Committee under the National Security Advisor for macro-level planning, the government has also announced a Defence Production Policy in 2018, revised offset guidelines and incorporated a 'Make-II' procedure to simplify private-sector participation in indigenous defence equipment manufacture. The setting up of two defence industrial corridors in Uttar Pradesh and Tamil Nadu are both welcome steps towards achieving a cohesive, self-reliant defence estate.

These improvements are piecemeal in front of the larger picture of an indigenous defence industrial complex. Several potent problems still lie unaddressed. First, the procurement cycle within the sector continues to be extremely time consuming, hence becoming inefficient. More importantly, the absence of a level playing field for private-sector players is the second problem facing the sector. As the major orders continue to sway in the direction of a 'nomination' basis to the defence public-sector undertakings (DPSUs), the private sector, bereft of any external stimulus, has witnessed no major order in the last four years, barring the K9 self-propelled gun won by Larsen & Toubro (L&T). Finally, the Strategic Partner (SP) Policy, a positive move towards including private players in building major defence platforms such as aircrafts, guns and armoured vehicles, lies stagnant. The policy, riddled with inactivity and delay, suffers from a lack of policy clarity and a failure of award-announcement for private firms to be selected as an SP.

The stark reality of the resource-starved defence sector is undeniable. After the inclusion of GST since July 2017 and custom duties since April 2017, additional outflows from funds allocated to the Ministry of Defence have cut the capital allocation to defence in real terms. Consequently, after factoring for inflation, the 2019–20 budgetary allocation is comparable with the allocation for the financial year 2016–17. As highlighted by Parliamentary responses and Standing Committees, India's defence modernization budget has not even been sufficient to cover the liabilities over the past couple of years. This drop in funds occurs alongside a stark reduction in the number of orders placed on Indian companies and a rise in imports. Subsequently, this has contributed to very low order placements—only about ₹77,000 crore—on the Indian industry for the past three years.

To further expand the defence sector in India, the underlying causes preventing foreign companies from setting up base in India need to be addressed. Ease of doing business, strengthening intellectual property laws, FDI norms and offset rules are all roadblocks that need to be identified and done away with. This is particularly critical in ensuring that India does not lose the companies that are viewing us as a long-term investment market for a permanent foothold. A culture of research and development (R&D) coupled with healthy competition must be promoted amongst public and private players. Within the defence technology and cyberspace ecosystem, we need to support entrepreneurs and defence start-ups in India with the right clarity and a long-term vision in mind.

Conclusion

With the cataclysmic shift in the world post COVID-19, India must take bold steps to become a leading Asian power. This goal will be achieved if the country's focus is on economy, defence, diplomacy and human capital. In every area, the government must respond to the needs of local enterprises, entrepreneurs and MSMEs. Working in this direction will also help sustain regular foreign investment. The road to managing conflicts within Asia will be complicated, but as a leading Asian power, India will need to be aggressive on terror and be strategic with rising powers. A deglobalized world will test India's diplomatic skills, but the world will need an India for its contribution to the global security and economic growth.

◆

Gaurav Gogoi is a member of the Indian National Congress and a Member of Parliament (MP) from the Kaliabor constituency (Assam). He worked in an NGO before joining politics.

6

ADMINISTRATIVE REFORMS: VISION FOR THE FUTURE

APARAJITA SARANGI

Every nation has a message to deliver, a mission to fulfil, a destiny to reach.

—Swami Vivekananda

India's tryst with destiny started in 1947, when its progenitors envisioned it as a developed country, with a strong welfare foundation underpinned by social and economic reforms in the years to come. Democratic India's edifice is built on a continuum of structural reforms and on the functionality of the organs of its government.

I remember vividly the day I got into the coveted Indian Administrative Service (IAS), way back in 1994. I was allotted the Odisha (then Orissa) cadre and got posted to Hindol in the Dhenkanal district, one of the remote subdivisions in the state. With every person that I met in my subdivision and beyond, I learnt something new about the nuances of the administration. Moving from village to village, looking into the quality of the implementation of government programmes, uplifting the morale of the government officials at the ground level and spending many a night in villages to comprehend rural lives better became a way of life. From being a district magistrate/collector to a municipal commissioner and secretary (Education and Rural Development departments), to being the joint secretary in the Ministry of Rural Development, Government of India (GoI), these challenging assignments as an administrative officer made me learn as well as unlearn several things. After 25 years of a very fulfilling career as a bureaucrat, I can say with all humility and absolute clarity that policies cannot transform the lives of people unless they are implemented effectively.

Recently, I came across an old cover story in a leading Indian magazine titled 'Bloated Babudom', which noted that bureaucracy 'is worse than a corpse, as it resists change, fails to deliver even elementary services and costs too much'.[1] This made me wonder as to what went wrong and where, that a leading magazine was compelled to have a cover story on inefficient bureaucracy! Over a period of time, bureaucracy has come to be perceived as bloated, self-serving, corrupt, apathetic and indifferent to the needs of the common man. This perception is further reinforced by various instances of harassment, indifference and corrupt practices in various public offices—from the police station to the patwari's office[2], from the forest department and the transport office to various tax departments. It is certainly time to think things through and go for mid-course corrections.

Today, India is one of the fastest-growing economies in the

---

[1]Sumit Mitra and Prabhu Chawla, 'The Babu Burden,' *India Today*, 5 February 2001.

[2]'Patwari' is a term used commonly in north and central India. It refers to an individual in the local authority who maintains the ownership records for a specific area as well as undertakes the collection of land taxes.

world. Its geopolitical influence is growing rapidly, and the views of India's leaders and the actions of its citizens are increasingly becoming instrumental in shaping the future of a global society.

At this juncture, when we are aspiring to be a US$5-trillion economy by 2025, our aspiration to become the third-most powerful economy in the world, after the United States (US) and China, is hinged on the successful implementation of the policies formulated.

Public administration in India is a British legacy and has several goals. What is tricky is that every time the government changes, so does its goals and priorities. Sardar Vallabhbhai Patel, India's first home minister, famously referred to the administrative services/civil servants as the 'steel frame of India'. He, along with many other stalwarts, perceived the administration as one of the most solid bedrocks on which the rest of the bureaucracy was built, and it has always been expected that it would execute public policies, deliver services to the last man in the hierarchy and be impartial.

It is pertinent to mention here that India's civil services is not overly large by global standards. Table 1 compares it with its international counterparts.

TABLE 1

India's Civil Services vis-à-vis its International Counterparts

Country and Region	Central Government Employees	Non-Central Government Employees	Total Civilian Government*
South Asia Region			
India	0.4	0.4	1.2
Bangladesh	0.4	-	0.6
Pakistan	0.4	0.6	1.5
Sri Lanka	2.8	0.6	4.5

East Asia			
China	0.1	1.6	2.8
Indonesia	0.7	0.3	2.1
Korea	0.6	0.7	2.2
Malaysia	2.3	1.1	4.5
Asia Average**	**0.9**	**0.7**	**2.6**
OECD (Organisation for Economic Co-operation and Development)			
Australia	1.3	2.3	7.6
France	2.7	2.2	7.0
Japan	0.7	1.2	3.2
United Kingdom	1.3	2.2	7.0
United States	1.2	3.2	7.1
OECD Average*	**1.8**	**2.5**	**7.7**

Source: The World Bank

* In addition to Central and non-Central government employees, Total Civilian Government includes employees from the education and health sectors.

** The Asia and OECD averages are region-wide and include other countries in addition to those cited here.

In order to reform its public administration system, the Indian government constituted the first Administrative Reforms Commission (ARC) in 1966 and reconstituted it in 2009, to recommend changes that could be incorporated to make the administrative system fit for fulfilling the social and economic policies of the government. The pay commissions set up by the government to make necessary improvements in the salary structure have also emphasized the need for reforms and efficiency in our administrative machinery.

Administrative Reforms in Future

As India enters the threshold of a middle-income economy, it is imperative that its public institutions play a more proactive role in governance and the officials manning these institutions display the highest levels of professional competence and probity. Many of our public institutions such as the Election Commission of India (ECI) and the National Disaster Response Force (NDRF), among others, have shown tremendous ability to deliver despite all odds and I am quite optimistic that with the right vision and the right direction, all our public institutions can show exemplary results. I would consider the following interventions as key to administrative reforms.

Merit-based Selection Process Combined with Continuous Capacity-building

The importance of merit-based entry into public services cannot be overemphasized. While the Union Public Service Commission (UPSC) has managed to keep the standard of the selection process fairly high, the same cannot be said for other selection agencies at the central and state levels which may be recruiting more than 95 per cent of the officials for various public offices. Bringing a certain degree of rigour, transparency and honesty in the selection process at each level is crucial. Equally important is the fact that many officials tend to lose motivation and commitment for public service after getting recruited. Therefore, a system that is capable of an objective evaluation of an officer's performance—one that provides the required training and capacity-building in his/her area of competence and offers the right kind of non-financial incentives—is crucial for maintaining competency levels in public services. Laying emphasis on smart governance by redirecting the focus to human resource development (HRD) and training is an important step to bring about the requisite change in the system. Skilling its employees and their skill upgradation at regular intervals will help ensure consistent performance that enables accomplishing of the desired objectives in a time-bound and efficient manner.

Measurable Standards for Performance Evaluation

Given the large number of public officials, measuring the standards of performance is often difficult. Therefore, the typical bell curve, which is common in any organization, is not very evident in the governmental system, where more than 80 per cent of the officials are found to be highly competent during the annual performance appraisal by their superiors. This provides a distorted picture of the real standards of the officials and tends to provide a platform wherein they have the comfort of an assured career progression without having to strive too hard for it. This can demotivate some of the high-performing officers, who find colleagues with ordinary competence and high dishonesty progressing equally well, or at times, even doing better career-wise. Thus, bringing in true measurable standards and strict adherence by reporting authorities in performance appraisal of administrative officials is crucial.

The Use of Technology

The use of technologies such as Artificial Intelligence (AI), blockchain, Internet of Things (IoT), virtual reality and augmented reality is becoming ubiquitous in the present-day world. The professors sitting in Washington DC are able to interact with students in San Francisco or Berkeley in a real classroom environment despite the geographical distance. Machine learning and AI are able to customize the educational requirements of specific students in accordance with his/her learning levels and accordingly, deliver educational materials that a person can absorb.

Blockchain technology is taking financial services to a level where the integrity of financial transaction is absolutely secure and trustworthy. It is essential for us to use technology for various kinds of service delivery to ensure transparency and to bring in the much-needed efficiency in public services.

Technology, if used correctly, has the capability to transform public-service delivery, and also to fill in the absence of a large number of extension officials or field officials in sectors such as health, education, agriculture and so on. Pilots in India have made use of drone-based technology to capture images of standing crops. They also analyse the hyperspectral images using AI and provide advisory to the farmers about the pesticides to be used and the intervals at which pesticide spray and irrigation are to be done. All of this is being done without anybody having to visit the agricultural field. Thus, creating the required infrastructure for these kinds of emerging technologies (e.g., implementation of 5G platform to allow AI and IoT to be more effective), creating the required manpower that is trained in the use of these technologies and customizing these technologies to address some of the important socio-economic gaps in our society will be key components of administrative reforms in future.

Quantity and Quality Aspects in Public Service

Public officials have taken an unfair share of the criticism in spite of the fact that we have a disproportionately low number of public officials to deliver different kinds of services. India compares poorly with many developed economies when it comes to nurses, doctors, agriculture scientists and police officials per lakh of population. In the health sector, our doctor–population ratio (1:1,457) is lower than the World Health Organization (WHO) norm of 1:1,000[1]

[1]PTI, 'India has One Doctor for Every 1,457 Citizens: Govt,' *Business Standard*, 4 July 2019, https://www.business-standard.com/article/pti-stories/india-has-one-

and we are short of approximately 1.94 million nurses[1]. The shortage of staff further aggravates the problem in day-to-day implementation of programmes, resulting in a long-term crisis. Our police personnel number is also not very promising. We have 151 police personnel per lakh of population, which is 71 less against the ratio prescribed by the United Nations (UN).[2]

Similarly, many departments are so overburdened with different responsibilities without having corresponding budget that the major share of allocation goes in establishment expenses (e.g., the school and higher-education departments in most states end up spending the lion's share in salaries and establishment expenses) and consequently, the quality of service delivery becomes a big casualty. There is an urgent need to bring out some degree of rationalization in the establishment expenses of the departments and the need for apportioning certain percentages of the allocation to improve the quality of infrastructure and the service delivered. A rationalization exercise in this regard must put an upper limit on the establishment expense for different categories of public service delivery, while earmarking the balance for improving the infrastructure and quality of services.

Higher Accountability of Public Servants

Many anecdotes, newspaper articles and complaints from public representatives as well as common people refer to the indifference,

---

doctor-for-every-1-457-citizens-govt-119070401127_1.html, last accessed on 28 August 2020.

[1]IndiaSpend, 'India Short Of Nearly Two Million Nurses,' NDTV, 12 May 2017, https://everylifecounts.ndtv.com/india-short-nearly-two-million-nurses-13129, last accessed on 28 August 2020.

[2]PTI, 'There Is a Shortage of Police Personnel, Govt Tells Lok Sabha,' *The Hindu*, 6 March 2028, https://www.thehindu.com/news/national/there-is-a-shortage-of-police-personnel-govt-tells-lok-sabha/article22946907.ece, last accessed on 28 August 2020.

apathy, sloth and dishonesty among public officials. The need for greater accountability cannot be overemphasized and an exercise in this regard has been done in various countries. Apart from the use of technologies, citizen's charters have been brought out by many departments specifying the timelines within which specific services will have to be provided.

As commissioner of the Bhubaneswar Municipal Corporation, we released a citizen's charter with 21 activities and prescribed time frames. The implementation of this charter brought about a very high degree of accountability in the system.

Although many departments and agencies have come up with citizen's charter, in the absence of monitoring and supervision, implementation of such promises has been observed only in breach. We need to look for mechanisms through which accountability is monitored on a real-time basis and public officials are forced to provide an account for delay, negligence or ulterior motive in not performing an assigned duty. A few instruments were designed to bring in greater accountability and transparency, but they have led to unnecessary demands on public officials. For instance, it has been seen over time that the Right to Information Act (RTI) has burdened public officials with innumerable requests for information, without really serving the purpose for which it was enacted in the first place.

While working as secretary in the School Education department in Odisha, we operated a 12-hour student helpline, which was professionally managed and had a clear-cut target. Meant for both students and parents, the goal of the helpline was to ensure higher accountability of teachers, punishment-free classrooms, joyful learning and a safe environment for children in school. This was a much-needed and a widely acclaimed initiative in improving governance in school education.

Strengthening of Financial Management and Social Audit

Public officials have to always keep in mind that government expenditure is done with taxpayers' money and hence, the need for them to maintain the highest levels of probity. The fact that they are spending taxpayers' money will have to be reinforced at each level of the government. The recent instances of many banks lending to doubtful projects on the basis of overvalued/inflated project cost, inflating the value of collaterals and taking a kickback for lending huge amounts in spite of knowing that it will become a non-performing asset, is a gross injustice to the trust of depositors, who deposit their hard-earned money with the bank. Similar is the case of public officials who expect returns in cash or kind for providing services/benefits, a legitimate work for which they get a salary as public servants.

I recollect my team's efforts in the Ministry of Rural Development, GoI, towards bringing in the concept of social audit in the implementation of the Mahatma Gandhi National Rural Employment Guarantee Scheme (MGNREGS) across the states in 2015. We introduced the National Electronic Fund Management System (NeFMS), through which all payments—wages and material components—were directly transferred to the accounts of labourers/vendors and all these payments were in the public domain. These reforms facilitated the implementation of MGNREGS.

Thus, streamlining the financial management systems, ensuring digital transaction and an uncompromising stand against corruption will lead to increased transparency and honesty in administration. Similarly, for many of the government schemes under implementation, a properly conducted social audit would ensure selection of the right beneficiary and proper implementation of the schemes.

Harmony between the Legislative and Executive Wings of Administration

The history of public service is replete with references to political interference and issues of committed bureaucracy, which refers to subservience to the ruling political masters instead of serving the rule of law. This tug of war between the political masters and permanent bureaucracy has resulted in deteriorating public services' quality, rather than improving it. Over the years, the political representatives, whose primary mandate was to focus on legislations and raising the issues of their constituents at the right forum, have come to play a more expansive role in view of rising public expectations. Consequently, their interface with different wings of public services has kept on increasing and, at times, has been construed as political interference. I think the time has come to harmonize political expectations with the roles and responsibilities that permanent civil servants have to perform, and identify the common limited denominators which prioritize the interests of the nation and its citizens.

Strengthening Local Governments

While speaking about administrative reforms in our country, it is important to focus on the third tier of governance, which is our local self-government. We have nearly two lakh rural and urban local bodies, of which more than 90 per cent are rural. While we are moving in the right direction with a massive devolution of funds to these bodies as per the recommendations of the 14th Finance Commission, the real challenge lies in improving the capacity of these bodies to deliver a variety of public services and empowering them with regard to the subject areas which they are meant to supervise and monitor. Apart from just funds, our country would also need to capacitate these bodies with trained human resources and create a cadre of professionals that is well-equipped to take on these mounting responsibilities. This is equally true for our urban local bodies, which are few in number in comparison to the rural bodies, but have to tackle multiple pressures of growing migratory population and choked infrastructure. Therefore, administrative reforms would mandatorily need to cover ground on bringing about transformative governance in our gram panchayats and urban local bodies in the modalities of carrying out the functions. These would span across budgeting, provision of services, outreach to households, enhancing accountability, improving community participation and so on.

Conclusion

I strongly believe that India is blessed with the right blend of ecological and human resources and is definitely on the path to emerging as a global economic power. However, this is not possible without aligning a strong political vision with effective implementation processes by the administrative machinery.

While I have listed above some of the key reforms required in the governance sector in India, I would like to reiterate that a strong, impartial and efficient administration is a prerequisite for ensuring socio-economic development, equity and fairness in our society. The requirement of a very robust recruitment system, measurable performance indicators, a continuous capacity-building exercise along with incentives for good performance and disincentives for corruption and inefficiency will have to be built at all levels of administrative hierarchy.

Our governance structure will have to be prepared for the disruptive nature of technologies and take all necessary steps to ensure that administrative machinery is geared to the use of technology for greater public good. An assessment of the areas where government presence is vital and subsequent ceding of the areas to the private sector will also be a key component of the reform measures. This will also be in line with the honourable prime minister's call for 'minimum government, maximum governance'.

The essence of all administrative reforms has been appropriately articulated by our prime minister, Narendra Modi. In his words, '"Citizen-First" is our mantra, our motto and our guiding principle. It has been my dream to bring the government closer to our citizens, so that they become active participants in the governance process.'[1] We all need to collectively strive to actualize this basic 'mantra' of governance.

◆

Aparajita Sarangi is a former Indian Administrative Service officer from the Odisha cadre. Affiliated with the Bharatiya Janata Party, she currently represents Bhubaneswar in the Lok Sabha.

---

[1]https://www.narendramodi.in/mobile/pms-message-to-the-nation-on-good-governance, last accessed 28 August 2020.

7

PROMOTING ENTREPRENEURSHIP IN THE MANUFACTURING SECTOR

LAVU SRI KRISHNA DEVARAYALU[1]

The COVID-19 pandemic and the emerging new economic order have made India acutely aware of its economic vulnerabilities. It is, therefore, a 'do-or-die' situation for India's manufacturing sector. The government needs to assist this sector on a war footing, if it needs to increase blue-collar jobs and insulate its industries from the internal and external fallout of the pandemic. We must approach this issue in the same manner as we tackled the lack of personal protective equipment (PPE) by becoming the world's second-largest manufacturer in a matter of weeks.

India has done well in the field of services. It has been able to produce global brands. Investors and the government have continuously looked to the services sector for profits and job creation, respectively. It is now time that a similarly conducive environment is made for India's manufacturing industry

[1]Assisted by Noel Therattil, Legislative Assistants to Members of Parliament (LAMP) Fellow.

and replicate the success story. The contribution of India's manufacturing sector at just over 16 per cent of India's gross domestic product (GDP) is much below its potential and a cause of concern, especially in the context of other Asian countries in similar stages of development. This calls for a government and policy intervention; therefore, the National Manufacturing Policy must be revisited and updated. Importantly, however, there must be renewed focus on shifting labour from agriculture to the manufacturing sector. The employment of semi-skilled workers in the manufacturing sector would ensure the most efficacious use of human resources and also reduce the dependence on agriculture. Perhaps this way, the government may also address multiple issues in one fell swoop.

Banking and Credit Flow

The government has taken many measures to ensure credit availability to most sectors, including to street vendors. However, other issues are to be addressed. Do public-sector banks have adequate liquidity to fund these schemes at a time when some government establishments are struggling to pay salaries? Are these loans enough to inject liquidity over and beyond what was already required in pre-COVID India? Finally, are banks in a position to cope with the certain increase in non-performing assets (NPAs)?

The availability of credit has been a major hindrance to the micro, small and medium enterprises (MSME) sector, which has been the leading contributor to Indian exports even before the pandemic. According to a June 2019 report of the Reserve Bank of India (RBI), the MSME sector's total addressable demand for external credit has been estimated to be ₹37 lakh crore; however, the overall supply of finance from formal sources is estimated to be

₹14.5 lakh crore. According to the 2019–20 Economic Survey, key industries such as textiles, coal, petroleum, food processing, etc., have seen negative growth in bank credit. The barriers to acquiring credit that have been identified by the RBI are namely lack of risk mitigation for MSMEs, cost to serve and lender coverage. These issues and their solutions are well-known and often discussed, but addressing them requires institutional changes. Identifying credit-worthy entrepreneurs in the MSME sector, especially in areas with low lender coverage, should be the first step. It will also assist in restoring confidence in both lenders and entrepreneurs. Losses to financial institutions from certain credits are to be expected, but they can be addressed by risk-mitigation measures and by the government absorbing some of the initial losses of entrepreneurs, especially from the micro and small sectors.

Pragmatic approach of the financial institutions, for instance in the form of cash flow-based lending or continuous monitoring of data for early warning signs can reduce the chances of creating NPAs and will increase the availability of credit. Unfortunately, the cut in the repo rate to 5.15 per cent, the lowest in nearly a decade, has failed to translate into greater access to credit. A greater proportion of the reduction in repo rate has gone to make NPA-laden banks buoyant.

Quality Manufacturing

Manufacturing in India needs to not only address institutional reforms and achieve economies of scale, but at the same time, be in a position to compete in international markets. Industries need to address quality and phytosanitary standards. Keeping in mind the MSME sector, the government has launched numerous schemes to promote quality and standardization in manufacturing. The Zero Defect Zero Effect (ZED) scheme to develop an ecosystem for quality, upgradation and professionalism is welcome, as it will promote an entrepreneurial ecosystem. The certification process under the scheme for use of quality tools, processes and standardization also gamifies the system to increase competition within the industry. It will permit India to enter a niche market for quality products, thereby becoming competitive and export high-value products.

On the same note, the government introduced the National Manufacturing Competitiveness Programme (NMCP) and ASPIRE in light of the importance of technology in producing standardized quality products. Under the NMCP, capital-linked subsidy schemes seek to provide 15 per cent subsidy for additional investment of up to ₹1 crore for technology upgradation of micro and small enterprises, thereby promoting the use of state-of-the-art technology, which can in turn, increase the productive capacity of these enterprises and also ensure standardization of products.

For India to play 'catch up', it will need to stand apart. Therefore, in the long run, continued and aggressive emphasis must be laid on quality management standards and quality technology tools.

Ease of Doing Business

In a post-COVID world where both protectionism and competition will increase, companies will look to creating multiple hubs. India must, therefore, make itself an attractive destination. It must not only prove itself as a cheaper alternative but as a market-friendly, liberally regulated and quality destination.

India was among the most notable countries to improve its Ease of Doing Business rankings in 2019. It jumped 14 places to be ranked 63rd in the World Bank ranking with a DB score of 71. However, there are certain areas where India must do better to create proper institutions and strengthen existing procedure. For instance, India has been lagging behind in 'starting a business'. The plethora of tedious nuances and obstacles has not permitted the development of an atmosphere conducive to doing business. The marginal improvement has largely been attributed to the government's decision to abolish filing fees for the electronic pro forma for incorporating a company, memorandum of association and article of association. Similarly, India has fared poorly in paying taxes. This would also explain the government introducing an optional new tax regime in the recent budget. Whether creating new tax slabs for those foregoing exemptions and deductions will incentivize potential taxpayers to come forward and pay taxes, needs to be watched carefully.

India also fairs poorly on 'enforcing contracts' primarily. Firstly, this is due to the high pendency rate in courts. In fact, nearly 88 per cent of all pending cases are in the subordinate courts. To address this, 100 per cent clearance rate must be achieved, which would be possible after the addition of nearly 2,300 judges in the lower courts and 100 in the higher courts. The fact that it takes over 1,400 days for a contract to be enforced in India is counter-intuitive to the government's initiatives to open doors to businesses.

The government has sought to address the apprehension amongst entrepreneurs by introducing the Nirvik scheme, which seeks to prove export credit insurance. Whether it will truly be able to revive exports and reassure entrepreneurs is unclear. The uncertainty surrounding other export schemes, especially the Merchandise Exports from India Scheme (MEIS), is likely to deter investors and entrepreneurs from establishing or conducting business from India. This is also symptomatic of the many flip-flops in India's trade policy, which is often difficult to anticipate and dissuades entrepreneurs from making long-term investments in the country. Further, reforming the lower bureaucracy will ensure that policies are implemented as envisaged and smoothly executed.

Research and Development

Research will boost every aspect of the Indian economy. Unfortunately, India has been lagging behind in research and development (R&D). It has largely been remitted as an outsource destination rather than an innovator. Unlike in advanced countries, funding for R&D has primarily been secured from public expenditure. According to the 'R&D Expenditure Ecosystem Report', despite the fact that R&D in India is heavily reliant on public funding, funding has been stagnant at 0.6 per cent to 0.7 per cent of GDP.[1] In comparison, the US and China spend 2.8 per cent and 2.1 per cent of their GDP on research respectively. To make up for this, the government must aggressively pursue technology transfer agreements while using its huge market potential as a bargaining chip. The government must hardball potential investors to share technology. At the same time, it must also restore their confidence by enforcing intellectual property (IP) rights. Technology transfer will allow India to attain international manufacturing standards and provide support for other allied industries while reducing the need for excessive capital and R&D.

The government must focus on promoting R&D in areas which can have a multiplier effect and assist Indian entrepreneurs develop indigenous solutions to sui generis issues. Finally, if India is to compete in the global market in the near future, it must

[1]PTI, 'India's R&D Spend Stagnant for 20 years at 0.7% of GDP,' *The Economic Times*, 29 January 2018, https://economictimes.indiatimes.com/news/economy/finance/indias-rd-spend-stagnant-for-20-years-at-0-7-of-gdp/articleshow/62697271.cms?from=mdr, last accessed on 14 October 2020.

adopt the Chinese example. The government needs to bite the bullet and sufficiently protect its entrepreneurs, incubate their ideas and create an atmosphere that is conducive to their growth. In times where protectionism is at a high, to take the moral high ground would be akin to playing the role of the greater fool.

◆

Lavu Sri Krishna Devarayalu is a first-time Member of Parliament from the Narasaraopet constituency of the Yuvajana Sramika Rythu Congress Party.

8

TECHNOLOGY AND DIGITAL INDIA

SAPTAGIRI SANKAR ULAKA

When the lockdown was announced in March 2020 as a response to contain the spread of COVID-19, many of us were stuck in Delhi, not knowing what's in store next. Being a Member of Parliament (MP) representing the constituents, it was important to continue business as usual, and reach out to the constituents and the administration, ensuring that we support people and keep the machinery running. Within a couple of days, it all settled down with a new norm of work, which would likely be a permanent feature for some in the future. Social distancing, video messages, video conferencing, work from home (WFH), social media, coordination on WhatsApp and so on have become the 'new normal'. The wheels running this business are evidently the advancement of technology and the various facets of Digital India. During the lockdown, the Indian information technology (IT) industry made employees WFH as per the government's mandate, resulting in about 90 per cent of employees working remotely.

We intervened in parliament and asked Prime Minister Narendra Modi (during his reply to the Motion of Thanks on the President's address) to talk on how he plans to address the problem of unemployment. He responded that the quantum computing allocation of ₹8,000 crore in the budget would help address this issue, amongst other things.[1] The government's response looked questionable and was devoid of details. Not too long ago, Rajiv Gandhi had come up with a computer and telecom road map and there were similar doubts in the minds of the principal Opposition. Gandhi was ridiculed, especially by the opposition parties when he stressed on the importance of computers. However, the naysayers were proven wrong with time.

We don't want to be seen in the same lenses as Gandhi's then opponents in the future, as people would then judge us for being short-sighted. As a young parliamentarian connected to the grassroots, coming from a tribal region with aspirational districts, the primary issue for me is not the sagging economy or the gross domestic product (GDP) numbers, but rather the huge unemployment prevailing in my constituency. Technology has always been an enabler in solving important problems and I'm sure that this would help in the long run, as we have seen in the past. However, technology itself without thoughtful policy interventions is as good as having a vehicle without fuel—a non-starter. The computer and telecom revolution of the 1980s was followed by the liberalization policies of the 1990s that enabled IT giants with a global delivery model and helped other industries thrive. Successive governments understood the importance of science and technology and laid the foundation for this transformation, which is being leveraged in building a New India—an India that is at the forefront in all spheres. This would attract not only

[1]Mohana Basu, 'What is Modi Govt's "Quantum Mission" that Has Been Allocated Rs8,000 cr in Budget 2020,' The Print, 1 February 2020, https://theprint.in/economy/modi-govt-allocates-rs-8000-crore-for-high-risk-quantum-mission-in-budget-2020/358208/, last accessed on 15 October 2020.

investors across the globe, but also the best minds doing research and providing solutions to global problems.

In his address at the Indian Science Congress on 26 December 1937, Pandit Jawaharlal Nehru stated: 'It is science alone that can solve the problems of hunger and poverty, of insanitation and illiteracy, of superstition and deadening custom and tradition, of vast resources running to waste, of a rich country inhabited by starving people… The future belongs to science and to those who make friends with science.'

As we got Independence, there was an absolute necessity to build infrastructure from scratch to harness science for the benefit of society at large. Nehru galvanized important scientists of the time, including Homi J. Bhabha, Sir C.V. Raman, Satish Dhawan, J.C. Ghosh, Meghnad Saha and S.S. Bhatnagar, and gave them a free hand in setting up institutes such as the Atomic Energy Commission (AEC), which subsequently became the foundation stones of India's scientific research and temperament. It was his vision that saw the inception and establishment of some of the most important and socially relevant technology hubs of the country. Five Indian Institutes of Technology (IITs) were established on the recommendation of the Sarkar Committee throughout the length and breadth of the country. Steps were also taken to increase India's capacity in the production of defence equipment, so that India could gradually become self-sufficient. The Defence Research and Development Organisation (DRDO) was set up for research in the manufacture of missiles, armaments, explosives and other defence-related inventory. India was one of the first nations to recognize the importance of nuclear energy.

Similarly, Rajiv Gandhi gave a lot of importance to science and technology. He brought in computers and spoke of liberalization. The telecom industry witnessed a breakthrough under his government with the initiation of the Mahanagar Telephone

Nigam Limited (MTNL) in 1986. He was hailed as the father of the IT and telecom revolution of India, as it was during his time that the Centre for Development of Telematics (C-DOT) and public call office (PCO) booths were established. With the initiation of economic liberalization in 1991—with the goal of making the economy more market- and service-oriented, and expanding the role of private and foreign investments—essential policy interventions with technology levers became proponents of high economic growth for the country.

Technology and Digital India have found prominence in the policies and intent of the current government. The Government of India has initiated the Digital India programme with the vision of transforming India into a digitally empowered society and knowledge economy. Of the 22 schemes that were announced to transform India into a digitally empowered country, some have clicked, some have not. BharatNet (also known as Bharat Broadband Network Limited) is one such ambitious initiative to trigger a broadband revolution in rural India. This project aims to connect all the 2,50,000 gram panchayats in the country and provide them 100 Mbps connectivity. Aadhaar provides a 12-digit biometric and demography-based identity that is unique, lifelong, online and authenticable.

The Common Services Centres, which are kiosks for delivery of G2C services such as birth certificate, marriage certificate, etc., are being opened at each of the 2,50,000 gram panchayats. So far, 3.05 lakh such centres are functional and are providing eServices, including services related to banking and finance to rural citizens.

Cloud computing is another area that is being explored. The government embarked upon an ambitious initiative known as MeghRaj to utilize and harness the benefits of cloud computing. This will ensure accelerating the delivery of eServices in the country and optimizing information and communications technology (ICT) spending of the government. To fast-track the adoption of cloud computing, the government has empanelled cloud service offerings of the 13 cloud service providers under different deployment models viz. public cloud, virtual private cloud and the government community cloud. Digital Locker provides an ecosystem with a collection of repositories and gateways for issuers to upload documents in the digital repositories. As of 2019, 2.36 crore documents have been uploaded by 1.91 crore registered users of DigiLocker,[1] yet we see that documents uploaded are hardly utilized in various services/institutions—be it universities or banks, as many still depend and rely on a paper trail. Direct benefit transfers (DBTs) are showing tremendous results. An amount of more than ₹6.06 lakh crore has been transferred through DBT and the ministries/departments have reported savings of ₹1,09,983 crore in the last three years due to the implementation of schemes in DBT mode.

Online Registration System (ORS) under e-Hospital, Open Government Data (OGD) platform, eTaal web portal, Government e-Marketplace (GeM), e-District Mission Mode Project (MMP), digital life certificate for pensioners known as Jeevan Pramaan, National Scholarships Portal (NSP) and the National Center of Geo-informatics (NCoG) project are various other digitization initiatives of the government.

The Digital India Land Records Modernization Programme (DILRMP), the erstwhile National Land Records Modernization Programme, seeks to improve the quality of land records in the country and make them more accessible and also develop a centralized land record management system. Karnataka was the first state in India to computerize land records, under the Bhoomi

[1]Ministry of Electronics and Information Technology, Government of India, http://loksabhahindiph.nic.in/Members/QResult16.aspx?qref=78895, last accessed 15 October 2020.

Project, followed by Andhra Pradesh and Tamil Nadu. By January 2020, the government had achieved over 90 per cent of digitization of land records. Out of the identified 6,55,959 villages, land records have been computerized in 90.1 per cent or 5,91,221 villages across the country. For continuous feedback and participatory governance, the Rapid Assessment System (RAS) and MyGov have been conceived. The RAS is leveraged for continuous feedback for e-Services delivered by the central and state governments. MyGov aims to facilitate a dialogue between citizens and the government, thus bringing them closer to each other.

UMANG has been developed as a single mobile platform to deliver major government services with a core platform integrated with Aadhaar, DigiLocker, PayGov India and RAS. Also, the government has implemented two schemes for digital literacy, namely National Digital Literacy Mission (NDLM) with a target of training 10 lakh persons and Digital Saksharta Abhiyan (DISHA) with a target of training 42.5 lakh persons, covering one person per family. These schemes were implemented concurrently across the country and a total of 53.67 lakh candidates have been trained and certified. The Pradhan Mantri Gramin Digital Saksharta Abhiyan (PMGDISHA) was introduced to usher in digital literacy in rural India by covering 6 crore rural households (one person per household). These schemes were envisioned to provide training especially in rural areas and bridge the digital gap.

If we look at the COVID-19 situation, it is heartening to see that states are leveraging technology to combat the pandemic. They are mapping COVID-19 positive cases using geographic information system (GIS), tracking healthcare workers using global positioning system (GPS) and finalizing containment plans with the help of heat mapping technologies. Tamil Nadu, for instance, has hired Garuda, a Chennai-based start-up, for the sanitization of hospitals through drones. The state-built Aarogya Setu app is supposed to be a game changer in helping citizens identify the risk of contracting the novel coronavirus. However, in the absence of meaningful anti-surveillance, privacy or data protection laws, it raises many questions rather than helping achieve its objectives. The main concerns lie around the data—how it will be handled, on sunset clauses for the data and assurance that it will not be repurposed post the pandemic. With the new digital landscape, we would need to be careful about data being shared, lest it's misused. The 1885 Telegraph Act is still in use; the questions around spyware Pegasus haven't been answered completely and it's really important for the government to urgently come up with robust data protection laws that will douse speculations on data protection, privacy violations and surveillance.

Most of the initiatives have not been successful due to the massive requirement of overhauling infrastructure, implementation issues, involved behavioural change and the digital divide in the country.

According to some estimates, nearly 80 per cent of our graduates (churned out in lakhs every year) lack essential skills and are unemployed. We are talking about one nation one grid, but huge losses are suffered by power firms during transmission across the various grids in the country. Research and development (R&D) is one area where the country is lagging even as the best brains in the country are contributing to research and industrial development outside the country. Our educational institutes and universities are not in sync with industry requirements; we lack entrepreneurial instincts; and students are let down due to poor infrastructure, opportunities and a secured future. Connecting the dots, bridging gaps and unleashing our true potential need to be prioritized. Technology, research, digital infrastructure, nurturing entrepreneurship, increasing risk appetite, access to resources and bridging the digital divide are some of the key areas that will shape the country's growth story.

In this world of connectivity, internet and mobile connectivity should be declared as part of a fundamental right—the right to connectivity. Universal access to mobile connectivity, broadband for rural and urban areas and public internet access programme under the National Rural Internet Mission are some of the key areas for the current government to focus on. However, we have seen little progress on that front with low teledensity in most of the rural areas. Unless right to connectivity is enacted as an act of parliament, we would continue to proceed at a slow pace with no accountability. Like right to food and right to education, right to connectivity should be enacted to ensure rapid progress and timely allocation of necessary funds to achieve the same. Connecting rural citizens digitally and providing internet access to every nook and corner of the country should be the basic foundation to build on in the next set of innovations.

Our education system needs a complete makeover. Creativity, innovation, problem-solving and, most importantly, relevance to the ecosystem should be prioritized. Even in top universities, we hardly find any substantive research, the curriculum is outdated and science becomes more of a cramming exercise rather than understanding the concepts in depth. We have thousands of mediocre and namesake schools, colleges and now universities that do not even meet the minimum standards. We need to embrace internet and technology to teach our huge population, the majority of which is located in remote villages. Even today, as a response to the COVID-19-induced lockdown, there are many initiatives to ensure continuity in education/studies and to minimize the impact on education. Various e-learning portals and apps have been launched such as DIKSHA portal, e-Pathshala, Swayam, STEM-based games, etc. We will need to invest heavily in technological infrastructure and shift more towards the e-class model, leveraging smartphones and computers connected by a high-speed internet connection. In our engineering colleges and research universities, one glaring feature is that the curriculum or the research material is irrelevant at times and most of our graduates need additional training to make them productive in jobs. The curriculum should be redone and inputs should be sought from industry leaders, businesses and/or target job markets, so that the students are industry-ready when they graduate.

The medical tourism industry is growing at an 18 per cent compound annual growth rate (CAGR) year on year and was expected to be worth US$9 billion by 2020, almost 20 per cent of the global medical tourism market share. We are one of the earliest countries to adopt medical technology. Recently, the Hyderabad-based Indian Institute of Chemical Technology (CSIR-IICT) has synthesized the key starting materials (KSMs) for Remdesivir, the first step to developing the active pharmaceutical ingredient in a drug. Remdesivir, manufactured by Gilead Sciences, is the first drug to treat COVID-19, which has been approved for emergency use in the US based on clinical data. KSMs for Remdesivir are readily available in India and we can manufacture these while sourcing other reagents. India is part of the World Health Organization's (WHO) Solidarity Trials for the cure of COVID-19 and has received 1,000+ doses of the drug for testing. Several Indian technology companies are actively harnessing analytics and artificial intelligence (AI) to simulate drug trials for a faster turnaround. Also, to accelerate the rate of testing, the Indian Institute of Technology (IIT) Alumni Council has launched a test bus that can reduce the cost of testing by over 80 per cent without compromising on testing capacity. This involves e-Vehicles for contactless sample collection, telemedicine, AI-based teleradiology, algorithm-based pooled genetic testing and mega labs capable of 5 million tests per month. During the government-organized hackathon, Team 132, a start-up, developed a UV disinfectant robot that can autonomously disinfect surfaces using UV light while another team designed a remotely operable ventilator system built from consumer durable components. Highly skilled doctors and medical professionals, world-class hospital infrastructure, cost-effective treatment and personalized care are some of the reasons for the fast growth of the medical tourism industry in India. On the other hand, we have seen a shortage of doctors and hospitals in many rural areas, which is a cause of concern. While we have the right and cost-effective talent, we would need to connect our hospitals and medical fraternity and share best practices and data to work on a comprehensive policy to make India the medical destination of the world.

The Smart Cities Mission leverages digital and information technologies, urban planning's best practices, public–private partnerships and policy change to make a difference. The objective is to promote cities that provide core infrastructure and give a decent quality of life to its citizens, a clean and sustainable environment and application of 'smart' solutions with a focus on sustainable and inclusive development. This sets examples that can be replicated and encourages the creation of similar prototypes in various regions and parts of the country. This has huge potential and the way forward would be to hand over the blueprint or development to local entrepreneurs through the request for proposal (RFP) process with the necessary allocation of funds and a free hand in developing the city. In addition to this, Smart Panchayats would enable the development of rural areas and at the same time encourage the crowdsourcing of ideas, an innovation that is community-driven and based on localized problem-solving.

The way forward would be to actively encourage the industry–academia collaboration and build on various policy interventions from successive governments as well as leverage available infrastructure to build a New India that is a leader and go-to destination in science and technology. Unfortunately, we are a country that has a large digital divide and unless we come up with a comprehensive plan to close the gaps, the true potential will be difficult to realize. Collaboration, crowdsourcing and making everyone partners in the technology success journey are the keys to progress on this front. We have great minds who have already established their credentials outside the country, and if we could attract them back with opportunities, it would help expedite our development.

One solution doesn't solve all—the same applies for education, employment issues and technology adaptation. Necessary policy interventions, adequate infrastructure and resource availability are crucial. We should try and leverage the available assets and large pool of human resources to work towards continual innovations, skill development and goal-oriented programmes to achieve the India that we are envisioning. Most of the achievements this far have been due to individual brilliance, but imagine what we will be able to achieve if we can collaborate our vast resource pool clubbed with technology/policy interventions and make it a mass movement. 'India Tomorrow' would then not only exceed our expectations, but we would be global leaders in solving problems, improving productivity and contributing to inventions. We should aspire to be an India where we build the best of satellites, become pioneers in astronomy and every citizen is able to avail technology benefits, be it to increase productivity in farming or use smart solutions for our daily needs.

The only challenge is that we tend to get lost in blueprinting and storytelling; we should rather work from scratch to come up with a comprehensive plan to achieve our goals. With our talent pool and time-bound policy interventions from successive governments, we would definitely be able to achieve our goals.

◆

Saptagiri Sankar Ulaka was elected to the Lok Sabha from Koraput, Odisha in the 17th Lok Sabha as a member of the Indian National Congress.

9

INDIA'S TRYST WITH SPORTING EXCELLENCE

KIREN RIJIJU

If we were to rewind to an era when the Indian men's hockey team remained unbeaten in the Olympic Games six times in a row, one would have to admit that India showed early signs of promise to dominate certain parts of the international sporting landscape. We were ambitious in hosting the first-ever Asian Games in 1951, just four years after Independence. These games were largely driven by the idea of decolonized states, led by India, marching forward to take their rightful place. Significant infrastructure was developed for the games that had 11 countries, with around 500 athletes taking part. These games were the gateway for India to be noticed at the international stage. In 1982, India once again became host to the Asian Games, which became a seminal moment for India and the Asian sporting fraternity.

In the layered build-up of our sporting culture, the 1982 Asian Games would act as the much-needed foundation. Appu, the Games mascot, who also played the role of the daily messenger on Indian national television, literally took sport to Indian drawing rooms. As host broadcaster, the information and broadcasting ministry was forced to introduce colour television broadcasting that revolutionized the way Indians consumed sport and television. Delhi was infused with immense amounts of world-class infrastructure: five new stadiums, seven new flyovers, two luxury hotels and around 300 km of roads renovated. At a time when getting a phone connection was a rare privilege, Delhi got 12,000 new phone lines; power distribution was upgraded and Delhiites began getting an extra 15 million gallons of water daily with the Ganga–Yamuna Link. In just 14 days of the competition, 33 countries took part with close to 3,500 athletes, and an incredible 74 Asian Games and Asian records were shattered.

Keeping the 1982 Asian Games as a reference point, I would like to draw attention to some crucial data points to throw light on how Asian countries such as China, Japan and South Korea have emerged as sporting powerhouses. Between the 1982 and 2014 Asian Games, China increased its medal count from 153 to 345 (125 per cent), Japan from 153 to 200 (30 per cent) and South Korea from 93 to 228 (145 per cent), whereas India has remained at 57 medals. The essential point to note here is that the number of sporting events had nearly tripled in the 2014 Asian Games, in comparison to the 1982 Asian Games and India could not capitalize on the opportunity of expansion provided. Thus, in 2014, when Prime Minister Narendra Modi got a resounding mandate, sports was made a key area of focus, and structural changes in India's sporting ecosystem were devised with the vision of making India a sporting superpower.

The pivotal point in ensuring that India becomes a sporting superpower is to increase participation at the grass-roots level. A wide participation base will ensure that there is a good number of children who continue to play sport professionally. Sports currently being a state subject, the central government has encouraged states to take initiatives to ensure that awareness on sports percolates down to the last household and that they incentivize participation in sports. The Government of India is working closely with all the states on a state-specific sports plan, where each state is being promoted to identify sports in which athletes in the state excel naturally. Another necessary step is developing high-quality teachers and coaches to engage with children taking up sports from across the country. The Sports Authority of India (SAI) is in the process of developing a coaches' curriculum to be used as a standard guideline for teachers and coaches across the country. This curriculum will be up to date with the best practices from across the world and is going to be designed such that it is easy to understand and adopt.

Our government understands that for India to do well at tournaments such as the Olympic Games, Asian Games, Commonwealth Games, etc., there needs to be a transformation in the way we accept and understand sports. Culturally, Indians must engage with sports at a very intimate level, if we want to gain presence at the global stage. Though we have a long way to go, it is pleasant to note that a lot has changed for the better in the Indian society. There is a heightened awareness amongst parents, who encourage children to take up sports. Thanks to television and social media platforms, sports other than cricket have gained popularity in India. We now have many sporting celebrities over and above cricket. Athletes from sports such as shooting, weightlifting, boxing, wrestling, hockey, archery, athletics, table tennis, etc., have emerged from small towns and become household names.

The Khelo India Scheme, with the objective of infusing a sporting culture and achieving sporting excellence in the country, has played a vital role in the past three years. Not only has the scheme provided a platform for raw talent to emerge from across the country, it also aims at identifying talent from the grass-roots level. Providing financial assistance to meritorious athletes, it has assisted in setting up of over a hundred sports academies and provided support to increase access to good-quality sports infrastructure in rural and urban areas of India. The blueprint for a multi-tier academy system is in its final stages, where beginner and intermediate-level athletes will be trained in SAI centres and Khelo India academies, and advanced-level athletes will be trained at National Centres of Excellence (NCOEs). The citizen-driven Fit India initiative, which was launched in August 2019 by the honourable prime minister, has gained extreme popularity. The initiative has a 34+ crore organic reach digitally and over 6.5 crore people participated in the recently concluded Fit India Freedom Run. This goes to show that awareness towards an active and fit lifestyle is on the rise in India. Thus, the starting point for becoming a sporting superpower rests on creating a cultural understanding and acceptance of sports, which we are rapidly enhancing through the Khelo India and Fit India schemes.

The Tokyo Olympics and Paralympics have been postponed to July 2021; it will soon become the most-talked-about event in newsrooms as well as our drawing rooms. Achieving success at the Olympic Games requires a very targeted and technical approach, which cannot happen overnight. The SAI's Target Olympic Podium Scheme (TOPS) focuses on high-performance sports where we provide the best assistance to our elite athletes. International training exposure, world-class physical and mental conditioning, scientific research, day-to-day monitoring and counselling and ample financial assistance have been provided to the 179 athletes covered under TOPS (95 in the core group, 84 in the developing group), so that the athletes can channelize all their efforts towards winning Olympic gold medals. The TOPS team, which consists of subject matter experts such as sports data analysts, sports science specialists and athlete relationship managers, has also formulated a plan called TOPS Junior, where the youngest of the athletes showing potential will be identified and groomed for the 2024, 2028 and 2032 Olympics Games. Sports science centres being established across the country will provide state-of-the-art technical assistance to our athletes, to take their performance to the next level. Synergy between various national sports federations (NSFs), the Indian Olympic Association, SAI and the Ministry of Youth Affairs and Sports has been on point and an athlete-centric approach has been adopted for all governance and management matters. Corporate houses will be made to complement our efforts and adopt a sport under the One Sport, One Corporate initiative so as to ensure our athletes have the best shot at achieving success at the Olympic Games.

The COVID-19 situation did not deter our government from continuing to actively support the sporting community. About 3,000 of our Khelo India athletes were provided with ₹30,000 each as out-of-pocket allowances during the lockdown (amounting to ₹8.25 crore). Our athlete relationship managers have been in constant touch with each of the TOPS athletes to cater to any kind of difficulty faced by them due to the pandemic. Periodic mentoring and counselling have been provided to every TOPS athlete to navigate through these challenging times. The ministry and SAI, in collaboration with the NSFs, have organized national camps in a bio-bubble environment, keeping the safety of our athletes as the highest priority. Special standard operating procedures (SOPs) have been drafted in consultation with experts for the timely restart of sporting activity (training) across the nation.

The sports fanatic in me must admit that India's sporting future looks bright, with the government adopting a two-pronged approach of creating an enhanced cultural awareness and acceptance towards sports, along with a focused preparation and planning for high-performance sports. The day is not far when India will be considered a sporting superpower at the global stage. I am positive that to get to this stage, our society will truly embrace sports and physical activity such that we march ever closer to the great Olympic ideal of '*Citius, Altius, Fortius*'—Faster, Higher, Stronger.

◆

Kiren Rijiju serves as the Minister of State (MoS) for Youth Affairs and Sports, and MoS for Minority Affairs in the present government. He represents the Arunachal West constituency in the Lok Sabha as a member of the Bharatiya Janata Party.

10

MEDIA MANTRA

VIVEK GUPTA

Before serving as a Member of Parliament (MP), I led an active career in the media sector. That experience gives me an understanding of the ins and outs of how the media functions, what are the hurdles facing the sector and the things that different stakeholders must keep in mind when operating in a dynamic and fast-paced world. Now, as an MP, I am on the other side of the sector and have an understanding as a policymaker to expound on the responsibilities that the media networks need to exemplify, if India is to succeed as an important player in the global arena.

History of Media in India

India has had a rich history of information dissemination, with elaborate systems involving huge groups of people with specified tasks in the information-sharing process. These evolved from singing mendicants of ancient times, who walked from place to place reciting stories of moralistic warriors and great battles, to the 'harbole' of the medieval era, who recited poems of kings' valour.

After the advent of colonizers in India, we also witnessed the adoption of the printing press from the late 1700s onwards. By the 1900s, India had several publications that played a significant role in disseminating critical information and creating a socially cohesive country from what, up until then, was a group of princely states and fragmented populations. From there on, media has played a vital role in our vibrant democracy and will continue to do so.

The Role Media Plays

Media refers to the main medium of communicating to a large audience. By the virtue of it being an activity dealing with hundreds, if not millions, of people, media attains an essential role, often of a watchtower or that of a regulator. In an age flooded with information influx from all sides, media frequently needs to play the role of a content filter, to ensure that only relevant, necessary and factual content is put out for consumption.

Media has been regarded as the fourth estate of democracy, the fourth pillar that doesn't have the constitutional backing like others, but plays an indispensable role in a democracy. Whether it is keeping an eye on the other estates, or shedding light on injustices in society, media dons many hats. It is also the duty of the media that they hold accountable the people who are responsible for the well-being of society.

Media also plays an imminent role in imparting social change in society because any large-scale social change cannot be achieved without disseminating ideas to the public. This responsibility falls squarely on the media's shoulders. Media, thus, has immense power to influence change.

Personally, it is the flipside that 'absolute power corrupts absolutely', which worries me about the kind of responsibility that media has come to shoulder. It is the duty of the government, the bureaucracy and the media stakeholders themselves as to how they aim to utilize this power for the greater good and without antagonizing each other. Whether through legislation, advisories, coercion or cooperation, media's power must constantly be kept in check, so as not to be harmful for the nation. On the other hand, these regulations must also not be so stringent that they impinge on the media's freedom to report. There must be a fine balance that ensures that this fourth pillar neither has a free reign to behave irresponsibly, nor is it choked to the extent of not being able to dispense its duty.

Ownership of Media

An oft-quoted adage on journalism goes: 'If someone says it's raining, and another person says it's dry, it's not a journalist's job to quote them both. Their job is to look out the window and find out which is true.' Thus, no one underestimates the value that good journalism and media as a whole brings to the table. People have come to rely on the news media to not only gain information, but also to form opinions. Consequently, there also exist high chances that the reportage might be compromised by the ideals of its owners.

In my opinion, there must be a clear demarcation between the ownership of the channel and ownership of the thoughts that are put on the channel. When it comes to news media that can severely impact the opinions of the public, there must be specific principles that it adheres to. There are numerous instances where the owners of the channel start imposing their views and opinions on a news network. It becomes increasingly problematic because the public expects news channels to be fact-based and not opinion-based. Biases of the owners thus contribute to increasingly opinion-based journalism, disguised as facts.

Role of an Editor

The editor occupies an immensely significant role: that of deciding what is worthy of the audience's attention, what is right or wrong. However now, because even the news networks operate in a 'marketplace', it sabotages the rationality and principled approach that an editor needs to practise. Instead of deciding what is 'right' for the audience, the editor ends up chasing what the audience desires. This translates into clickbait news stories and titillating news coverage.

Like everything else, media has also become a 'commodity' to be profited from in this marketplace. And the editor, thus, should be more in sync with what the readers' perceptions of right and wrong are, rather than being an objective watchtower. The editorial policy is severely affected by this consideration. When editors are expected to deliver high target rating points (TRPs), they might end up compromising on quality for extra views.

Tackling this challenge rests solely on the shoulders of the media network owners and editors. They must take responsibility to ensure that facts, rationality and, ultimately, the truth become the basis of any news report and not clicks generated or eyeballs grabbed.

Governance

The directly elected members of the legislative branch are obligated to represent the electors' views, ideas and aspirations in parliament. However, when they reach parliament, the party ideology clouds their judgement and even if they want to exercise their judgement, there exist tight 'reins' in the name of party line/party discipline. This prohibits them from having a broader vision and often conflicts with what is the best course of action for the public's needs. Even in this conflict, the media has a great duty to play. It is responsible for holding accountable those elected to carry the hopes of the citizenry to the highest echelons of policymaking.

On the other hand, with evolving technology, even the relationship between governments and citizens is undergoing change. It is not merely a one-sided relationship, but through the use of technology, citizens can easily partake in governance and make their opinions count. There exist many avenues where technology can actually help the government function better. Extending it further, the government has also maintained an open-minded approach when drafting new policies, which have been open for comments by experts and the general public alike.

Hence, even in a broader sense, media and technology play a notable role in improving the lives of the public and making a difference in society, both at the micro and macro levels.

The Future

I believe that our approach as policymakers must be future-forward. We shouldn't overlook the problems plaguing our lives right now, but our focus should be on preparing for the future and plan for the curveballs that we might have to endure.

As India approaches a century of gaining independence in 2047, it would transform into what experts call 'a mature democracy' with an informed electorate, a robust Constitution, with a system of checks and balances between stable institutions and a sense of freedom. At this juncture, one must discuss what the media industry might look like in the future and how it ought to function to dispense its duties responsibly.

In my vision, there are two possible scenarios of what our media might look like.

First scenario: The media would become too fragmented and

we will have a 'niche media', where people of different ideologies can cherry-pick the kind of news/information they prefer, from the source they prefer. These echo chambers have already developed on social media, where the 'timeline' of each person is filled with posts that one agrees with, and hardly is one confronted by views of a person from an opposing ideology. This is in part due to intelligent learning software that tracks user behaviour to quickly learn what pleases one person and offends the other.

In the future, print media and electronic media might follow the same track and resort to creating their own little 'bubbles', where each consumer could pick and choose what they prefer to expose themselves to, and subsequently, believe. It might not be surprising to see hundreds of newspapers, each catering to the specific needs/interests of less than 5,000 consumers. This model can be exported to other mediums such as news channels or the internet, with several thousand microcosms catering to the needs of small groups.

Second scenario: The situation could also turn out to be how the western media is organized currently—heavily consolidated, with a few all-powerful actors controlling everything.

Consolidated media is just not restricted to traditional TV news moguls or print media owners, but in this new age, it also raises doubts on the obligation of giants such as Google, Facebook, YouTube, etc., who may not have intended to become media-owners but have inadvertently become extremely influential as media platforms. With the backing of a vast amount of real-time data which can present a clear picture of what the public is searching for, or what is piquing their interest, these digital behemoths have quickly become more influential than traditional platforms. These new-age platforms can easily manipulate data by artificial intelligence (AI) to formulate marketing strategies and serve their own profit. Even right now, big tech companies have hordes of software developers, behavioural psychologists and experts who are tasked with improving software that manipulates you into spending more and more time on their apps, which translates into more and more dollars in advertising revenue.

If trends in 2020 are anything to go by, by the next few decades, there will be numerous media outlets that focus on individualized content, for which consumers pay premium prices. This is in line with a user-focused approach to everything, from online shopping to consumption of news.

In the future, news platforms will also have at their disposal highly efficient technology such as predictive analysis, quantum technology and metadata to accurately predict the kind of content users prefer to engage with.

Post-Coronavirus Changes in the Media Industry

The year 2020 will forever be etched in the minds of people as the year that drastically altered how society was arranged, how industries functioned and how the government reacted to challenging scenarios. During the novel coronavirus pandemic, all industries (including the media) found themselves inept and perplexed by the disease. It could be described by the Sanskrit phrase: '*Na bhuto na bhavishyati*' (something we've never experienced in our lifetime) and hopefully something we can avoid in the future. Because of its novelty, the pandemic brought with itself fake news, rumours and conspiracy theories. Thankfully, after initial hiccups, the media bounced back and has become a vital player during these tough times.

Newspapers, in particular, have come to be our most trusted and fact-checked repository of information. The lockdown has been hard-hitting for the industry due to loss of advertising revenue for the newspapers. Several senior journalists tweeted to inform that they had been laid off due to budget constraints. *The Times of India* shut down its 'Sunday Magazine' and let go of all the staff associated with it.

It is a sobering fact that revenue models of print journalism have been stretched to their core. Media, at the end of the day, functions as a business and cannot afford to be a loss-making venture. This holds true for news channels on TV who face similar difficulties unless backed by powerful and influential parent companies. Unfortunately, this is our new normal. Sustainability and profitability of all media outlets will be put to the test due to falling advertising revenue.

Post COVID-19, the public, too, will realize the distinction between different mediums of information dissemination. TV news channels function more on bold headings and attention-grabbing sensational clips. Social media continues to churn out baseless theories disguised as facts and is a breeding ground for vast amounts of 'unverified' news. In these trying times, print media can be relied on for in-depth coverage and opinion pieces by distinguished authors that give the reader a balanced perspective rather than focusing on sensationalism. I believe, the media industry as a whole will undergo a massive change in the coming months and the pandemic will impact the industry in more than one negative way.

Harnessing the Power of Media

Since 2018, India's working-age population (people between 15 and 64 years of age) has grown larger than the dependent population (children below 14 and elders above 65 years). This phenomenon is defined as the demographic dividend of a country and has helped countries such as Japan, South Korea and China transform into high-growth nation's. India will experience this bulge in the working-age population till 2055 (or 37 years from its beginning).

Moreover, India has one of the highest number of active internet users and those using social media every day for not just networking but also for gaining information and sharing it. This number is bound to go up in the coming years, with newer generations being exposed to technology at a much younger age.

Therefore, it becomes imperative that in an age when information can be disseminated so quickly and so widely, media behaves in an accountable manner while dispensing its duty of an information broadcaster. In conclusion, now is the time to actively emulate well-established values and principles that become the basis of an influential and efficient media sector in the country. It is the shared obligation of public policy architects, bureaucrats and media stakeholders themselves, to actively engage in devising the solid principles that ought to guide the sector and hold it accountable without choking its freedom.

◆

Vivek Gupta is a Member of Parliament representing the All India Trinamool Congress in the Rajya Sabha from West Bengal. He is the editor and founder of the Hindi newspaper, *Sanmarg*.

PART III

PILLARS OF PROGRESS

11

CHANGING INDIA'S ENERGY LANDSCAPE: STRIVING FOR ENERGY JUSTICE FOR ALL

DHARMENDRA PRADHAN

Energy functions as a universal currency, thereby defining the material possibilities of a civilization. Global energy systems are complex structures circumscribed by geopolitics, and cultural and economic scaffoldings. Historically, the drive to control energy resources has both built and destroyed regimes. Therefore, it is one of the most important constituents of a nation's progress.

India is home to 18 per cent of the world's population, but uses only around 6 per cent of the world's primary energy. This is despite it being the third-largest energy consumer in absolute terms after China and the United States (US). While India's per capita consumption of energy is one-third of the global average, the country's energy appetite is bound to grow by leaps and bounds with its fast-growing economy and an aspirational society.

The Prime Minister of India, Shri Narendra Modi has set a target of transforming India to a US$5-trillion economy by 2024–25. Achieving this target requires a gradual and measured energy transition by deploying all sources of energy. India's energy consumption is expected to grow at 4.2 per cent annually up to 2035. It is projected that India's share of the total global primary energy demand is set to roughly double to about 11 per cent by 2040.

Prime Minister Modi has envisioned a clear road map for India's energy future, which rests on five key enablers:

i) Energy availability and accessibility
ii) Energy affordability to the poorest of the poor
iii) Energy efficiency
iv) Energy sustainability for combating climate change as a responsible global citizen
v) Energy security in the age of global turbulence.

Accordingly, we are consistently taking policy initiatives, revamping them and constructing next-generation infrastructure based on these five guiding principles.

Inspired by the idea of '*Sabka Saath, Sabka Vikas, Sabka Vishwas*' (Together with all, for the development of all and with the trust of all), there has been a significant push during the last five years to ensure that people have access to clean, affordable and reliable energy while pursuing a green path to progress.

Availability and Accessibility

The story of Abraham Lincoln studying under street lights as a child is well-known. When asked by a policeman during his night patrol as to why he was taking such trouble to read, little Lincoln is said to have replied, 'If I don't read, how do I become the President of the United States?' This story exemplifies how energy is an enabler of the vast, untapped potential of a population. In that sense, the Ministry of Petroleum and Natural Gas is not just a ministry for abstract trade numbers, but can be used as a primary tool for enhancing the well-being of the people and pushing up social indices of a nation state.

Availability of uninterrupted supply of energy sources and access to energy by all sections of the population have been an overriding goal of our government. Our government has spearheaded a number of policy reforms to remove obstacles to infrastructure investment in the oil and gas sector on the lines of ease of doing business, minimum government maximum governance and also to promote the Make in India initiative.

During the last five years, significant policy reforms have been introduced to revitalize the exploration and production (E&P) ecosystem and establish an environment that is conducive to business. We launched the Hydrocarbon Exploration and Licensing Policy (HELP) and the Open Acreage Licensing Policy (OALP), along with a National Data Repository (NDR), Uniform Licensing Policy (ULP) and Discovered Small Fields (DSF) policy. We also removed contractual rigidities in Production Sharing Contracts (PSCs), allowing marketing and pricing freedom for sale of natural gas, and industry-friendly policy for exploitation of unconventional hydrocarbons. Additionally, we incentivized the Enhanced Recovery/Improved Recovery (ER/IR) policy and the National Seismic Programme (NSP) to increase exploration interest in Indian fields.

Under OALP, four rounds have been completed and a total of 94 blocks covering an exploratory area of approximately 1,36,800 sq. km over 16 Indian sedimentary basins have been awarded. During the last five years, the acreage under exploration has increased from 90,000 sq. km in 2014 to 2,27,000 sq. km in 2019-end.

DSF policy was undertaken to monetize the discovered hydrocarbon potential in small and isolated fields of national oil companies. Till date, two bidding rounds have been completed in which 53 contracts were awarded with an estimated investment of around US$1 billion by 2023. We are exploring avenues for private participation in 66 of the oil and gas fields of Oil and Natural Gas Commission (ONGC) and Oil India Limited (OIL) to infuse more capital and new technology.

As part of the reforms under the New Exploration Licensing Policy (NELP), focus has shifted from 'revenue' to 'production maximization'. Revenue-sharing has been dispensed with in the upstream sector as a conscious step to boost exploration and production, except in cases involving windfall profits. With a view to further liberalize the E&P ecosystem, our government has allowed complete pricing and marketing freedom for gas discoveries after February 2019. It has also carried out 2D Seismic survey of 48,000 line km in unexplored areas for prospectivity analysis.

We are also promoting other forms of gas production, including through Coal-bed Methane (CBM) and in-situ coal gasification. The government provides marketing and pricing freedom for CBM and streamline operational issues.

Oil and gas infrastructure has a direct bearing on the entire economy and facilitates growth through its forward and backward linkages. Infrastructure is also the key for ensuring easy access to petroleum products in every corner of the country. Our government has laid down the road map for a massive US$100-billion investment in the next five years in the oil and gas sector. Moreover, investment in energy in particular and the oil and gas sector in general has a multiplier effect across the economy.

Under the Conference of the Parties (COP) 21, also known as the Paris Climate Conference agreement, the government has made voluntary commitments to reduce the emission intensity of the gross domestic product (GDP) by 33–35 per cent by 2030 as compared to the 2005 levels. Moving towards a gas-based economy is a critical step towards achieving this target. We are working on an 'One Nation, One Grid' plan. We have already laid over 16,800 km of gas pipeline network while an additional 14,700 km gas pipelines are under different stages of construction. An estimated investment of US$60 billion is lined up in developing gas infrastructure, which includes pipelines, city gas distribution and liquefied natural gas (LNG) regasification terminals.

Apart from cross-country pipelines, the LNG infrastructure in the country is also being expanded rapidly. Six LNG regasification terminals are operational, with a capacity of over 39 million metric tonne per annum (MMTPA) on both the east and west coasts of the country and an additional capacity of 18 MMTPA is at an advanced stage of development. India is the world's fourth-largest LNG importer after Japan, South Korea and China.

The largest-ever roll-out of city gas distribution networks across India has been undertaken to enable inclusive growth and to provide cleaner fuel to the remotest parts of the country. Plans have been chalked out to provide compressed natural gas (CNG) and piped natural gas (PNG) infrastructure in most parts of the country. Till 2014, only 66 districts of the country were covered under CNG and PNG infrastructure. In the last five years, we have worked to strengthen this infrastructure in a planned way. The CNG and PNG infrastructure will be provided in 407 districts. The number of PNG connections for households has increased 'from 25.4 lakh [2.54 million] consumers in 2014 to 50.43 lakh [5.04 million] consumers in 2019'[1]. The target is to add

[1]Bureau, 'Work on CNG, PNG Infrastructure Begins in 50 More Places, *The Hindu Business Line*, 26 August 2019. Available at: https://www.thehindubusinessline.com/news/work-on-cng-png-infrastructure-begins-in-50-more-places/article29259100.ece, last accessed on 1 September 2020.

another 40 million households by 2027.[1] Similarly, the number of CNG connections has increased from 938 in 2014[2] to 1,989 stations in January 2020[3] and will be further expanded to 10,000 by 2030[4]. After expanding these facilities, almost 70 per cent of the population will get clean energy.

We are actively encouraging the use of LNG, among other forms of energy, for long-haul trucking along expressways, industrial corridors and inside mining areas, and for marine applications. We are also making natural gas easily available, reaching users' doorsteps through mobile dispensing.

India is the fourth-largest refiner in the world. Our refining capacity exceeds the demand. We have been able to set up complex and efficient refineries and petrochemical complexes in India. India is already a major refinery hub. We are, in fact, net exporters of gasoline, naphtha, jet fuel and gas oil. Whatever be the scenario of growth of electric vehicles, India would still need higher refining capacities. Consumption of petrol and diesel in India is growing in excess of 5 per cent per annum. With increasing demand and consumption, we are in the process of increasing our refining capacities through several brownfield refinery expansions and

---

[1]Rajeev Jayaswal, 'Govt Seeks to Bring States on Board for Piped Gas Project,' *Hindustan Times*, 19 January 2020. Available at: https://www.hindustantimes.com/india-news/govt-seeks-to-bring-states-on-board-for-piped-gas-project/story-qHjyqXIYSLBbt8OvN4NrZM.html, last accessed on 1 September 2020.

[2]PTI, 'Rs 1.2 lakh cr Investment Planned for CNG Network Expansion: Pradhan,' Auto.com, 26 August 2019. Available at: https://auto.economictimes.indiatimes.com/news/industry/pradhan-says-rs-1-2-lakh-cr-investment-planned-for-city-gas-network-expansion/70841012, last accessed on 1 September 2020.

[3]CNG Stations, Ministry of Petroleum and Natural Gas. Available at: https://pib.gov.in/PressReleasePage.aspx?PRID=1606550, accessed on 1 September 2020

[4]PTI, 'Rs 1.2 lakh cr Investment Planned for CNG Network Expansion: Pradhan,' Auto.com, 26 August 2019. Available at: https://auto.economictimes.indiatimes.com/news/industry/pradhan-says-rs-1-2-lakh-cr-investment-planned-for-city-gas-network-expansion/70841012, last accessed on 1 September 2020.

setting up new greenfield refineries. India's refining capacity has increased from 215 MMTPA in 2014 to 249 MMTPA and is being further expanded to 438 MMTPA by 2030.

The Pradhan Mantri Ujjwala Yojana (PMUY) has proved to be a game changer in drastically ramping up access to clean cooking fuel. Under the Ujjwala programme, the target to provide LPG connections to 8 crore households was achieved seven months ahead of the target date (in 2019). LPG connections are now available to almost 97 per cent of the population, which was just about 55 per cent in 2014. Similarly, thrust has been given to the expansion of LPG distribution network. The number of LPG distributorships has increased from 13,896 in 2014 to 24,382 as on 1 January 2020.[1] Similarly, the network of retail outlets has expanded in the country from 56,000 in 2014 to more than 65,000.

Various multilateral agencies and governments have lauded the successful implementation of PMUY. We also successfully implemented Pratyaksha Hastaantarit Laabh (PAHAL), the world's largest cash transfer programme for household LPG subsidies, which has been recognized by the Guinness Book of World Records. The 'Give it Up' initiative inspired people to voluntarily give up LPG subsidies. The savings from this were used to fund connections to poor households.

Power demand is expected to increase by 53 per cent by 2022 and 100 per cent by 2027. We have introduced the '24×7 Power for All (24×7 PFA)' initiative. Keeping in view the role of electricity in human development, we have launched the Pradhan Mantri Sahaj Bijli Har Ghar Yojana (SAUBHAGYA) to provide electricity connections to unelectrified households in rural as well

---

[1]LPG Profile, Petroleum Planning and Analysis Cell, Ministry of Petroleum and Natural Gas. Available at: https://www.ppac.gov.in/WriteReadData/Reports/202002260532483115107WebVersionLPGProfile26Feb2020.pdf, last accessed on 1 September 2020.

as urban areas. We are in the process of establishing a Green Energy Corridor project with an investment of US$6.5 billion to integrate renewable energy (RE) into the national grid to set a target of 19,000 MVA capacity substations by 2020. We have taken the Ujwal DISCOM Assurance Yojana (UDAY) for the financial turnaround and revival package of electricity distribution companies of India (DISCOMs). India is now leading the global movement in embracing RE sources. The country has an ambitious plan to increase RE capacity to over 175 GW by 2022 and up to 450 GW by 2030. The share of renewables in the electricity mix has gone up from around 10 per cent in 2014–15 to over 22 per cent currently.

Energy Efficiency

We are keen on creating a functioning energy market, which will ensure energy efficiency in the management of coal, gas and power sectors. Implementation and scaling up of efficiency improvement measures in residential, commercial, transport and industrial sectors could drive energy demand reduction of 160 to 200 megatoe (Mtoe/one million toe) by 2030.

Recently, the government has opened up the coal sector completely for commercial mining for all local and global firms after easing restrictions on end-use and prior experience. Today, there are proven technologies that use coal in a cleaner and more sustainable manner. We are setting up a fertilizer plant in Odisha, which will be the first of its kind in terms of the coal gasification technology being used. We had earlier opened the oil and gas retail markets and also took lead in the global energy transition efforts by promoting the International Solar Alliance (ISA), which was set up on the lines of the Paris Climate Conference.

On 5 January 2020, Unnat Jyoti by Affordable LEDs for All

(UJALA) and LED Street Lighting National Programme (SLNP) marked their fifth anniversary. Under the SLNP initiative, within a time frame of five years, around 1.03 crore smart LED street lights were installed. This helped in reducing greenhouse gas (GHG) emissions by 4.8 million tonnes annually. Under the UJALA programme, 36.13 crore LED bulbs have been distributed so far. This helped in reducing GHG emissions by 38 million tonnes annually. The scheme has brought down the prices of LED bulbs to one-tenth that of 2015. Also, they have helped in reducing customer bills by 15 per cent.

The SLNP programme's aim to replace 1.34 crore street lights with smart LEDs by March 2020 was to help reduce peak demands by 1.5 GW and reduce GHG emissions by 6.2 million tonnes. The implementing agencies of the scheme have planned to invest another ₹8,000 crore by 2024 to install more than 30 million LED street lights.

One of the most effective ways to bring about greater environmental sustainability and flexibility in India's energy system is through the rapid deployment of natural gas. We are, indeed, moving towards developing natural gas as a transition fuel in our national energy transition process. Our government is working towards increasing the share of gas in the energy mix from 6.2 per cent to 15 per cent by 2030.

In our resolve to curb vehicular pollution, we introduced Bharat Stage (BS)-IV (equivalent to Euro-IV) fuels all across the country in April 2017. The next step has been to usher in BS-VI (Equivalent to Euro-VI) fuels from 1 April 2020, to be at par with global standards. Oil marketing companies have invested over ₹32,000 crore to upgrade their refinery processes to produce BS-VI grade fuel. This shows India's resolve to cut down on emissions.

Our government's efforts in making energy efficiency a prime policy priority has been extolled in various reports, which recognize the efficiency achieved due to the government's relentless march in undertaking tectonic reforms in the energy sector and its continued pursuit of market-based solutions.

Energy Sustainability

Greater use of cleaner fuels and renewable energy resources has been a priority in our pursuit to chart a green path to progress. Alternative fuels such as ethanol and bio-diesel are being given high priority in our energy mix. The National Biofuel Policy of 2018 focuses on giving impetus to advanced biofuels. We are well on our way to meet the target of 20 per cent blending of ethanol in petrol and 5 per cent blending of biodiesel in diesel by 2030. The ethanol blending percentage has risen from 0.67 per cent in 2012–13 to now close to 6 per cent. We are also working towards the conversion of used cooking oil (UCO) to biodiesel in select cities. We are advancing our collaboration with countries such as Brazil and the US to improve blending technologies in the transport sector.

Indian Oil has tied up with the Delhi government to introduce 50 hydrogen-enriched CNG buses. This will be India's first hydrogen-powered buses to be rolled out on Delhi roads this year.

Given the abundance of biomass in the country, the use of Compressed Biogas (CBG) will be promoted in a big way in automotive, industrial and commercial uses in the coming years. Sustainable Alternative Towards Affordable Transport (SATAT) is an important initiative of our government, which targets to set up 5,000 compressed biogas plants with a target of 15 million metric tonne (MMT) per year, mostly by private entrepreneurs who are assured price and offtake guarantee by oil-marketing companies. These plants will help tackle the problem of burning of agricultural waste. These plants will also bring monetary benefits to farmers with an estimated production of 15 MMT CBG per annum by 2023.

India is among the select few nations in the world which successfully operated a flight running on biofuel in August 2018. We are keen to expand the use of biofuels in the aviation sector to meet the new International Civil Aviation Organization (ICAO) standards.

Energy Security

As the centre of gravity shifts from the oil-producing countries to the consuming nations, India has emerged as a crucial centre in the world of oil and gas as the third-largest energy consumer in the world, after the US and China. This has resulted in India asserting its market influence in the global arena to reorder the anomalies currently existing in the global energy markets.

Our energy diplomacy has become an integral part of India's overall foreign policy. Given the high levels of interdependence of countries on energy security, we are taking active part in bilateral, regional and international fora to secure our energy interests. We are developing energy corridors with our neighbouring countries as part of the Neighbourhood First policy of Prime Minister Narendra Modi. We have been developing strategic energy partnerships with key countries, such as Saudi Arabia, the UAE, Russia and the US, while continuously expanding outreach to countries in Asia, Africa and Latin America.

The government has been actively engaged in oil diplomacy for diversifying India's energy imports, acquisition of oil and gas assets overseas and to attract foreign investments into the hydrocarbon sector. We have firmly established the global energy landscape by acquiring stakes in overseas projects. The share of equity oil and gas for the year 2018–19 for Indian public-sector undertakings (PSUs) from these assets was around 21.91 MMtoe. We have adopted a balanced portfolio approach and maintain a combination of producing, discovered and exploration assets.

During the last three years, Indian companies have acquired strategic stakes in overseas assets in the UAE, Oman, Israel and Russia. For FY 2018–19, the share of equity oil and gas for Indian PSUs from these assets was approximately 24.72 MMtoe, which is worth US$5007.73 million. From April to November 2019, equity oil and gas from overseas assets was 16.416 MMtoe.

In line with the government's diplomatic approach of 'neighbourhood first', the prime ministers of India and Nepal jointly inaugurated South Asia's first cross-border petroleum products pipeline from Motihari in India to Amlekhgunj in Nepal through a video conference on 10 September 2019. The 69-km pipeline, having a capacity of 2 MMTPA, is the first transnational petroleum pipeline from India and the first South Asian oil pipeline corridor. The pipeline will ensure smooth, cost-effective and environment-friendly supply of petroleum products to Nepal.

India is also constructing a 130-km Indo-Bangla Friendship Pipeline (IBFPL) from Siliguri (India) to Parbatipur (Bangladesh) which will supply 1 MMT of diesel to the Bangladesh Petroleum Corporation for 20 years. This pipeline will put in place a mechanism for assured, long-term, uninterrupted and eco-friendly supply of petroleum products to Bangladesh. India and Bangladesh also jointly inaugurated a project to import bulk LPG from Bangladesh to ensure sustained and affordable supply of LPG to the north-eastern region of the country.

Taking advantage of geographical proximity, Indian PSU refineries, that is, the Indian Oil Corporation Limited (IOCL) and Numaligrah Refinery Limited are also working with Myanmar companies to supply petroleum products to Myanmar. GAIL and Indraprastha Gas Limited (IGL) are also working with Myanmar government agencies to establish city gas distribution in Yangon. ONGC Videsh Limited (OVL) increased its presence in a gas field by continuing its additional investments in their exploration and production asset.

India has already built strategic oil reserves of 5.33 MMT capacities in a bid to enhance oil security and protect supply disruptions. The government has approved the construction of another 6.5 MMT of Strategic Petroleum Reserve (SPR) under phase II at Chandikhol in Odisha and Padur in Karnataka.

Given the high level of vulnerability of our energy security to developments in the Middle East, we have been diversifying our import sources of crude oil and LNG away from the region. As a result of our persistent efforts, we have been able to reduce crude oil import from the Middle East to 56 per cent during the current year as compared to 65 per cent in 2016. We now have more sources of LNG that extend beyond Qatar. In the last three years, Russia, Australia and the US have emerged as important sources of LNG.

Our strategic energy partnership with the US has assumed greater salience in the last three to four years. In a short period, the US has become one of the top 10 sources of crude oil and also an important source of LNG. Energy has been featured as an important commodity in our merchandise trade and has been an important bridge to narrow the trade deficit. Total import of petroleum products, including LNG in 2018–19 stood at US$7.2 billion. So, energy is increasingly becoming one of the most important elements of the India–US bilateral trade.

Russia and India too have a bilateral hydrocarbon engagement—an 'energy bridge' between the two countries. Russia is our largest oil and gas investment destination, with over US$15 billion investment so far. Indian oil and gas PSUs have stakes in various strategic oil and gas projects in Russia, including in Sakhalin-1, Vankorneft and Taas-Yuryakh. On the other hand, Rosneft's investment of nearly US$13 billion in the Vadinar refinery is the largest foreign direct investment (FDI) in the Indian oil and gas sector. GAIL has contracted 2.5 MMTPA of LNG from Gazprom on a long-term basis. The first cargo of Russian LNG was received on 4 June 2018 at Dahej in Gujarat. Indian oil and gas PSUs are also pursuing a number of business opportunities in Russia, including getting stakes in oil and gas projects in the Russian Arctic and the Far East region and exploring sourcing of crude oil from eastern Russia to the eastern coast of India via the eastern sea route. A Memorandum of Understanding (MoU) was signed recently between our Ministry of Petroleum and Natural Gas and Russia's Ministry of Energy on the use of natural gas for transportation. Indian Oil has recently signed a term contract for importing 2 MMT of Russian Urals crude oil for 2020. This is yet another concrete action to diversify our crude sources and to reduce our vulnerability to the developments in the Strait of Hormuz.

Challenges and the Way Forward

The winds of change are evident in the global energy arena. Energy sources, energy supply and energy consumption patterns are changing rapidly. The contours of India's energy transition are also changing fast in sync with global challenges and opportunities. India will chart its own course of energy transition in a responsible manner, even as it will become the key driver of global energy demand in the coming decades. No single source can meet energy demand given the fact that India is in a particular phase of its development cycle. We are preparing for a low-carbon energy economy.

India has seen unprecedented reforms in the energy sector in the last five years. There is still the need to work on innovation, research and induction of new technologies through collaboration, particularly in the areas of deep water exploration, enhanced oil recovery, coal gasification, coal-based methanol through joint ventures, technology transfer and technical innovations to exploit the vast coal reserves located in the country, which require development.

The research priorities for us are in the areas of bioenergy, biomass and biofuel, including production of compressed biogas from organic waste, agri-residue, municipal solid waste (MSW) and press mud, value-added chemicals to improve commercial viability of 2G technology, indigenous enzyme production scale-up for 2G technology, development of new feedstock for biodiesel, biodiesel production from UCO, castor oil to biofuel jet, algae to biodiesel, drop-in fuel from plastic waste and CO2 capturing to lipids technology, to name a few.

There is a need to work on different pathways to march towards a hydrogen economy. Therefore, there is a need to focus on developing technologies for the production of hydrogen from non-fossil source and electrolysis using renewable electricity as well as demonstration of fuel cell technologies.

Energy saved is energy produced. Therefore, we must work towards energy conservation and efficiency improvement in whatever we do, from manufacturing to its end use.

Conclusion

Petroleum, natural gas and coal will continue to remain vital for India's energy security in the foreseeable future. Our commitment to decarbonize energy is unwavering, as is amply evident through various policy reforms and concrete initiatives taken.

Concerted effort is required among all stakeholders to ensure that India is appropriately positioned to take advantage of the existing opportunities. This will require end-to-end planning, synergies and trade-off across sectors. India has taken the initiative to change its energy stance at a global level and to enhance collaboration with the best of minds in the sector.

Under the leadership of Prime Minister Modi, we are working relentlessly to ensure that everyone has access to clean, affordable and reliable energy and India becomes a welcoming haven for investments across the energy sector.

◆

Dharmendra Pradhan is currently Minister of Petroleum and Natural Gas and Minister of Steel at the Centre. He is a member of the Rajya Sabha from Madhya Pradesh from the Bharatiya Janata Party.

12

RENEWABLE ENERGY

JAMYANG TSERING NAMGYAL

Ever since humans invented fire, energy has been at the heart of human civilization—and it has been ever changing. The quest for energy in different forms has led humans to explore the environment in many ways. With rapid progress in each civilization, humans have made use of different sources of energy to move things faster, with ever-expanding inventions and innovations. This, in turn, has impacted the environment around us. A balance between the two is—and will be—the way ahead.

The consumption patterns of Homo sapiens have changed over time. Once he learnt to make tools, they helped him to keep reaching new frontiers. When he finally discovered how to make fire and use it to cook his food, his life changed. He no longer depended solely on eating raw food. Fire hence became the first exterior form of energy, giving him the comforts of life.

However, fire as a simple form of energy had its own impact on nature. Since the very evolution of humans, there has been a need to strike a balance—while fire could help man cook his food, it could also destroy the whole of the forest around him. There were both positive and adverse impacts, right from the earliest form of energy.

Over time, man started domesticating animals, using them for either agriculture or transportation. Ever-expanding needs, and consequently the need for a more diversified reservoir of energy, led to the discovery of coal. This set off the transition/conversion of one form of energy to others, each with its own set of advantages and effects on nature.

Over the last few decades, we have moved on from coal to natural gas, petroleum, nuclear power and sustainable energy sources such as wind, hydroelectric power, solar energy and biofuels. While the earlier ways of using non-renewable natural resources such as fossil fuels have resulted in drastic imbalances in nature, the modern sources of clean, renewable energy have been transformative, with highly reduced ill effects.

As of 2016, global energy consumption, by source worldwide, stands at: coal 9,863,339 gigawatt hours (GWh), oil 8,41,878 GWh, natural gas 5,882,825 GWh, biofuels 4,81,529 GWh, waste 114043 GWh, hydro 4197299 GWh, geothermal 8,53,48 GWh and wind 1,127,319 GWh.[1]

Major countries such as the US generate 4.01 trillion kilowatt-hour (kWh) of energy per year, of which coal constitutes 30 per cent, nuclear 20 per cent, natural gas 32 per cent and renewable energy 17 per cent (the last comprises hydro 7.5 per cent, wind 6.3 per cent, biomass 1.6 per cent, solar 1.3 per cent and geothermal 0.4 per cent). According to the US Energy Information Administration (EIA), coal, oil and natural gas will still account for 77 per cent of our energy in 2040. Fossil fuels will continue to account for a predominantly high proportion,

[1]'Shaping a Secure and Sustainable Energy Future for All,' International Energy Agency (IEA). Available at: www.iea.org, last accessed on 8 October 2020.

despite the disadvantages associated with them. Fossil fuels are formed by a natural decomposition process of the remains of dead animals and plants over millions of years. One of the main by-products of fossil fuel combustion is carbon dioxide (CO2). The ever-increasing use of fossil fuels in industries, transportation and various sectors has added large amounts of CO2 to the earth's atmosphere, which in turn, is a major factor contributing to global warming. Most air pollution deaths are due to fossil fuels. Data levels show that fossil fuel reserves left as shown in 2015 would last as follows: oil 50.7 years, natural gas 52.8 years and coal 114 years.

The World Economic Forum (WEF) reported a few key points from the EIA's report on the sources of energy in future, including:

i. World use of petroleum and other liquid fuels will increase from 95 million barrels per day (b/d) in 2015 to 104 million b/d in 2030 and 113 million b/d by 2040.
ii. Liquid fuels will continue to provide most of the energy consumed by the transportation sector and will rise by an average of 0.7 per cent a year to 2040. Transport will account for 60 per cent of the total increase.
iii. Natural gas will account for the largest increase in world primary energy consumption after renewables. It burns more cleanly than coal or petroleum and as more governments begin implementing national or regional plans to reduce carbon dioxide (CO2) emissions, they may turn to it more.
iv. Global coal production is likely to remain steady at about 9 billion short tons from 2015 to 2040, and consumption is likely to rise by 0.2 per cent a year between 2015 and 2025, and then start declining.

With ever-increasing needs and developing countries wanting to reap benefits of their youth dividend, the need for energy consumption is bound to grow manyfold in future. Energy demand in India has been on a steady rise. India is one of the top five consumers of energy in the world, with its largest source of energy being coal, followed by petroleum and others. There is, therefore, an urgent need to transition from hazardous sources of energy to renewable, sustainable and eco-friendly forms.

The 2019 WEF Energy Transition Index (ETI), which benchmarks countries on their energy system, as well as their readiness for transition to a secure, sustainable, affordable and reliable energy future, shows India's ranking at 76, with 51.3 per cent readiness for transition ahead of China, which is ranked at 82, with 49.6 per cent readiness. Renewable energy which can be naturally replenished has started playing an increasingly important role in augmenting grid power, providing energy access, reducing consumption of fossil fuels and helping India pursue its low-carbon development path.

Over the years, at the national level, India has successfully created a positive outlook necessary to promote investment in, demand for and supply of renewable energy that includes solar, wind, biofuels and hydel. In 2010, India launched the National Solar Mission (NSM), the first to be operationalized under the National Action Plan on Climate Change (NAPCC). Using a three-phase approach, the mission's objective is to establish India as a global leader in solar energy, by creating the policy conditions for solar technology diffusion across the country as quickly as possible. The mission's initial target of installing 20 gigawatts (GW) of grid-connected solar power plants by the year 2022 has been enhanced to 100 GW.

In the year 2015, the Government of India announced a target of 175 GW cumulative renewable power-installed capacity by the year 2022. India has set its goals, increasing its power generation capacity from renewables from 80 GW to 175 GW by 2022 and then to 450 GW in coming times.

With 'data as the new oil', digital transformations, and the rapid use of technologies across the globe as well as in India, energy needs are bound to grow exponentially. The National Energy Policy (NEP) aims to build an integrated energy policy, providing access at affordable prices and greater sustainability. A number of initiatives are being taken to scale up access to clean energy. Some of these are the Solar Park Scheme, grid interactive rooftop and small power plants programme. Other such initiatives include loans and international funding, off-grid solar photovoltaics, the Ministry of New and Renewable Energy's (MNRE) scheme of introducing 7 million solar study lamps and the Atal Jyoti Yojana (AJAY), among others.

Ladakh, too, has been playing its role in contributing to this sustainable goal, in the form of the Ladakh Renewable Energy Development Agency (LREDA). It is one of the largest off-grid renewable energy projects in the world. LREDA has a number of projects in the pipeline, such as 11 micro hydro projects with a total capacity of 11.2 MV, 125 solar photovoltaic power plants of varying capacities and others.

Ladakh, which has the highest intensity of solar radiation, is posed to be at the forefront of India's mission of achieving a renewable energy state. The Solar Energy Corporation of India (SECI) aims to install 7,500 MW of solar energy by 2023 in Ladakh. This will be transformational. In his 2020 Independence Day speech, Prime Minister Modi has announced that he would strive to make Ladakh carbon-neutral by 2050 and thereby, set a precedence for the whole of India. Also, new initiatives by the Modi-led government on solar energy generation on barren agro lands is a step towards generating income for farmers as well as a contribution in maintaining ecological balance.

In terms of power from other renewables, India is forging ahead in the wind energy sector too with manufacturing based at about 10,000 MW per annum. India currently has the fourth highest wind-installed capacity in the world, with total installed capacity of 35.62 GW as of 2019 and 62 billion units were generated from wind power during 2018–19. Hydro energy has also been a great source of energy for India. States in the higher Himalayan ranges, such as Arunachal Pradesh, have been at the forefront in this area. India is also taking steps to expand biogas generation by implementing biogas-based schemes such as decentralized power generation in the capacity range of 3kw to 250 kw.

India has been playing a leading role in encouraging the establishment of a solar-based economy across the globe. In partnership with France, it has promoted the establishment of the International Solar Alliance (ISA) in 2015. Even as a developing economy, our country is transitioning towards clean, sustainable forms of energy.

With rising global population and advances in modern technology, our dependency on energy sources is set to rise in the coming decades. However, one cannot turn a blind eye to the harms caused by traditional sources of energy. In this regard, renewable energy becomes essential for developing nations, especially, India, which is one of the largest energy consumers in the world. India has been proactive when it comes to utilizing resources to produce greener fuels. I am sure that under the able guidance of Modi, Ladakh will become a pioneer in harnessing the power of solar energy and set precedents for the entire nation to follow. In conclusion, India has tremendous potential to lead the world towards a greener and more sustainable future.

◆

Jamyang Tsering Namgyal is a first-time Member of Parliament and represents Ladakh in the Lok Sabha as part the Bharatiya Janata Party. He is also the youngest chief executive councillor of the Ladakh Autonomous Hill Development Council, Leh.

13

WATER MANAGEMENT AND SANITATION

MEENAKSHI LEKHI

The World Health Organization (WHO) defines the term 'sanitation' as: 'Sanitation generally refers to the provision of facilities and services for the safe disposal of human urine and faeces. ...The word "sanitation" also refers to the maintenance of hygienic conditions, through services such as garbage collection and wastewater disposal.'[1]

Poverty and sanitation are closely linked with each other. The World Bank has conducted a study that correlates poverty with water, sanitation and hygiene (WASH). In the Republic of Niger, one of the poorest countries of the world, 90 per cent of the rural population has no access to toilets and 51 per cent is without access to improved water. In Tanzania, 49 per cent of the population does not have access to basic water services. In July 2018, World Poverty Clock, a Vienna-based think tank, reported that a minimal 5.3 per cent or 70.6 million Indians lived in extreme poverty. According to United Nations Development

[1]https://www.afro.who.int/health-topics/sanitation, last accessed on 10 September 2020.

Programme (UNDP) administrator Achim Steiner, India lifted 271 million people out of poverty in just a 10-year time period, from 2005–06 to 2015–16. However, when it comes to sanitation, India still has a long way to go.

The issues related to WASH affect every person in the world. In India, even the middle class and upper middle class face water shortage situations, including in the urban settings. With groundwater levels falling exponentially with every passing day, the issues are only getting bigger and more critical.

Extensive urbanization has also led to a decline in groundwater levels. Chennai ran out of groundwater in the summer of 2019, leaving millions of people to fight for this basic necessity. The situation was such that people were getting as little as half-an-hour supply of water on alternate days. India's capital city is now on its way to lose out on groundwater in the near future.

Everyone needs clean water to drink. Everyone needs a safe and clean place to do their personal business. And everyone needs to be able to clean themselves. For the privileged few like us, these concerns are taken for granted and their combined impact on life isn't always appreciated.

However, for millions of others, water, sanitation and hygiene are constant sources of stress and illness. The quality of water, sanitation and hygiene in a person's life is directly correlated to poverty, as it is usually accompanied by lack of education and opportunity as well as gender inequality.

Poverty means lack of infrastructure and often leads to open defecation, which in turn, gives way to water-borne diseases such as cholera, dysentery, typhoid, malaria, diarrhoea, etc. Inadequate sanitation generally means open defecation. When people defecate in the open without a proper waste management system, the faeces generally seeps into and contaminates water systems. The problem is concentrated in Maharashtra, Rajasthan, Punjab, Haryana and

Tamil Nadu. New Delhi and Mumbai also have issues related to poor sanitation due to patches of underdeveloped slums existing within these uber-sleek modern cities.

Poor sanitation also leads to gender inequality, as primary schools lack proper sanitation services, and girls drop out of school due to stigmas associated with periods. Also, when families don't have enough water, girls are generally forced to travel for hours to gather some, leaving little time for school. This lack of education then contributes to higher poverty rates for women. Water scarcity is so severe in parts of western Maharashtra, which is a rocky terrain, that some villages have adopted polygamy as a solution. It is learnt through news reports that in a village named Denganmal in Maharashtra, there is acute dearth of water during summer months. The only source of drinking water are two wells at the foot of a nearby rocky hill, which takes hours to reach. Since men are out working in the fields and women are out fetching water, there is no one to take care of the children. Consequently, men marry multiple women for the sole purpose of fetching water from far-flung places. They are called 'paani bai' in Marathi, which translates to 'water wives'. Even though polygamy is illegal under the Hindu Marriage Act of our Constitution, the practice is rampant due to the prevailing water crisis.

Forty-five per cent of India's children are stunted and 6 lakh children under five years of age die each year, largely because of inadequate water supply and poor sanitation. According to a WHO study, in 2002, unsafe water and poor sanitation contributed 7.5 per cent of the total deaths and 9.4 per cent of the total disability-adjusted life years in India. About 73 million working days are lost in India due to water-borne diseases each year. Many or almost all of these deaths can be prevented by providing clean drinking water to children and adequate sanitation. There are a lot of health risks associated with inadequate hygiene systems. Just imagine what it would be like if you were drinking contaminated water and everyone in your community defecated in the open.

In terms of water stress level, Punjab, Rajasthan, Uttar Pradesh, Chandigarh, Gujarat, Uttarakhand, Madhya Pradesh, and Jammu and Kashmir, all scored between four and five on a scale of zero to five, with five being the worst.

The demand for water has increased across domestic and industrial sectors, as well as for irrigation, leading to severe water scarcity. This is supported by the government-run Central Water Commission's 2019 report, which states that there are more than 20 million borewells pumping out groundwater across India.

Sewages are directly dumped in the rivers which contaminate the water and make them unfit for drinking. However, unlike African countries, India's major problem is water management rather than lack of water. Our country's water scarcity, according to the report, stems not so much from a deficit, but from severe neglect and a lack of monitoring of water resources. Needless to say, we are blessed with rivers and glaciers with abundant natural resources of water. Mismanagement has led to the situation that we see today.

The government's own think tank, the National Institution for Transforming India (NITI Aayog), the successor to the country's Planning Commission, says that 600 million Indians face high to extreme water stress. About 200,000 people die every year due to inadequate access to safe water[1] and 21 major cities are expected to run out of groundwater by 2020, affecting around 100 million people.[2] Seventy-five per cent of households do not have drinking water at home, 84 per cent rural households do not have piped water access and 70 per cent of India's water is

[1]As per the Composite Water Management Index (CWMI) report, released on 14 June 2018.

[2]As per NITI Aayog's 2018 report.

contaminated, with the country ranked 120 among 122 in the water quality index as of 2019.

According to the NITI Aayog database, 54 per cent of wells in India are declining in level due to unsustainable withdrawals for irrigation. Of the 24 states from which data was collected, 20 have established a legal and regulatory framework for participatory irrigation management through water user associations (WUAs), but progress on the ground is inadequate, with 10 states having WUAs involved in maintenance activities in less than 20 per cent of the irrigation command area. The report calls for states to establish WUAs across the majority of irrigated areas and ensure they are allowed to retain a significant portion of irrigation fees and are thus empowered to govern local irrigation systems.

Throughout India, the big problem is that water quality remains a major issue, with several populous states reporting no reduction in quality incidents. State governments can support entrepreneurs in piloting and scaling promising decentralized technologies for measuring and improving water quality, NITI Aayog had suggested.

Thousands have lived without love, not one without WATER!

—W.H. Auden

Constant efforts are required to deal with water management issues. The Union government recently formed a new Jal Shakti ministry, which aims at tackling water issues with a holistic and integrated perspective on the subject. The ministry has announced an ambitious plan to provide piped water connections to every household in India by 2024.

We can do much better if we make existing state and central pollution control boards effective. We need to worry about what happens when latrine pits fill up and who empties them. Even as the government is facilitating the use of a technology that allows the pits to decompose before they need to be emptied, the rural population still sees it as manual scavenging. The lower castes don't want to clean others' toilets, not even of those belonging to their own community, and people from upper and intermediate castes don't want to associate themselves even with the emptying of decomposed pits. Thus, the government needs to focus on Panchayati Raj Institutions (PRIs) and use them as a platform to encourage villagers to adopt sustainable sanitation practices and facilities through awareness creation, health education, and creating public-supported frameworks of disposal and utilization.

Urban access can be improved by reducing the approximately 40 per cent of water lost due to leakages in urban areas through smart technologies, such as sensors. Further, building treatment capacity can enable reuse of water, thereby increasing the utility gained out of every drop.

Environmental problems have the most basic solutions. Reading a seventh-standard book about water conservation would give you a simple, basic solution. Plant more trees. It's the most basic solution because in a forest area, fallen tree leaves (litter) acts as a huge sponge. This absorbs rain water and prevents runoff and soil erosion. The absorbed water percolates to the groundwater and recharges it over a period of time. The effect of deforestation on water dynamics has been proven by various studies. However, in some low-lying areas (inland basins), the groundwater becomes overcharged and rises up to the soil surface. This causes waterlogging and salinity and renders the landscape unfit for cultivation. Planting of trees here causes biodrainage, i.e., the evapotranspiration loss of water by the trees that lowers the groundwater. Trees thus help to prevent waterlogging. However, planting of non-native trees such as eucalyptus on shallow water table areas may cause a fall in water table due to biodrainage.

This may become harmful for the shallow-rooted native flora on the ground.

However, in most places, afforestation is a positive and effective solution to the water problem. The central government had approved the National Mission for Green India in February 2014 as a centrally sponsored scheme for a total cost of ₹13,000 crore, having a plan outlay of ₹2,000 crore for the 12th Five-year Plan. The central government also provides assistance to state governments and union territories under a centrally sponsored scheme called the National Afforestation Programme (NAP) for the regeneration of degraded forests and adjoining areas through people's participation. The scheme is being implemented through a decentralized mechanism of the state Forest Development Agency (FDA) at the forest division level and joint forest management committees (JFMCs) at the village level. The budget allocation for 2015 under the NAP was ₹100 crore.

Major amount of deforestation occurs for expansion of economic activities. Development and expansion need to be planned as a homogenous mix with respect towards environment.

The year 2020 is witnessing the global COVID-19 pandemic that has shaken the world to its core. It's a virus believed to have originated in the Chinese city Wuhan. The symptoms are akin to common cold and flu, except that it is highly fatal and attacks the respiratory organs, thus leading to difficulty in breathing and eventual death in severely infected patients. The world is witnessing an economic shutdown to contain the virus and there is no vaccine as yet. It is a communicable disease and the only prevention prescribed by scientists and doctors is washing the hands with soap and water frequently, wearing masks and maintaining social distance. There is a direct connection between the prevention of this pandemic's transmission in India and water management. Access to clean water is the most important preventive measure against illness. We are told to wash our hands at least five to six times a day for at least 20 seconds. Twenty seconds of handwash means consumption of approx. 2 litres of water. This is critical. More washing translates to increased sewage. Sewage should be treated and reused. According to the WHO, COVID-19 is 'not robust'—it is less stable in the environment and more susceptible to oxidants such as chlorine. Conventional methods of cleaning sewage can kill the virus and prepare water to be reused. During this crisis, proper treatment of sewage becomes all the more important. Buying packaged water should be discouraged as plastic waste produced is way too high. We can direct funds towards replenishment of water resources through proper sewage systems in the city.

The National Policy on Faecal Sludge and Septage Management (FSSM) was launched in 2017 by the Union government with an objective to address synergies between FSSM and sewerage systems or municipal solid waste (MSW) management, e.g., co-treatment of faecal sludge and septage at sewage treatment plants or co-treatment and management of faecal sludge and septage, and MSW. The Government of India recognizes that sanitation is a state subject and onground implementation and sustenance of public health and environmental outcomes requires strong city-level institutions and stakeholders.

Interlinking of rivers (ILR) is a new initiative taken up by the government's Jal Shakti Mantralaya. Hon'ble Minister for Water Resources, RD & GR, is monitoring the progress of the ILR scheme from time to time. The mission of this programme is to ensure greater equity in the distribution of water by enhancing the availability of water in drought-prone and rain-fed areas. This is a major step in equal distribution of water resources in India. We see Maharashtra suffer from drought year after year and Assam faces floods year after year.

The government has taken modern initiatives to curb both the situations. The Ken-Betwa Link Project, the country's first river interlinking project, has been declared as a national project by the government. The Damanganga-Pinjal Link Project and the Par-Tapi-Narmada Link Project are twin links that benefit Maharashtra and Gujarat, respectively. The detailed project reports of both links are ready. The Central Water Commission has completed techno-economic appraisal of the Damanganga-Pinjal Link Project while the techno-economic appraisal of the Par-Tapi-Narmada Link Project is in its advance stage.

The Mahanadi-Godavari link is the first and critical link of a nine link system of Mahanadi-Godavari-Krishna-Pennar-Cauvery-Vaigai-Gundar under the Peninsular Component of the National Perspective Plan (NPP).

The overall implementation of the ILR programme under the NPP will benefit 35 million hectares of irrigation, raising the ultimate irrigation potential from 140 million hectare to 175 million hectare and the generation of 34,000 megawatt of hydropower, apart from the incidental benefits of flood control, navigation, water supply, fisheries, salinity, pollution control, etc.

Based on joint proposals received in mission, third-party monitoring visits would be planned in such a way that such reports are available before the release of the next instalment. Further, the visits of the third party shall be planned keeping in view the visits that shall be made by the CWC.

India is currently in the process of an unprecedented water, sanitation and hygiene investment programme. At the 2014 Global Citizen Festival, Prime Minister Narendra Modi committed to end open defecation in the country and has since mobilized substantial resources with the help of the World Bank.[1] This will bring about

[1]Murphy McAnulty, 'Impact Report: World Bank Makes $1.5 Billion Loan to Support Sanitation Efforts in India,' Global Citizen, 3 February 2016, https://

holistic development for the country.

While the numbers are daunting, a lot is being done. And the economic benefits of WASH investments make the likelihood of future investments and future progress much higher. Some investments are small scale, others are large scale. On the smaller side of the spectrum, investments can be directed towards water purification methods, community wells or sources of water and the construction of community latrines.

Let us talk about sanitation and water management issues at an international level.

As per data of the Sustainable Development Goals (SDGs) Council of the United Nations (UN), one in four healthcare facilities lack basic water services.[1] Three in 10 people lack access to safely managed drinking water services and six in 10 people lack access to safely managed sanitation facilities. At least 892 million people continue to practise open defecation. Women and girls are responsible for water collection in 80 per cent of households without access to water on premises. Between 1990 and 2015, the proportion of the global population using an improved drinking water source has increased from 76 per cent to 90 per cent. Water scarcity affects more than 40 per cent of the global population and is projected to rise. Over 1.7 billion people are currently living in river basins, where water use exceeds recharge, and 2.4 billion people lack access to basic sanitation services, such as toilets or latrines. More than 80 per cent of wastewater resulting from human activities is discharged into rivers or sea without any pollution removal.

---

www.globalcitizen.org/en/content/impact-report-world-bank-makes-15-billion-loan-to/, last accessed on 14 October 2020.

[1]World Health Organization (WHO), '1 in 4 Health Care Facilities Lacks Basic Water Services – UNICEF, WHO,' 3 April 2019, https://www.who.int/news-room/detail/03-04-2019-1-in-4-health-care-facilities-lacks-basic-water-services-unicef-who, last accessed on 14 October 2020.

Each day, nearly 1,000 children die due to preventable water- and sanitation-related diarrheal diseases. Approximately 70 per cent of all water abstracted from rivers, lakes and aquifers is used for irrigation. Floods and other water-related disasters account for 70 per cent of all deaths related to natural disasters.

The leaders of all UN members pledged to achieve the sixth goal of the coveted SDGs, i.e., ensure access to water and sanitation for all.

6.1 By 2030, achieve universal and equitable access to safe and affordable drinking water for all

6.2 By 2030, achieve access to adequate and equitable sanitation and hygiene for all and end open defecation, paying special attention to the needs of women and girls and those in vulnerable situations

6.3 By 2030, improve water quality by reducing pollution, eliminating dumping and minimizing release of hazardous chemicals and materials, halving the proportion of untreated wastewater and substantially increasing recycling and safe reuse globally

6.4 By 2030, substantially increase water-use efficiency across all sectors and ensure sustainable withdrawals and supply of freshwater to address water scarcity and substantially reduce the number of people suffering from water scarcity

6.5 By 2030, implement integrated water resources management at all levels, including through transboundary cooperation as appropriate

6.6 By 2020, protect and restore water-related ecosystems, including mountains, forests, wetlands, rivers, aquifers and lakes

6.A By 2030, expand international cooperation and capacity-building support to developing countries in water- and sanitation-related activities and programmes, including water harvesting, desalination, water efficiency, wastewater treatment, recycling and reuse technologies

6.B Support and strengthen the participation of local communities in improving water and sanitation management.

The governments within India and all around the world are innovating and implementing policies to provide this basic necessity to all our citizens. However, it is a social responsibility of every individual and the large corporations alike to consume water judiciously and ensure that each human has access to this essential elixir of life!

◆

Meenakshi Lekhi represents the New Delhi constituency in the Lok Sabha and she is a National Spokesperson for the Bharatiya Janata Party. She is also a practising lawyer in the Supreme Court of India.

PART IV

CULTURE AND SOCIETY

14

CULTURAL NATIONALISM

K. KANIMOZHI

Nationalism as a modern concept emerged from the Treaty of Westphalia signed in 1648, after a civil-religious war. The major feature of this development is the separation of state and church, whereas the church hitherto was head of the state. European nationalism later developed into a kind of monocultural, monolingual nation state concept after the Napoleonic wars and the French Revolution. The American Revolution and the Switzerland model of national state brought forth the idea of multicultural, federal national states which differed from the archetypical nation states of Europe. During the colonial period, the oppressive nature of British rule in India led to the awakening of national consciousness through the ideas of various scholars, freedom fighters and political leaders. The whole of South Asia as we know now was under British rule and each region with its different culture and language countered British oppression through protests and various creative arts such as dramas, cinema, folklore, etc., in their independence struggle. Throughout the struggle for independence, the idea of civic nationalism with various institutions such as democracy, voting rights, rule of law, etc. were increasingly adopted by the masses and, at the same time, the regional, cultural and linguistic traditions were revived, through which the consciousness of nationalism was kindled.

Dravidian Nationalism

The Nationalist movement in India consisted of people from different ethnicities, cultures and languages coming together for the cause of Independence. The major political organization which had a pan-India presence was the Indian National Congress, which supported the idea of language-based provinces during the national movement. However, immediately after the religion-based partition, the Congress, which ruled at the national level, then became wary of the language-based reorganization of provinces. But ultimately with the States Reorganization Act, 1956, states were created based on linguistic criteria. Many scholars believe that the language-based classification of the Indian Union has led to effective governance and successful nation-building of India in the postcolonial era.

The Dravidian movement, which spearheaded the idea of Social Justice and brought significant social changes, was at the forefront along with, and often at odds with, the Congress during the national movement in South India. The Dravidian consciousness initially appeared among some backward-caste scholars in the second part of the nineteenth century, which has become a mass movement in the first half of the twentieth century with the formation of the Justice Party and the Self-respect Movement by Periyar E.V. Ramaswamy.

As per the author Jacob Pandian, the early 'Dravidian' ideology was developed and refined in social milieu which exhibited, among others, three important features: (1) the near-monopoly over the public administration of the Madras

Presidency exercised by the English-educated upper-caste individuals; (2) the privilege of Sanskrit as their distinct cultural marker and the simultaneous inferiorization of Tamil culture/identity by them; and (3) the efflorescence of a kind of orientalist scholarship which offered a picture of glorious Tamil/Dravidian past/identity as distinct from Sanskrit/Aryan past/identity.[1] The culmination of constant interaction between these closely related aspects resulted in the founding of the Justice Party and the Self-Respect Movement, which furthered the core principle of Social Justice in South India and laid a strong foundation for inclusive progress of Indians both during the British rule and after Independence.

The Revival of Dravidian Language and Culture

The Dravidian politics evolved into an inclusive ideology associating the Dravidian community with Tamil language and culture. As a scholar of Tamil movement, Pandiyan says, 'Tamil re-ethnogenesis and re-invention of tradition of the late 19th and 20th centuries proclaimed the boundary between the "Dravidian south" and the "Aryan north," and the Tamil literary tradition, once again, became the vehicle for boundary-maintenance, which affirmed the distinctive linguistic-cultural heritage of Tamils, providing them with the Dravidian identity.'[2]

Ahead of the revival of Tamil literature, the autonomous nature of Tamil and other South Indian languages belonging to the Dravidian language family has been established by scholars

[1]M.S.S. Pandian, 'Notes on the Transformation of "Dravidian" Ideology: Tamil Nadu, c. 1900-1940,' *Social Scientist*, Vol. 22, No. 5/6, 1994, pp. 84–104. JSTOR. Available at: www.jstor.org/stable/3517904, last accessed on 23 February 2020.

[2]Jacob Pandian, 'Re-Ethnogenesis. The Quest for a Dravidian Identity among the Tamils of India,' *Anthropos*, Vol. 93, no. 4/6, 1998, pp. 545–52. Available at: http://www.jstor.org/stable/40464849, last accessed on 10 September 2020.

at the beginning of the nineteenth century itself. One of the pioneers in this area was a British civil servant named Francis Whyte Ellis, who published about the Dravidian language family in 1816.[1] In his work, he established that the Dravidian languages are interrelated and are not derived from Sanskrit. Subsequently, the work of Robert Caldwell, *A Comparative Grammar of the Dravidian or South-Indian Family of Languages,* was published in 1856. After this, the Dravidian language family and its autonomous nature have been acknowledged and well-documented by scholars and popular figures alike. Though there were concerted attempts to establish the supremacy of Sanskrit over the rest of the Indian languages by a certain group, the main reason behind this Sanskrit supremacy push was to establish Manudharma, which divides people into four varnas based on their birth and establishes the superiority of the upper castes. This Sanskritization was vehemently opposed in the South and Western India as early as the second half of the nineteenth century by Dravidian scholars in the South and reformists such as Jyotirao Phule in the West. Movements such as the Tanitamil Iyakkam (Pure Tamil Movement) opposed the Sanskrit imposition, but it was often at odds with Periyar E.V. Ramaswamy's Self-respect Movement. The difference between them has to do with the former's Shaivite tradition and the latter's atheistic pronunciations.

In the literary world, there was a resurgence of Tamil classics during this period. Amongst the Indian scholars, Vedanayagam Pillai, Tamotharam Pillai, P. Sundaram Pillai and U.V. Swaminatha Aiyer undertook notable works in Tamil literature. Particularly, Swaminatha Aiyer had edited *Chivaka Chinthamani*, *Silappathikaram*, *Manimekalai*, *Pattupattu* and *Purananuru*[2],

---

[1]Thomas R. Trautmann, *Languages and Nations: The Dravidian Proof in Colonial Madras.*

[2]*Chivaka Chinthamani* is a story about a king who becomes an ascetic.

among his other works. Apart from them, *Parithimar Kalaignar* and *Dravida Sashtri* traced the history of Tamil Language. All these enabled the development of a larger Tamil consciousness, which can be witnessed post the 1910s and these works have been taken to the masses by the Justice Party, Self-respect Movement, Dravidar Kazhagam and later by the Dravida Munnetra Kazhagam (DMK).

The Dravidian movement used the power of theatre and cinema to spread the ideology of the movement among the masses. The Self-respect Movement had seen the emergence of theatre for propaganda and towards the late 1940s, the Dravidian movement captured the imagination of Tamil people through movies. The founder of DMK, Perarignar Anna, and Kalaignar Karunanidhi were scriptwriters and there were film actors such as K.R. Ramaswamy, S.S. Rajendran, Shivaji Ganesan and M.G. Ramachandran. Perarignar Anna's first film, *Nalla Thambi* (1948), featuring the popular comedian of those times, N.S. Krishnan, advocated cooperative farming, zamindari abolition and socialism. Movies such as *Parasakthi* and *Ratha Kanneer* were radical in their times as they were against the social hierarchy of the caste system. They also highlighted injustice within the society and propagated social reform ideas such as women's rights, widow remarriage and labour rights.

Their simple rendition of such historic literary pieces paved the way for the immersion of Tamil classics amongst the common people. The film *Poompuhar* (1964) took the classical Tamil epic *Silappathikaram*, which is a story about Kannagi and the Justice system of ancient Tamils, to the masses.

Silappathikaram (a Tale of an Anklet) is a story about *Kannagi*, which signifies the Tamil values and justice of ancient times. *Manimekalai* is a story about a Buddhist nun and is a sequel to *Silappathikaram*. *Pattupattu* means 'Ten Lays', which is a collection of 10 longer poems. *Purananuru* means '400 poems of Puram'. All these epics belong to Sangam literature, which traces back to the first century CE.

Justice Party and Social Reformation

The early Dravidian consciousness in a way culminated in the formation of the South Indian Liberal Federation and later transformed itself into the Justice Party in 1917. The Montagu-Chelmsford constitutional reforms of 1919 enabled more Indians to participate in the government. This enabled the Justice Party leaders to compete in the elections held in Madras Province and form the government in 1921.

The Justice Party, after coming to power in 1921, laid a strong foundation of social justice by bringing about reforms in the administration and to society at large. The notable achievements include voting rights for women; abolition of the devadasi system; the Communal G.O., which provided reservation for the backward community in the administration, considered as a first step towards affirmative action policies in modern India; introduction of the mid-day meal scheme in corporation schools and removal of the requirement of knowledge in Sanskrit to become a doctor.

These foundational policy steps proved to be an invaluable contribution to the better socio-economic status of the people of the present state of Tamil Nadu. There is enough literature and academic studies indicating socio-economic policy decisions taken during the Justice Party rule and later during the DMK rule, starting from 1967, to be the reasons for the better Human Development Indicators (HDI) currently in the state of Tamil Nadu.

Self-Respect Movement

The Self-respect Movement started by Periyar played an important role in taking the Dravidian consciousness to the masses. Periyar started a Tamil newspaper *Kudi Arasu* in 1925 and an English journal *Revolt* in 1928, both of which he used to disseminate the ideals of the Self-respect Movement. Periyar considered it as a movement to liberate the intellect. The ancient Tamils considered self-respect (*Than Maanam*) as an integral virtue and valued it. Periyar's self-respect philosophy is based on reason, critical intelligence, analytical thinking, intellect, empirical evidence and scientific approach. Periyar rejected the idea of division based on birth as dictated by the varna system, and thereby vehemently opposed the upper-caste domination in society and strived to establish a casteless society. He believed that self-respect is a prerequisite for achieving swaraj and that people must be freed from the shackles of caste, superstitions and blind faith in God before achieving swaraj.

Periyar spoke out against all forms of oppression. Not only did he oppose the caste oppression, but also gender discrimination. Women's rights were an inalienable part of Periyar's movement. He not only wrote and promoted these ideas, but he also put them to practice as well. He organized many self-respect marriages, widow remarriages and inter-caste marriages. Periyar inspired women to step out of their homes and participate in public life to liberate themselves. He welcomed the Simon Commission's recommendation of a 5–10 per cent reservation for women in politics.

The major point of action of the Self-respect Movement was the anti-Hindi Agitation of 1938. A year before that, the Congress formed the government in the Madras Presidency after winning elections held under the Government of India Act, 1935 and C. Rajagopalachari became the premier of the Madras Presidency. He introduced Hindi as a compulsory subject in schools of the Madras Presidency. In October 1938, Periyar organized the Anti-Hindi Propaganda League. Periyar condemned the Hindi imposition as he considered it a means to sideline Tamilians and felt it would ultimately lead to the destruction of the Tamil language and culture. The Tamil Nadu Women's Conference was convened in November 1938, in which prominent women leaders of the Self-respect Movement participated to mark their protest over the Hindi imposition. Periyar made a specific call to women to participate in the agitations. He said, 'It would be proper if the women went to jail and the men congratulated them in turn.' He also asked women to, 'fight for the cause of Tamil Language and culture with determination.'[1] Periyar was arrested for instigating women to participate in the anti-Hindi agitation and was punished with one-year rigorous imprisonment.

Periyar was invited to form the government in the Madras Presidency many times, but he refused to take those offers. Instead, he gave preference to his goal of improving the living conditions of the backward castes. In 1944, Periyar merged his Self-respect Movement with the Justice Party and formed a new organization called Dravidar Kazhagam, also known as the Dravidian Federation. The main objectives of this new organization were to abolish caste and superstitions and to strive for the retention of proportional representation of the depressed class people. He asked his followers to renounce all titles conferred by the British in protest against their atrocities.

Formation of the DMK and Tamil Nationalism in post-Independence India

In 1949, the DMK was founded by a group of Periyar's young followers who parted ways with him and broke away from the Dravidar Kazhagam. The two most prominent founding leaders are C.N. Annadurai and Kalaignar M. Karunanidhi. Both of them were renowned orators and used popular arts such as drama and cinema to propagate the ideals of the Self-respect Movement and

---

[1]K. Nambi Arooran, *Tamil Renaissance and Dravidian Nationalism 1905–1944.* Koodal, Madurai, 1980.

the objectives of Dravidian nationalism and Tamil language.

Tamil as a language was promoted as a medium to unite the masses irrespective of caste. The people of Tamil Nadu increasingly identified themselves as Tamilians rather than by their religion or caste. There were no Hindus, Muslims, Christians and so on; there were only Tamilians.

The DMK had spearheaded various causes of Tamils, immediately upon its formation. In 1952, when the Congress government, headed by C. Rajagopalachari, brought the Kula Kalvi Thittam, an educational policy that would require children to be schooled in the occupation of their parents, both DMK and Dravidar Kazhagam opposed it vehemently. The underlying principle of Varnashrama dharma in this education policy was taken to the masses and protests were organized to educate people about the need to oppose such policies.[1]

The DMK contested in the 1957 elections and established itself as the second-most powerful party in the state of Madras. The DMK manifesto issued ahead of the 1957 elections had socialist policies. The party continued its fight for social justice, both in and out of the legislative assembly. In the 1962 elections, the DMK went on to win seats all over Tamil Nadu and again became the second-largest party in Tamil Nadu.

The Anti-Hindi Imposition movement of 1965 was started by DMK in response to the central government's announcement to make Hindi the sole official language from 26 January 1965. This went against the assurances given by Jawaharlal Nehru in parliament.[2] During the movement, many cadres of DMK and

---

[1]R. Hardgrave, 'The DMK and the Politics of Tamil Nationalism,' *Pacific Affairs*, 37(4), 396–411. doi:10.2307/2755132, 1964.

[2]On 7 August 1959 and again on 4 September 1959, then PM Jawaharlal Nehru assured the parliament that, 'I would have English as an alternate language as long as the people require it, and I would leave the decision, not to the Hindi-knowing people, but the non-Hindi-knowing people.'

students were killed due to police excesses.[1] Though the situation returned to normal after then PM Lal Bahadur Sashtri assured that English will continue, the people of the state were deeply anguished by the actions of the government and this reflected in the 1967 elections.

DMK Government and Revival of Social Justice Policies

In 1967, the DMK won the election and formed the government in the state of Tamil Nadu and Perarignar C.N. Annadurai became the first DMK chief minister of the state. Ever since then, the DMK has been at the forefront of implementing social and economic policies to promote social justice and to eradicate inequality in society. Tamil literary and cultural elements were promoted. The two-language policy was adopted by the state government, which continues to be the language policy of the state even today. The one-kilogram rice per rupee through ration cards distributed by the DMK government was one of the first of its kind. The whole relationship between a common man and the government underwent a monumental change after the DMK came to power. The government was made more accessible and receptive to the voices of the common man and that reflected in the policies implemented.

After Perarignar Anna's untimely death in 1969, Muthuvel Karunanidhi became the face of the party and the chief minister of Tamil Nadu. In 1969, the DMK government undertook several key measures such as establishing the Slum Clearance Board to provide housing for the underprivileged living in slums. The public distribution system (PDS) was expanded to cover the

[1]In the memory of the people who lost their lives during the Anti-Hindi Agitation for the cause of Tamil, DMK observes Veera Vanakka Naal (day of saluting the martyrs) on 25 January every year.

whole state by 1976 and they also provided sugar, wheat and kerosene to each cardholder. There were need-based schemes for widows and pensioners, which were also implemented during this time. To promote agriculture, small farmers were exempted from land taxes. In 1971 and 1972, the Tamil Nadu Land Reforms Act was amended, reducing the ceiling of land ownership per individual from 30 standard acres to 15.[1] These welfare measures taken up during the DMK government's period have become the stepping stones on which the governments that came to power subsequently, have built the idea of social justice and welfare measures.

In 1969, the DMK government constituted a committee to inquire about the Centre–state relations under the chairmanship of P.V. Rajamannar. In 1974, the Tamil Nadu Legislative Assembly passed a resolution urging the Union Government to implement the Rajamannar committee recommendations to uphold federalism. The DMK has been a consistent driving force for greater autonomy of the state governments in the Indian political space till today.

The first backward class commission established by the DMK government submitted its report in 1970. Based on the recommendations of the commission, the backward class reservation was increased from 25 per cent to 31 per cent and that of the scheduled castes (SCs) and scheduled tribes (STs) from 16 per cent to 18 per cent by the DMK government in 1971. Subsequent governments that came after the DMK increased the reservation and at present, the reservation for other backward classes (OBCs) stands at 50 per cent and that of SCs and STs is 19 per cent. The successful reservation policy of Tamil Nadu democratized the public sphere and has proved to be a major reason for the more than satisfactory performance of the state

---

[1]S. Narayan, *The Dravidian Years: Politics and Welfare in Tamil Nadu*. Oxford University Press. ISBN: 9780199488179.

in the Human Development Indicators.

Another notable reform undertaken during this period (1969–76) was an amendment to the Hindu Religious and Endowments Act, which enabled any person, irrespective of his caste or creed, to become a priest in the temples. Again, in 2006, the DMK government had issued a G.O., which enabled any person having necessary training to become an *archaka* (a priest) in Hindu temples, irrespective of the person's caste.

A social movement that emphasized on cultural nationalism and preserving its language culminated in the movement being able to form the ruling government in the state of Tamil Nadu. Once it came to power, the DMK was able to use a bottom-up approach in administration and effectively listen to the public and address their grievances. It extended the welfare schemes and benefits for the downtrodden and oppressed classes such as the Arunthathiyars, transgenders, differently abled, women and children. The strong foundation was laid in all aspects of governance, including industrial development by bringing global technology companies to Tamil Nadu, developing small-scale industries and providing support to new entrepreneurs by establishing SIPCOT complexes and TIDEL Parks for IT. The Tamil Nadu state and its politics show us that having a strong cultural affiliation and subnational ideology can be used to practise good governance and bring revolutionary transformation to the lives of common and oppressed people alike.

At present, the power in Indian polity is heavily tilted towards the central government even in case of the subjects that feature on the State List. Slowly, the government at the Centre is trying to bestow upon itself all the powers, by reducing the state governments' power and autonomy and therefore, undermining the true federal structure. The threat of 'Hindi imperialism' has been revived with the New Education Policy brought out by the present government. Various state governments have already opposed the policy and been increasingly demanding more federal autonomy. The government's push for a monocultural, monolinguistic identity among all the Indians living in this diverse country will not succeed. The multicultural and multilingual identity of this nation is being put to the test once again. It is necessary to respect the regional, cultural and linguistic aspirations of all in this diverse country and give greater autonomy to the state governments.

◆

K. Kanimozhi is a Member of Parliament from the DMK party and represents the Thoothukudi constituency.

15

ROLE OF INDIAN CULTURE IN THE TWENTY-FIRST CENTURY

LOCKET CHATTERJEE

The twenty-first-century world system is defined by a horde of newly formed nations in the wake of decolonization after World War II. India, along with many other nations of Asia, Africa and Latin America, started their journeys towards building a nation from what were essentially fragmented groups and sects. Many other countries failed to do what India achieved—forming a fully functional democracy and granting adult franchise to all citizens. This feat could be achieved because of an essentially Indian culture that emerged through centuries.

Culture is one of the many signatures that lend a nation its distinctive existential ambiance. Any nation needs a culture of its own to hold it together. It is culture that fosters a sense of national togetherness. And it's the cultural atmosphere and values which build a national sense of belonging. What we understand by the love for one's country and nation has much to do with the value we set to national culture. Our national leaders at the time of the struggle for Independence were successful in channelling this national culture to get fragmented groups motivated to come together and persist for sovereignty.

Each nation has its own cultural narrative, which keeps changing down the years. This stands even truer for nations that trace their existence back to centuries such as India, Europe, China, Egypt, etc. These nations have had a dynamic history to say the least, starting off as primitive societies based on kinship, to becoming a region with a bunch of monarchically ruled areas. These nations also saw several decades of just one power controlling an entire area and many were colonialized by foreign powers and carry those influences to this date. In the twenty-first century, these ancient civilizations have emerged as democracies and espouse the ideals of a free and equal society.

However, despite the inevitable cultural metamorphoses, the basic cultural values continue to flow as the undercurrent. Whatever cultural and value changes keep happening, they do not or cannot change the basic cultural codes of a nation. This holds especially true for states such as France, the US and even India. Although the first two are 'newer' civilizations as compared to India, they have existed as nations since the 1700s. French nationalism is an interesting concept to understand how the culture of a region can be channelized to form a strong nation. French nationalism emerged from the continuous warring between France and England. There were numerous conquests through which the French were able to take back territories that make up France. These wars also gave the country their symbol of French nationalism in Joan of Arc. She was a peasant girl who led the French army in a momentous victory at the battle of Orleans against the English army, during the Hundred Years' War.

France was also influenced by Catholicism, which strengthened the cultural bond in the society, especially after the Protestant Reformation of the sixteenth century. However, what gave French nationalism a massive reinforcement was the 1789 French Revolution, which saw dedicated action by different groups of the society, across the country. The calls of 'Liberty, Equality and Fraternity' became the basis of the movement that helped form a coherent feeling among all people who shared the culture. French nationalism gained an 'expansive' quality under Napoleon Bonaparte, who justified military campaigns on the claim that France had the right to spread the enlightened French nationalist ideas across Europe and expand its 'natural borders'.

However, culture changes and evolves over time, to imbibe values from different cultures and ideas. Mostly, it is a way to include more people in the fold and thereby increase its sphere of influence. However, whenever a cultural change occurs (mostly when it is sudden), it creates an ideological crisis. Whether the change is only limited to the upper echelons of the propagators of the culture (the elite who have massive influence over the culture) or among the lower levels (the masses), it brings about tension and conflicts.

The new ideological values, brought about either by crisis in politics or by various implications of emerging societal philosophies, create a totally new narrative of culture, which we may call a new frontier of post-modernism. Or maybe we can even describe it as a sudden cultural liquidity—a state of continual cultural flux. As described earlier, most cultures are continually evolving and have a dynamic character to them where change occurs, but at a slower pace. This helps in proper acceptance of the change by all levels of the society, so that the change permeates the psyche of the population.

In the words of Dr S. Radhakrishnan, 'Over the past 5,000 years, Indian culture has responded differently to different influences and it has preserved, absorbed and assimilated elements from different cultures which is the secret of success of Indian culture and civilization.'

This is exactly what has created a cultural climate of incredible uncertainty in India. Due to its ancient existence, the civilization of the subcontinent has seen so many changes and influences that it is almost impossible to discern between the 'real culture' and the influences from 'outside'. This societal and cultural liquidity has served to give us an extremely diverse citizenry, but it is also the basis for our greatest crisis creating a precarious hiatus between us and our glorious cultural past. Many believe that we enjoyed a much better status in our past than what we enjoy currently. This gives rise to several questions. How much of our culture is homogeneous? And can we hope to solve our cultural problems in a homogenous cast? Can our cultural homogeneousness provide an answer to the collapse of ideologies around us? These are pertinent questions that require deep analysis and introspection.

We sometimes think that the collapse of ideologies in Indian societies is born out of ironic recasting of old values. Some of us glibly call it 'modernity'. Further, what many may understand as modernity is actually Westernization. There is a deep desire to chase modernity at the cost of discarding one's ancient culture and knowledge, but most of the third-world population ends up emulating western culture as a way to chase modernity. There is a stark difference between the two. Modernity is a focus on science and reason, which can coexist with one's cultural and societal practices; while the same cannot be said of blindly following western ideals.

In my opinion, the collapse of ideologies and old cultural values points to our increasingly precarious cultural stability. No doubt politics is closely woven into the texture of our complex cultural heritage. Politics is at the basis of not just how we organize ourselves, but also how we relate to one another.

The fast-changing political allegiance of individuals around us is definitely creating a cultural crisis. One often feels that people are now more divided than ever, with political ideologies trumping over personal relationships and respect for one another. Not just in India but worldwide, almost all nations are experiencing this age of great polarization. Voices are amplified and echo chambers crop up, especially due to social media. People from differing ideologies only focus on what makes them different rather than the numerous ways in which they are similar, thereby exacerbating the cultural crisis.

I understand this as a cultural crisis born out of political liquidity. Our failure to control the political flux has led to the collapse of old cultural values. And, therefore, we are fast losing cultural moorings. The only voice that is crying in the wilderness is the steady ancient voice of the Upanishads. 'Upanishad' comes from two words: 'Upa' refers to near or 'sameep', and 'Nisad' refers to sit-down or 'baithna'. It originated from the practice of pedagogy in ancient India where learned sages and peers who studied the Vedas, sat down with their students to disseminate the learnings and meaning of the Vedas. The Upanishads are a practical and detailed analysis of spiritual knowledge laid in the Vedas. These texts are the voice of the eternal and unchangeable truth, the voice of certainty that can show us the way out of the vast state of liquidity and flux.

I have little doubt that amid the collapsing values, India needs spiritual transformation and a Renaissance movement. The narrative now has to change thoroughly. The time has come for a significant cultural transformation bridging the hiatus between us and our philosophic and religious heritage. Let us unite as a nation to call for the spirit of religion and truth, to call for the old values and faith that we have lost in the blurred search for modernity (often Westernization) and new ethical principles. We have to rediscover ourselves in terms of our traditional national culture and traditional faith without having to make any compromise. We should not mistake regression for progress. The fundamental philosophy that binds Indian culture and nation together is our ancient philosophy of truth and spirituality. The cultural liquidity brought about by Western influence has created a mess. And it's high time we clear it. The only way out of the cultural mess is to embrace the spiritual culture of ancient India.

It's the culture of renunciation and not of greed. The culture of love and not of aggression. The culture of tolerance and control and not of vile propaganda. And the culture of vision, of inspiration, of faith. The culture of peace and prosperity.

◆

Locket Chatterjee is State President of Mahila Morcha, Bharatitya Janata Party, West Bengal and a Member of Parliament from Hooghly, West Bengal.

16

KALIKALAM[1] IS A BYGONE ERA: WOMEN IN THE POLITICAL SPHERE

S. JOTHIMANI

We have also seen that women are under-represented in Panchayati Raj Institutions. This is most unfortunate as it is women who undertake much more than half the economic activities of rural India. It is women to whom are entrusted the welfare and, often, the finances of the household. It is the women of rural India who are the main repository of India's great cultural traditions, of moral values which are fundamental to the survival and efflorescence of our civilization. Even we made reservation for Scheduled Caste and Scheduled Tribes in the upper tiers and are now bringing it down to the lower tier, should we not begin the process of reservations for women at the lower tier in the hope that it might in due course expand upwards to the higher tiers?

—Rajiv Gandhi

[1]'Kalikalam' is a Tamil word which denotes a belief in mythology that it is the end of the world.

I was just 14 years old, happily playing on the streets and beating up boys when Rajiv Gandhi made this historic speech at the Conference of Chief Ministers on Panchayati Raj, New Delhi on 5 May 1989. Neither that child nor her family could have ever imagined that this speech followed by its implementation (seventy-third and seventy-fourth amendments) would change the course of her life forever.

Exactly seven years later, in 1996, that child turned into a young lady. Just out of college, with crazy ideas and an uncompromising idealistic attitude, she aspired to contest the panchayat election on a seat reserved for women. It was a bolt from the blue for her family and also for her small idyllic village that had till then peacefully existed on the banks of the mystic river Amaravathi.

The tremors could be felt in the surrounding villages as well. 'How can someone from a decent family background, and that too a girl, even think of entering the stinking world of politics? Who will marry her?' The questions were never ending and eyebrows raised!

That child was me. When I broke my decision to contest elections, people started pouring into my home. They were in a state of shock. Many people were convinced that 'Kalikalam' (end of the world) has arrived, and wondered at the exclusive reservation for women. For them, the fact that men could not contest those reserved seats was a cultural shock.

After a month-long battle with kith and kin, I came to be seen as a stubborn, disobedient brat. I knew my family was concerned for me, but I still decided to venture out. I learnt my first lesson that I can convince people about my conviction with a smile and patient listening. Later, this proved to be one of the most essential qualities of a successful politician.

I had to go through another emotional hurdle—convincing

my mother. Amidst the stormy struggles of her life as a widow, she has brought me up as a happy, independent child who was unaware of gender discrimination—a blessing in disguise. She is the fulcrum of my life, on which my entire world revolves and vice versa. She had to withstand the criticism of rearing a girl child as a brat. Setting aside the criticism, her main concern was her only child's future. A young woman daring to enter politics where, it is said, angels fear to tread, was still a taboo for her. She spent sleepless nights worrying about her only child's plight. Yet, aware of her daughter's unyielding, decisive attitude even as a child, she had to finally relent. From that moment onwards, she has stood by me as a pillar of support.

Having crossed the obstacle of pitching myself in the elections, there were many more bridges to cross. At each crossroads, whenever I took up an issue to fight for, whether it was sand mining or water struggle for Dalits, I had to simultaneously fight two battles—one against gender discrimination and the other, standing up for an issue, which is the tough part of being a woman in public life.

From the panchayat to parliament, my journey has been punctuated with ebbs and flows, but I have never been dejected. I owe a great deal of my success to the landmark reservation policy which enabled one million women to be empowered politically as well socially through the panchayati raj. This is not my story alone, but that of one million women who have been brushed aside as subjects and not rulers! I am reminded of Neil Armstrong's quote when he landed on the moon, 'That's one small step for man, one giant leap for mankind.' We owe the credit to *the* man, Rajiv Gandhi, who as a great visionary had opened up a golden chapter for millions of women.

This silent revolution has transformed the ethos of the society in all areas, especially in rural India. There is an interesting empirical study which is worth sharing here. It pointed out that most of these women leaders, who haven't had even formal education, have concentrated with much vigour and interest on issues such as education, healthcare, sanitation, safe drinking water, community development, women's empowerment, environment, preservation of natural resources and transparency in administration, while their male counterparts prefer to pitch infrastructure and issues related to it. Also, these women leaders are known for fighting nightmarish battles. Ms Leelavathi, a corporator from the Madurai corporation (Tamil Nadu) was brutally murdered for her unstinting fight against water mafias. Another inspiring example is that of Ms Rani Sathappan from Rayapuram Panchayat (Tamil Nadu), who has emerged from being a docile housewife to a successful panchayat president (sarpanch). Although she was initially supported by her husband, she quickly learnt the ropes and became an efficient administrator. She played a pivotal role in the desilting of ponds and water bodies in her ward, thus making her panchayat self-sufficient in water management. She was also instrumental in making her panchayat a plastic-free zone. I am delighted to see this inspiring woman being recently re-elected for the third time.

The stories never end. I have heard the life story of the 55-year-old Panidevi, the sarpanch of the Bavdi village panchayat in Rajasthan. Born into the Dalit community and brought up in the feudal milieu of Rajasthan, her story is more like a fairy tale. Panidevi did not have any formal education, but through her commitment and zeal for learning, she made her dream a reality. Her life mission is to see every girl child in her panchayat empowered with education. She would tirelessly visit all the panchayat schools, ensuring literacy for all. Even though she bore the triple discrimination of illiteracy, poverty, and caste and gender inequality, she rose like a phoenix!

In my recent campaign for the local body elections in Tamil Nadu, a stunning fact was revealed to me. In many places, I could see the reservation bearing fruit. Women's reservation has gone up from 33 per cent to 50 per cent in 20 states, not to undermine the collective hard work, commitment and courage of thousands of brave women. When such is the ground reality, a fake image that 'all women are proxies to men' is being projected. My first-hand experience is that in many places, all three posts in a three-tier panchayat system—president, union councillor and district councillor—are occupied by women. It is not Kalikalam after all!

In a lighter vein, the lone male Member of the Legislative Assembly (MLA) who campaigned along with us remarked, 'It's high time I take a step back, as I have four strong women at the forefront'. Hope all other male counterparts acknowledge his opinion and pave the way for us women to lead from the front. Certainly this will make Rajiv Gandhi's dream a reality. Women emerging from the lower rung of the ladder to the top, from state assemblies to parliament, is definitely worth rejoicing. Yet, we have miles to go…

We women have proved our mettle as effective rulers and excellent decision-makers. And thus reservation is our right and not a concession. It has been a long wait—for 33 per cent reservation in state assemblies and parliament, while we actually deserve 50 per cent reservation. Aren't we fair in our demand?

◆

Sennimalai Jothimani represents Karur (Tamil Nadu) as a Member of Parliament in the Lok Sabha from the Indian National Congress.

17

REDISCOVERING INDIA

JYOTIRADITYA SCINDIA

Is India a country? Or merely a landmass embracing disparate aspirations, ethos, identities and ways of life? While these questions can be debated at great length, there isn't the slightest doubt about the fact that right from the pre-Independence era, India has shown the world the true meaning of diversity. Time and again, Indians have been vehement in the exhibition of their religious, linguistic and ethnic identities. Take, for instance, independent India's first cabinet, which had people from across regions and religions, and each carried his/her respective community's title with their name (such as Sardar Vallabhbhai Patel, Maulana Abul Kalam Azad and Rajkumari Amrit Kaur).

Yet, India has been held together, as much as by strong but invisible threads, as in our ancient sacred texts. 'Vasudhaiva Kutumbakam' (The World Is One Family) has time and again reminded us that the most consequential identity for us all, the umbrella of all other micro-identities, is the human identity. Although we are a collection of very distinct individuals, we prefer the Asian concept of 'we' rather than the Occidental notion of 'me'. So, if we look back through the ancient and medieval times coming up to the present, India has never considered itself to be distinct from the Homo sapiens of the world. Rather, we have always been a home for all. In some sense, our socio-cultural fabric is 'elastic' and 'osmotic'. 'All the convergent influences of the world,' wrote E.P. Thompson, 'run through this society: Hindu, Moslem, Christian, secular; Stalinist, liberal, Maoist, democratic socialist, Gandhian. There is not a thought that is being thought in the West or East that is not active in some Indian mind.'

Placing this fact at the very core of our values as a nation, our founding fathers gave birth to the Indian Constitution. In effect, pluralism is not a product of our Constitution; rather the Constitution captured the core, inherently pluralistic nature of the Indian society, which is also the essence of 'Indianness'.

In retrospect, most of India's successes can be attributed to its founding idea, which was anchored in resisting certain tendencies—the thoroughness of authoritarian politics and the temptations of a singular identity for all its citizens. Analogous to this, the most crucial element of our democratic system, what has prevented India from facing the same fate as many other postcolonial nations, is a unique kind of political invention, the intricate concoction of constitutional democracy entrenched by our founding fathers.

Therefore, not just developing countries, but the world as a whole has looked up to India's experiences of transitioning into a constitutional democracy—from building a legitimate and cohesive state to becoming an enduring democracy. Undoubtedly, as in the past, India is well-placed to take the lead in a currently changing world order. Perhaps, in a world that is today grappling with issues of identity, race and religion, and where the very fundamentals of pluralism are being challenged, India can usher in global policies that allow it to bridge these issues and foster a more plural world. As a confluence of civilizations, our nation has the ability to bridge many global divides.

This is not just true for India's cultural and nation-building prowess. Our country has shown that it is a remarkably intellectually progressive nation, and carries a glorious history of contributions that enabled massive intellectual and social transformations across the globe. There are plenty of examples. For instance, it was an Indian woman, Sophia Duleep Singh, the daughter of the exiled king of Lahore, Maharaja Duleep Singh, who led the movement for voting rights for British women. The Ghadar party in North America was the torchbearer of anti-imperialism and the right of self-determination for colonized nations. It is not merely by chance that so many of the Indian diaspora have secured leadership positions in governments around the world.

This is a great time for India to foster a balanced approach between redistributive public policies through appropriate government intervention on one hand, and the need to keep the economy open, as well as domestic capabilities intact and thriving on the other. There is huge merit in strengthening our domestic capabilities, as taught by the Gandhian economics of focusing more on production by the masses where jobs and, in turn, demand could be created, over mass production. One of the finest examples that come to my mind is khadi. Khadi was a symbol of emancipation and resistance against the colonial rule, but now, it is fashionable and much in demand worldwide. Thanks to Prime Minister Narendra Modi, the last five years under his able leadership have seen the widest acceptance of 'brand Khadi' in India. Khadi production has grown at an average of 19.45 per cent per annum since 2015–16, which was merely 6.25 per cent from 2004 to 2014.

However, it is a well-accepted notion that any economic transformation in India cannot happen in exclusivity.

The solution lies in enabling India's 'employable' (not defined on the basis of skill sets, but the potential of untapped human resources, and converting this potential into the ability to work) population to earn.

More than 50 per cent rural population needs to climb the upward mobility ladder. The surplus labour from the fields must transition into the factories. The Indian government has prioritized and invested in skill development—a growing avenue for India. With the path-breaking National Education Policy 2020, students will gain from vocational exposure at a young age. This approach is at par with the vocational training models employed by the UK and Germany, where educational institutes (schools and colleges) have been at the heart of vocational education.

For any movement up the ladder, our economy needs sector-specific plans for sustained growth and development across the primary, secondary, tertiary, quaternary and quinary sectors. Despite riding on the wave of the services sector, it is extremely crucial for the economy to revive expansion of the agricultural and manufacturing sectors, for they continue to hold the maximum potential to absorb a significant portion of our unemployed youth into the workforce.

Since decades, our system of agriculture has been marred by disguised unemployment, in addition to unproductive land sizes, low yields and natural disasters. The landmark farm bills passed this year by the parliament mark new thinking and a fresh approach to boost farmer incomes. This includes the fulfilment of the dream of 'One Nation, One Market', loosening the grip of middlemen and other bottlenecks, better market linkages, et al.

To reduce the burden on the agricultural sector, however, factories also need to flourish and for that, our industrial policies need to be consistent. Our policies must also incorporate environmental considerations because only if the environment is accorded topmost priority, will our development last.

We need to learn inexpensive manufacturing practices, by better synchronization in the supply chain. The export-led manufacturing model of China needs to be studied and may be adopted as per Indian conditions. Industrial townships such as Jamshedpur or textile manufacturing centres such as Tirupur in Tamil Nadu should be encouraged.

However, a lot is already in progress. With the Make in India initiative, India will truly 'open up' for greater business and ideas, thus making it the new global manufacturing hub in sectors such as electronics and defence. The Modi government is committed towards creating a robust ecosystem for defence manufacturers. The private sector's role has been expanded, licencing process reformed and domestic production has been incentivized. The government is treading on the path to realize India's potential to become a dependable supplier of defence equipment to many countries.

In the tertiary sector, boosting investment in infrastructure will have a multiplier effect on employment generation and ancillary industries. Banking, the backbone of the financial sector, must hold firm by ensuring credit availability and affordability. The increase in deposit insurance in this year's budget would surely improve public confidence in the banking sector. The problem of non-performing assets (NPAs) has been ailing the banking sector. The vigilance structure of the bank needs to improve with a proper know your customer (KYC) and background study of those seeking loans. Work culture of public-sector banks should be brought at par with private-sector banks, with customer satisfaction as the topmost priority, along with an effective grievance redressal mechanism for customers.

For governance to be truly effective, the poor must have a voice in the planning and implementation of schemes meant to help them. This, in turn, necessitates decentralization of key government functions. Mahatma Gandhi envisaged the villages of India as mini-republics and advocated that true democracy must begin at the grass-roots level, with gram panchayats (village councils) serving as the basic unit of governance. He firmly believed in the empowerment of these local government bodies as the only means to emancipate the country's rural populace.

Today, the government under the strong leadership of Narendra Modi is working on tackling the grave challenges facing rural India, pertaining to food security, quality education, healthcare, access to clean water and energy, sanitation and gender justice, among others, all of which fall within the realm of gram panchayats. The government is thus ensuring greater decentralization and empowering them by meaningful devolution of the 3Fs, that is, funds, functions and functionaries. The mantra is 'minimum government, maximum governance'. It is also about empowering the marginalized to participate in the development process. It is a matter of great pride that among the 3 million elected representatives across the 250 thousand gram panchayats in the country, 1.4 million are women. The largest representation of women in local governance in the world must translate into significant participation and empowerment of rural women.

I envision village councils, primarily in India but also across the developing world, as active quasi-autonomous bodies with enhanced transparency and accountability, equipped to prepare development plans for their villages in a participatory fashion. These bodies must also be facilitated with infrastructural upgrades in the form of teleconferencing amenities, computerized data management systems as well as solar panels for consistent supply of power. Through this pursuit, we must set out to structurally transfigure the Indian Panchayati Raj (local governance) apparatus that shall eventually alleviate the country's socio-economic troubles.

The road map should ensure awareness generation and capacity-building of stakeholders, especially the elected representatives of panchayats and officials, and people's participation and convergence at the gram panchayat level while practising transparency and accountability. As for all the other levels of governance, a blanket approach that focuses on outcomes rather than outlays should steer policies; with the Modi government's overarching 'Aatmanirbhar Bharat' (or self-reliance) vision, we have defined a common, long-term outcome for all, where our short-term goals, policies and laws will be set in line with this outcome. At the micro level, an outcome-based approach would also ensure that spending by governments at the lowest level is result-oriented. The Modi government realizes that just spending money on development is no longer a matter of pride. It strives to ensure that every rupee spent adds material value on the ground, thus differentiating between doing the job and doing it well.

That said, to govern a democracy like India is no easy task. We may have moved up on some economic and social indicators, but we have a diverse set of economic hurdles before us, and more so with the changing global economic order. The one constant, that is, India's diversity of communities (which also reside in other countries) is as much a challenge as it is an opportunity for India to foster connections globally, and even take the lead in establishing a shared global cultural order.

As for the vision for India, we must realize that there is no singular, all-encompassing Indian dream, but an amalgamation of multiple dreams our forefathers laid out for India's plural nature.

There is the Phule-Ambedkarite notion of social empowerment leading to actual economic empowerment of the backward communities. Or Verrier Elwin's idea of development of tribals while preserving their unique culture and lifestyle.

I believe that the Indian dream is most closely associated

with having the freedom and the means of authoring oneself into being. It is where differences are respected and assimilation is not considered a prerequisite for membership in the national community; where diversity is not a cause of disunity. It is a dream where one's caste, class, native place, religion and parent's occupation have no bearing on what one may aspire to be or seek to achieve.

At the bedrock of this dream is India's ability to transform differences into assimilation, and division into diversity. It is this idea of India that the Prime Minister Narendra Modi-led government has re-committed itself to. In the wake of a changing global order, the solid foundation of oneness built by our forefathers will also prove to be our greatest strength.

◆

Jyotiraditya Scindia is a Member of Parliament from Madhya Pradesh. Formerly a member of the Indian National Congress, he joined the Bharatiya Janata Party in 2020.

18

IS INDIA READY FOR HUGE POLITICAL AND SOCIAL SHIFTS?

RAM MOHAN NAIDU KINJARAPU

A lot has been written about India's demographic dividend and how it is going to transform the country economically. This was going to make it the world power that it was destined to be, but that destiny has eluded our grasp for decades now. From the days of being a middling economy but a moral giant, we have decisively left behind our Nehruvian legacies of non-alignment and moral politik. But have we truly arrived on the world stage as a superpower? Or are we still dependent on other economies for some of our major industrial needs in defence, pharmaceuticals, energy, etc.? In the age of PM Narendra Modi and the rise of a neoliberal political economy, are we even focusing on the right questions?

In the last two decades, India was focused on becoming an economic giant, but the focus has now shifted decisively to the remaking of its politics. Rather than economic reforms transforming our nation further, social engineering has been transforming our politics, and the burgeoning youth of the country has been playing an important role in these shifts. In my essay, I wish to throw light on how we must integrate these demographic shifts into our democratic set-up. Unless we are able to reshape our institutions to account for these changes, India's huge economic inequalities will be paralleled by huge political inequalities, where only one section wields power and patronage. Other groups will be forced to make demands through non-institutional means that may or may not be violent.

As an elected representative of the largely rural constituency of Srikakulam from the Telugu Desam Party, with its avowed adherence to social justice and good governance, I wish to focus on the bottom rung of our three-tiered democracy. While Indian democracy is successfully entrenched at the national and state levels, it is yet to root itself sufficiently well at the panchayat level. Ironically, the panchayat elections are closely fought affairs involving great prestige and huge sums of money, and attract high voter turnouts in Andhra Pradesh. Experimenting or reforming how these elections are fought at the grassroots, in consonance with our changing demographics and aspirations, might give us a better idea of how to emulate it at higher levels of our diverse federal polity.

Local Democracies: Grass without roots

Be it Mahatma Gandhi, M.N. Roy or Jayaprakash Narayan, some of our influential thinkers stressed upon the importance of democracy at the grass-roots level, beginning at the village and the panchayat. Gandhi's idea of democracy had the individual at the centre of expanding circles of political units, with villages making up the inner circle. Groups of villages (panchayats) come next, then groups of panchayats (talukas), and so on upwards. Each level was supposed to take strength from the level within it, while serving as a bulwark against centralization from outer levels of authority. Similarly, Narayan's idea of People's Committees and Roy's envisioning of a politics without political parties (radical humanism) aimed to foreground the last man, woman and child in their pursuit of a true democracy.

As the legacy of Gandhi and Narayan on our Constitution, the ideas of Sarvodaya and Antyodaya have had a powerful effect on the seventy-third and seventy-fourth Constitutional amendments. An example that shows their potential for empowerment is the fact that India has more women as elected representatives than the rest of the world combined! The setting up of rural and urban local bodies, thus giving India a unique three-tiered political structure, was to usher in an era of decentralized governance and diffused authority. However, these have remained on paper, with the failure of devolution in powers and finances from states and the Centre.

The main strands of my essay focus on the dialectical relationship between election funding and the presence of youth as the candidates, and the role of technology in the conduct of elections. The local bodies are famously said to suffer from the lack of three Fs: functions, functionaries and finances. I humbly admit that they also suffer from the lack of another crucial factor: youth under 35 years of age. Despite the age eligibility for contesting elections being 21 years and above, the number of youth under 35 who contest and win is surprisingly low. From my experience with political funding in Andhra Pradesh, local body elections frequently involve voter turnouts above 90 per cent, involve sums of ₹25–50 lakh on an average (ranging from ₹5–10 lakh to crores in extreme cases) and are closely fought affairs that mobilize the entire village or panchayat. Additionally, I raise the need to further empower the state election commissions, equipping them better to face challenges in local elections.

In my seven years of political journey, from my cycle yatra in

2014 till my recent campaign tours across the constituency, I have had the opportunity to visit more than 700 villages in Srikakulam. It's the northernmost district of Andhra Pradesh with the second-longest coastline in South India. It's also the poorest district in the state in terms of per capita income and gross domestic product (GDP), characterized by high outward migration among all sections and communities living here. I entered politics not just to build on the legacy of my father, the late Shri Yerrannaidu, but also because I was convinced of the ability of politics to restructure society into something more progressive and inclusive. This becomes crucial in an impoverished district as Srikakulam, which is blessed with natural resources and hard-working people. While its backwardness can partly be attributed to historical and geographical factors, its lack of progress over the decades can surely be attributed to the lack of political empowerment and non-delivery of public services to the last village and hamlet of Srikakulam. After its birth and quelling in Naxalbari, Naxalism emerged next in Srikakulam owing to conditions of extreme poverty and exploitation of peasants by landed classes.

A few good leaders in politics or a few great men in society might lead the society towards a better future for a while, but this becomes inherently dependent on their existence. Nor do such leaders have the wherewithal or resources to empower every individual and family of such a region. Sooner or later, the instruments for progress must be path-dependent and not person-dependent. They must be institutionalized so as to replace deeply unequal patronage networks. Citizens must be able to question their local representatives rather than depend on the mercy of great men and women. Reforming the way local politics is practised and the way local body elections are conducted is one such powerful measure to create an empowered citizenry. In fact, a direct link can be drawn between the complete non-legitimization of Naxalism as an ideology among the people of Srikakulam since the advent of Panchayat Raj Institutions from the 1990s, even in a limited manner. My own father, then MP of Srikakulam, survived an assassination attempt in 2004 by Naxalites in a last-gasp attempt to shore up the influence of their dying ideas.

Reforming Local Body Elections

Why focus on local elections and not on state or national elections? I believe that asking the right questions regarding local body elections and finding answers will give us an evidence-based road map to attempting reforms at the next level. Secondly, reforms at the grassroots could kick-start a virtuous cycle that might spiral into positive outcomes in state and national elections. Elections mobilize large parts of our society and political economy. Rather than attempting top-down reforms that might not account for the complexity of India, experimenting with reforms from a bottom-up perspective is more sustainable. While there have been several committees and commissions on Panchayati Raj Institutions since the noted Balwant Rai Mehta Committee of the 1950s, none of them examined the issues I have laid out previously, i.e., election funding, youth in local politics and the role of technology in campaigning.

Youth in Local Politics

In my interactions with local leaders as a young parliamentarian, I could see a consistent ignorance of young people being involved in politics. Even the few who are interested to fight for power or elected posts are met with huge challenges. India's current demographic dividend is simply not reflected in how it's being represented at its grass-roots level. This means that some of the issues that are important to the youth are not being highlighted by sarpanches (village heads) and ward members. Whether we like it or not, youth born in the 1980s and the 1990s will increasingly come to shape the nation's destiny and reshape its founding ideals. They have no lived experience of the freedom struggle, the Nehruvian era of socialist politics or the age of license quota and permit raj. All political parties must account for their aspirations and come up with institutional mechanisms for their participation. If not, their energies and ambitions might find expression on the street in ways that are wasteful and might not even be conducive to India's peaceful rise.

For decades, villages have witnessed high out migration to cities and towns, as they simply could not provide the kind of opportunities valued by the young for upward social mobility. Echoing the climax of the classic *Raag Darbari*, the youth solved the problems they faced in villages by simply leaving them for towns and cities. The seventy-third and seventy-fourth Constitutional amendments, coming into force in 1993, paralleled the ushering in of economic reforms begun in 1991. While this could be seen as a significant factor that accelerated rural–urban migration, state institutions also failed in developing villages as sites of opportunity or in reshaping cities as inclusive economies. The fact that the Mahatma Gandhi National Rural Employment Guarantee Act (MGNREGA) succeeded in stemming distress/seasonal migration and upended rural hierarchies reflects the ability of political institutions in empowering every community in a village. Another underappreciated measure was the liquidation of the karanam system in the 1980s by the then NTR-led government in Andhra Pradesh. This step broke the hold of feudal networks over state resources and public services, and gave power to local elected leaders.

While measures such as these were appropriate for their time, whether 10 or 30 years ago, they simply are not enough to satisfy the needs of our youth today. Nor do elected bodies in villages focus on skilling youth or encouraging educational institutions with disciplines centred on the demands of an agrarian set-up. Would this have been the case if young individuals participated enthusiastically in local elections, gained power and represented an influential lobby fighting for programmes and institutions focused on their economic mobility? People born after 1991 make up more than 60 per cent of our population. Few of these individuals can transcend local and state barriers to be elected on a national level at a young age. Most do not have the privilege of being from a political background as myself. Thus, involving youth as representatives from the bottom rung obviates the need for a political, caste or moneyed advantage for anyone to rise higher in a diverse democratic set-up as ours.

To reflect our changing demographic dividend, I propose that all political parties nominate a certain percentage of their candidates under 40 years in local body elections. Suppose all parties nominate 30 per cent of their candidates under 40. This would probably ensure that a much higher percentage of elected representatives will be under 40. Reservation of elected posts is not the panacea for youth under-representation since taking this to its logical conclusion might envisage reserving percentages for various age groups. Beyond implementing such a reservation within all parties, we must also explore barriers faced by the youth while contesting elections. Without tackling these, suggesting reservations becomes symbolism that preserves the prevailing dysfunctions. This brings me to the next area of reform—election funding, which is a significant barrier for political entry.

Election Funding

Given the continuing hold of caste and community networks in rural areas, panchayat elections are prestige-laden affairs, resulting in extreme expenditures. Even the average spending of ₹25–50 lakh per panchayat makes these elections a contest of the elites. Families sometimes end up selling their land and assets to win, even in cases of unanimous elections where potential candidates need to be pacified with promises of money or future patronage. The tensions are also more immediate owing to the personal and frontal nature of campaigning in a dense social sphere such as a village. Sometimes, these can be life-and-death affairs when one looks at the history of Rayalaseema factionism (Andhra Pradesh) in conjunction with its electoral cycles from the 1980s till the 2000s.

Elections, especially at the local level, are democratic festivals filled with meaning, a sense of history and the dilemma of voting for or against the party in power at the state level. This is important since funds received by local bodies, whether from the Centre or the Finance Commission, can become unstuck if opposing parties are in power at the local and state levels. The example of Ponduru, a census town and major panchayat in my constituency, is pertinent here. In the 2013 local body elections, Ponduru Gram Panchayat and Ponduru Mandal Parishad body were won by Yuvajana Sramika Rythu Congress Party (YSRCP)-backed leaders. This overlapped with a Telugu Desam Party-led government at the state level. In the year 2016–17, about ₹85 lakh was granted to the Ponduru Gram Panchayat (including ₹32.5 lakh left over from the previous year). Of this, only ₹5.7 lakh was spent. In the year 2017–18, ₹50 lakh was granted by the Finance Commission. Almost ₹80 lakh was left over from the previous year. Of the ₹1.3 crore of funds, barely ₹20 lakh had been spent in total. Politicization of development works has dealt a blow to its development with, as of May 2019, more than 80 per cent of the Finance Commission funds remaining unspent and more than 50 per cent of local revenues remaining unspent.

Thus, elections are double-edged affairs not just for the contestants but for the panchayat itself. You might win (or lose) after spending lakhs or crores. And if you win on behalf of a party that's not in power, you might not be able to ideate and sanction development works at all. Reforms in election funding must thus be two-pronged. How can excessive spending be curbed? This is directly linked to having better representation for the youth and minorities. State funding of elections has not been that effective when considering evidence from across the world. It could also make elections more expensive as established parties might still spend clandestinely, just as they spend above the limits prescribed by the Election Commission of India in assembly and national elections. To encourage youth participation, why not apply a model used in university elections? Can attempting the system of proportional representation minimize the flow of money? Let's unpack.

Like villages, universities are dense social spheres though they tend to be closed and controlled spaces. They are also closely fought affairs, with ideology replacing prestige as the driving factor for a candidate to win. Some of the practices from university elections can be emulated while conducting panchayat elections. First, draw lots on the places where each candidate can stick his posters. His or her leaflets, manifestoes and other campaign materials must be made available at the panchayat office and other public spaces. Posters must be handmade and not printed. Leaflets must be photocopied and not mass-printed. The philosophical point underlying these proposals is that of putting politics back to where it belongs—as political energies expended by the workers instead of money power expended by the candidates.

Elections must be driven by conviction and courage rather than consultants and commerce. Working to remove the power of money by starting at the bottom might give us valuable lessons on emulating the successful practices higher up. While the power of money and muscle can't be completely done away with, decreasing the scale will even things out. It would encourage not just youth but individuals from impoverished backgrounds to believe they have a chance, based on their convictions and volunteering energies of their supporters. Once you take out money, you are bringing in human power and devotion into play. When money isn't an issue, what becomes an issue is devotion to party or to the leader. There might still be quid pro quo situations and clientelistic relationships motivating some campaigns. However, these will not be the norm, unlike in the past, due to rising consciousness among the general public about their rights and dignity.

Role of the Election Commissions

Additionally, the state election commissions must be given the power to countermand elections when they find evidence of use of black money. The Election Commission of India had already made such a proposal to the Centre on multiple occasions. However, despite the central government's avowed fight against black money and corruption, this proposal was rejected. The state governments can take the lead in ushering in such a reform. For the Centre and the ruling party, losing a few constituencies due to countermanding might hurt its chances at the state or national level. While this proposal is based on first principles of fair electoral conduct, it might not affect anyone's chances politically either. For the governing party in Andhra Pradesh, having a few (or a few dozen) panchayat polls countermanded among more than 12,000 such polls might not hurt its chances as much. In fact, proclaiming itself as a champion of transparency and anti-corruption brings any political party far more electoral benefit than losing out on a few panchayats among thousands.

The role of the Election Commission becomes important not just with distribution of money or goods, but also with the dissemination of information. We must think afresh on how to devise ways and new bodies to specifically tackle the spread of misinformation and disinformation. Are the state election commissions in their current form equipped to deal with the creation and spread of fake news? Does fake news even have as much of a potent impact in largely closed spaces such as a panchayat, where the election is fought and where everybody knows everybody? It might be easy to believe when some public figure or community is falsely accused of something, but this might be a lot more difficult in an intimate space such as a village. Fake news needs to be created with an idea of the problems or issues in that particular village. Panchayat elections tend to foreground local issues over state or national issues, making the fake news phenomenon not as potent as it can be elsewhere.

Making a New India, Ground-up

Thomas Carlyle believed in the making of history as nothing but the actions of great men. From the time the country gained Independence, Indian politics and society have been obsessed with worshipping one kind of leader or other, hoping to find answers for their well-being from demigod-like figures who were far removed from their lived realities. This has had mixed results, to put it charitably. Invoking Swami Vivekananda, we must write our own destinies, and we must begin that by starting at the bottom of our politics. The remaking of a new India, with the kind of politics that foregrounds aspiration and opportunity above caste, community, ethnicity and religion, must necessarily begin through revolutionary changes in how local politics is practised and in how local elections are conducted. The achievement of Jawaharlal Nehru that I most admire is that he ensured democratic processes took root so strongly that India did not need any more Nehrus. I want our local politics to be so shaped that India will not need any more men gaining power using their inherited capital: caste, social, political or economic. Our politics must make space for youth, or they might make that space forcefully. The story of the rise (or fall) of youth in India will be the story of India in the twenty-first century.

Ram Mohan Naidu Kinjarapu is a Member of Parliament to the 17th Lok Sabha from Srikakulam, Andhra Pradesh, representing the Telugu Desam Party (TDP). He is also the national general secretary of the TDP and the leader of the party in the Lok Sabha.

PART V

THE FUTURE IS HUMAN

19

TAPPING INDIA'S DEMOGRAPHIC DIVIDEND

GAUTAM GAMBHIR

Ever since Independence, there have been constant debates and discussions around India's massive population—whether it is a boon or a curse. As in the case of most developing countries, India is also seeing an exponential rise in the size of its population. India is projected to become the world's most populous country by 2024, surpassing China. Due to the lack of resources and facilities in post-Independence India, this rise has been touted as the root cause of several problems. Be it malnourishment, high mortality rates, high morbidity or general poverty, it has always been challenging for the government to take care of so many people with such limited resources, no matter how judiciously they have been utilized. If one speaks with elders who lived through those times, they will always reminiscence about the shortage of medical facilities, modes of transport and even food supplies. Our country was not even able to produce enough food for the consumption of its own people, let alone for export. Furthermore, a very large section of our population, especially in the tribal areas, was left completely untouched by any kind of development.

The rise in India's population over time has also led to a shift in the demographic structure of the country. Currently, 65 per cent of our population is less than 35 years of age and it was projected that in 2020, the average age of Indians fell to just 29 years. India is set to become the youngest country in the world in terms of age. What this effectively means is that the size of productive population, i.e., the size of the workforce, has increased drastically. In simple words, we have more hands to develop our country and lift people out of poverty and into the middle class. This is the demographic dividend that our country can and should tap into. However, this cannot be a foregone conclusion. India cannot achieve its potential as a country just by having a large number of young people. We have to first invest in these youngsters, mould them and align their energies, talents and ambitions with the development of the country. If the foundation is not strong enough, the same youngsters could end up becoming a liability. For ensuring the holistic development of youngsters so as to make them become productive citizens, I believe that it is imperative for the society as well as the government to focus on the following five areas.

Nutrition

According to the World Bank estimates, India is one of the highest ranking countries with regard to the number of malnourished children. Studies indicate that one-third of the world's malnourished children live in India. The 2019 Global Hunger Index ranked India 102 out of 117 countries, identifying the situation as 'serious'. Child stunting and child wasting rates, especially in children under the age of five years, are also very high in our country. Uttar Pradesh, Tamil Nadu, Madhya Pradesh and Jharkhand rank highest in malnutrition. We can never have productive adults if the situation remains like this. Our Hon'ble Prime Minister Shri Narendra Modi has also stressed on the need to eradicate malnutrition completely. In furtherance of his vision, the government launched Poshan Abhiyaan to spread awareness about malnourishment in children and women, and to encourage the civil society to help the government in providing nourishing food to the underprivileged. There are several organizations that are coming forward with mid-day meal programmes and other such initiatives. The private sector as well as individuals will have to think of this as a social investment in the larger interest of the country or else this golden opportunity of reaping the demographic dividend will be wasted. Only a combination of efforts by the civil society, public sector and sponsorship through donations, investors, corporates and volunteers can successfully eradicate this problem and permanently end the scourge of malnutrition-based infant deaths. I have been conducting several awareness campaigns in my constituency and will be setting up community kitchens to provide nutritious food in those areas of the constituency where large sections of underprivileged reside. Ever since I have announced this initiative, several like-minded people have also come forward to contribute to the cause.

Revolutionizing the Education System

Although the literacy rate, which is currently 74 per cent, has been increasing consistently, the quality of education has not seen a substantial improvement. There is a huge gap between the infrastructure and facilities provided in government and private schools. For several courses, our country has been following the same curriculum which was set up by the British to colonize the population and create yes-men. The focus was never to encourage creativity, innovation and excellence, but to sow the seeds of obedience to particular thought processes. The situation in higher education is no better. Although courses offered by more than 500 government universities carry immense prestige and legitimacy, private universities, colleges and technical institutes cannot boast of the same. According to the *India Skills Report 2018*, a survey by Wheelbox, Pearson and the Confederation of Indian Industry, 1.5 million engineers graduate every year, but only 52 per cent are employable. Further, about 3.6 lakh MBA students graduate from 4,000 business schools in India, but only 61 per cent of them are unemployable due to skill gaps and less work experience. Many scholars and academicians have been saying that several private colleges and technical institutes mushroomed over the past few decades where the quality of education is abysmal. In 2017, the University Grants Commission (UGC) stated that the country has more than 23 fake universities, with 66 bogus colleges in the national capital itself. This situation is one of the major reasons behind growing unemployment in the country. We can never reach our true potential if the education being provided is not sound and useful. The government needs to invest more in building infrastructure for quality education and must also regulate private education with proper accreditation and regular assessments. Otherwise, we will end up having a very large number of young adults who are educated on paper, but their degrees and diplomas cannot facilitate them in acquiring two square meals a day.

Bolstering an Entrepreneurial Mindset

Third is the need to bolster an entrepreneurial mindset in the youth of this country. In the cycle of development, initially, a bulk of the population is engaged in the primary or agrarian sector. With increase in resources, the upper strata moves towards the secondary or manufacturing sector. Finally, when manufacturing reaches an optimum level, people start moving towards the tertiary or service sector. However, the development in India has been quite skewed in this regard. After leaving the agricultural sector, people started moving towards services, directly bypassing the manufacturing sector, which was in a shambles. Most of the youngsters whose parents were engaged in agricultural activities aimed at white-collar jobs instead of setting up manufacturing units. This also reflects the risk-averse attitude of youngsters in India as compared to their counterparts in developed countries. This led to stagnation in the manufacturing sector, a sector that is yet to attain its full potential.

India has to rely on imports from foreign countries for several essential products. What is to be analysed is that if everybody is out to get a job and nobody is creating more jobs, then it would result in the collapse of the job market. If there aren't enough factories and manufacturing units, what will so many engineers and managers who are graduating every year do? The central government under the leadership of our Hon'ble Prime Minister has time and again reiterated that India can only develop at a fast pace if the youth develops an entrepreneurial approach and aims at giving jobs rather than seeking them.

The central government has taken several initiatives to encourage budding entrepreneurs through easy loans, creating a start-up ecosystem in India and focussing on digitization to reduce operational costs. This is the only way to revamp the business world, where the concentration of economic power has been in the hands of a few families since Independence. In the last few years, we have seen many success stories. Be it OYO, Flipkart or Paytm, bright Indian minds have showcased that if a conducive environment is provided, they, too, can excel. As a society, we have to inculcate a sense of confidence in the minds of youngsters, so that they can bet on themselves and pursue their dreams and ambitions. Creation of sustainable businesses will be the key to development of our country and tapping into the demographic dividend.

Nurturing the Youth

Fourthly, we as a country, have to nurture our young and provide a stress-free environment. The National Mental Health Survey 2015–16[1], conducted by the National Institute of Mental Health and Neuro Sciences Bengaluru, under the purview of the Union Ministry of Health and Family Welfare, reveals that 9.8 million teenagers in the age group of 13–17 years suffer from depression and other mental health disorders and are 'in need of active interventions'. There have been several studies which suggest that youngsters who suffer from depression and other mental health issues are more prone to substance abuse. The suicide rate among young adults aged between 15 and 29 years in the country is more than three times the national average.[2] This makes us a country with one of the highest suicide rates among youth in the world. What is most shocking is the fact that in India, every hour, a student commits suicide.[3] Suicide mortality in India is higher among the

---

[1]National Mental Health Survey of India 2015–16: Prevalence, Pattern and Outcomes. Available at: http://indianmhs.nimhans.ac.in/Docs/Summary.pdf, accessed on 1 September 2020.

[2]Neeraj Kaushal, 'India's Youth Suicide Binge: Younger People, and Married Women, Are More Prone to Suicide in India,' *The Times of India*, 7 February 2019. Available at: https://timesofindia.indiatimes.com/blogs/toi-edit-page/indias-youth-suicide-binge-younger-people-and-married-women-are-more-prone-to-suicide-in-india/, last accessed on 1 September 2020.

[3]ET Contributors, 'A Student Commits Suicide in India Every Hour; How Can our Educational System Prevent this?' *The Economic Times*, 22 March 2018. Available at: https://economictimes.indiatimes.com/magazines/panache/between-the-lines/a-student-commits-suicide-in-india-every-hour-how-can-our-educational-system-

more educated, who are typically better off financially than the less educated. This is an extremely precarious situation, which has to be handled deftly. There is still stigma attached to mental illness and the number of psychiatrists, counsellors and mental health experts in the country is relatively low. Globally, a major factor contributing towards reduced suicide is better diagnosis and timely treatment of mental illnesses. It would have to be a societal effort and not just something left to the government. Even today, the initial reaction of most parents is to suppress such emotions in their children, instead of dealing with them. As a society, it is incumbent upon us to provide a safe environment to our young where they can express themselves, and share their concerns and fears. Educational institutions must also have psychological counselling programmes in place to help students deal with their issues in confidentiality and in a comfortable environment. If this situation does not improve, it would permanently damage the overall productivity of the country, thus leading to an increase in dependency.

Steering towards Sustainability

Lastly, we must steer the next generation towards sustainability. The debate around deterioration of the environment and its root cause is over. The biggest reason behind it is our insatiable greed. To fight poverty and lack of resources, several countries including those which we refer to as developed, engaged in rampant industrialization. This did help in increasing productivity and revenue, which led to a better life for the citizens. However, all this was not without any consequence. Our thirst for development and commercialization has had an extremely adverse impact on the environment. Growth is crucial, as without it, a growing population can never be accommodated. However, it is equally

---

prevent-this/articleshow/63411123.cms, last accessed on 1 September 2020.

important for us, as a society, to focus on sustainable development, especially for the future of our children. The younger generation must learn from their past mistakes.

According to me, the overuse of plastic has been the biggest fault of mankind in the past century. Initially, it was just a matter of convenience for people, but slowly and steadily, this deadly plastic penetrated each and every aspect of our daily lives. Surviving without it has now become difficult to fathom. On one hand, thousands of products would become unmarketable if we put an end to single-use plastic and several industries would suffer irreversible losses. On the other hand, our very existence is threatened if we keep using plastic in our daily lives. Not only does it pollute land, water and air, it is also known to increase cancerous elements in the environment which are ingested by all of us, day in, day out.

The second mistake that we have made in furtherance of achieving development is excessive deforestation. This has now been happening for thousands of years, arguably since man began converting from hunter-gatherer to agriculture-based societies and required larger, unobstructed tracks of land to accommodate domestic animals, crops and housing. However, it is only after the onset of the modern era that it has taken the shape of an epidemic. In the short run, deforestation means more land for the people and more resources such as fruits, vegetables, timber, wood, etc. However, in the longer run, it means increase in greenhouse gases, climate change, desertification of green belts, flooding, soil erosion leading to infertile land and loss of habitat.

Land reclamation, i.e., creation of land on sea is another major decision which has had an adverse impact on our environment. Several of our cities, including our financial capital, have been built through land reclamation. It has not only affected the ecology and marine life, but has also invited the wrath of the sea in the form of flooding and soil liquefaction. This has also made buildings and other infrastructure more susceptible to earthquakes. Fishermen and tribal population living in the coastal areas are forever in danger because of our reckless actions. The younger generation must be made aware of the price of those skyscrapers standing on the coastlines of our big cities.

Finally, the next generation must develop the habit of using renewable and non-polluting sources of energy from a very young age. The previous generations took a very long time to understand that pollution stemming from vehicles, burning of crops and from industry can choke entire cities such as Delhi and Beijing. The only way for the world to reduce its dependence on oil and gas and transition to eco-friendly sources of energy is by steering the new generation towards wind, solar, hydro and nuclear energy. These sources are inexhaustible, have lower maintenance costs and numerous environmental and health benefits. Although these sources have higher upfront costs, I believe that today's youth will do a much better job at developing technologies which would cater to the needs of the masses and make these affordable. Today, if we build the path towards sustainable development, our children will be able to reverse the losses that have been suffered by us and build a better tomorrow. Without teaching the youth about sustainable development, tapping into the demographic dividend will remain a far-fetched dream.

I am certain that if one looks deep into the system, one would find several problems pertaining to the development and well-being of the youth, which need immediate attention. However, the first step towards solving any major issue is chalking out a solid strategy. That is exactly why I have zeroed in on these broad areas. If we can come together and work on the above-mentioned five issues, we can transform our country by harnessing our biggest strength, i.e., the youngest population in the world, and achieve our long-standing dream of becoming a global superpower.

◆

Gautam Gambhir, a former cricketer, was part of the international cricket team of India. A member of the Bharatiya Janata Party and a first-time Member of Parliament, he currently represents East Delhi in the Lok Sabha.

20

THE GENDER IMPERATIVE: GENDER EQUALITY, GENDER SENSITIVITY AND GENDER NEUTRALITY

HARSIMRAT KAUR BADAL

So kyun manda aakhiye jit jamme rajaan?
(Why look down upon women who give birth to men, including the kings?)

—Guru Nanak Dev Ji, on female gender equality[1]

By quoting this verse by Shri Guru Nanak Dev Ji, I aim to draw attention to the state of gender imperative in our society. The need to treat women equally has been felt since time immemorial, but it has been faintly realized. Discussions around gender equality, gender sensitivity and gender neutrality are pertinent to ensure that the discrepancy in figures and facts relating to gender are addressed and the gap is narrowed with

[1]Upinder Swahney, 'Gurbani Reflects his Educational Philosophy,' *The Tribune*, 10 November 2019. Available at: https://www.tribuneindia.com/news/archive/features/gurbani-reflects-his-educational-philosophy-858136, last accessed on 3 September 2020.

the help of concrete initiatives.

Gender Indicators

If one analyses the difference between the status of women and men in our country, the revealing figures speak truth to power. For instance, as per Census 2011, the female literacy rate stood at approximately 65.5 per cent, whereas male literacy was 82.1 per cent. Although this gap has reduced over the years, the adult male literacy rate exceeds the adult female literacy rate by 17 percentage points.[1] The difference is a stark reminder that India is still away from attaining Goal 4 of the UN Sustainable Development Goals of ensuring 'inclusive and equitable quality education' and 'lifelong learning opportunities for all' by 2030.[2]

TABLE 1

Male and Female Literacy Rate Gap

	1993–94	1999–2000	2007–08	2014	2017–18
Male literacy rate	65.5	69.2	76.6	80.3	81.5
Female literacy rate	37.9	43.8	54.9	61.8	64.6
Gap	27.6	25.4	21.7	18.5	16.9

Source: National Sample Survey (NSS)

As per Census 2011, in a population of 121 crore, there were around 48.5 per cent females with a sex ratio of 949 females/1,000

[1]Tanushree Chandra, *Literacy in India: The Gender and Age Dimension*, ORF Issue Brief No. 322, October 2019, Observer Research Foundation (ORF). Available at: https://www.orfonline.org/research/literacy-in-india-the-gender-and-age-dimension-57150/, last accessed on 3 September 2020.

[2]*The Sustainable Development Goals Report 2019* (New York: United Nations, 2019).

males in rural India and 929 females/1,000 males in urban India. The United Nations (UN) report listed India at the 189th position out of 201 countries in terms of female-to-male ratio.[1] Among the Asian countries, India is at the 43rd position out of 51.

Health indicators for women have been a mixed bag, with the maternal mortality rate (MMR) sliding considerably from 301 in 2001–03 to a low of 130 in 2014–16. The total fertility rate has come down to 1.8 in 2016 as compared to 2.3 in 2015. The decline of fertility can be attributed to various factors, including modern lifestyles and external stressors, which also cause other female health issues such as polycystic ovary syndrome (PCOS), endometriosis and menopausal depression, among others. Female mental health is bereft of concrete attention and redressal. As per the World Health Organization (WHO), 'Unipolar depression, predicted to be the second leading cause of global disability burden by 2020, is twice as common in women'.[2] Also, depressive disorders are responsible for 41.9 per cent of the disability from neuropsychiatric disorders among women compared to 29.3 per cent among men.

Violence and physical and mental abuse against women are commonplace throughout the world. As per the WHO, at least one in every five women suffer rape or attempted rape in their lifetime. The National Crime Records Bureau (NCRB) registered a record high, as many as 3,59,849 cases of crime against women across the country in 2017, signifying an upward trend each year.[3]

---

[1]'List of Countries by Sex Ratio,' Statistics Times, UN (World Population Prospects 2019), World Bank, 4 May 2020. Available at: http://statisticstimes.com/demographics/countries-by-sex-ratio.php, last accessed on 3 September 2020.

[2]'Gender and Women's Mental Health,' World Health Organization (WHO). Available at: https://www.who.int/mental_health/prevention/genderwomen/en/, last accessed on 3 September 2020.

[3]Outlook Web Bureau, 'Crimes Against Women in India Continue to Rise,

This rise is of grave concern and deserves immediate attention.

When compared to men, economic participation of women is abysmal. A Deloitte report titled 'Empowering Women and Girls in India for the Fourth Industrial Revolution'[1] noted that female labour force participation had declined to 26 per cent in the year 2018 from 36.7 per cent in 2005, a corollary to lack of access to quality education and various barriers, be it social or economic, which in turn, limit work opportunities for women. Further, 95 per cent of women or 195 million are employed in the unorganized sector or are engaged in unpaid work.

Another pertinent issue that demands attention is that of women in leadership positions. As per the United Nations Women report titled 'Progress of World's Women: Access to Justice, 2011–12, UN Women,' 'On an average, women hold only 7 percent of ministerial positions and 15 percent in national parliaments in all the 9 countries of the South Asia region.'[2] Further, in India, only 10 per cent women occupy ministerial positions and 14 per cent occupy the national parliament.

These figures are startling, to say the least. Gender parity should be prioritized to ensure that these gaps are fixed, and the goal of women empowerment is attained at the earliest.

UP Most Unsafe: NCRB,' *Outlook*, 22 October 2019. Available at: https://www.outlookindia.com/website/story/india-news-crimes-against-women-in-india-continue-to-rise-up-most-unsafe/340881, accessed on 3 September 2020.

[1]'Empowering Women and Girls in India for the Fourth Industrial Revolution: Opportunity or Challenge?' Deloitte. Available at: https://www2.deloitte.com/content/dam/Deloitte/in/Documents/about-deloitte/UNGCNI_black_final%20v6%20web%20high%20res.pdf, last accessed on 3 September 2020.

[2]Available at: https://asiapacific.unwomen.org/en/countries/india/leadership-and-participation/fact-and-figures, last accessed on 7 October 2020.

Problem Statement

Women have historically been seen only as 'the second sex', which led to them being excluded from the decision-making process in not just the private sphere of their homes, but in the public sphere of politics, too. This oppressive structure has relied on women's unpaid labour and their role as caregivers, while simultaneously denying them any opportunities to transcend these roles. Examples of other developed nations make it abundantly clear that a country can develop only when it channelizes the talents of its female population, a goal that India is lagging behind in. The need of the hour is for India to ensure that women are provided with equal opportunities in the economy, polity and society.

None of these factors can be classified as definite causes because all of them contribute to making the condition of women what it is, and their secondary status in society. One kind of discrimination feeds off the other and creates even more difficult circumstances for women across class, caste and creed.

Political Representation

India is one of the few countries where women did not have to struggle for their right to vote, but got it at the time of Independence. To ensure that more women occupy the political sphere, the seventy-third and seventy-fourth amendments guaranteed a 33 per cent reservation of seats for female candidates in local-level government. Since then, 20 states have enacted a 50 per cent reservation for women at the local level,[1] thus providing a strong impetus to include more women in the

---

[1]Available at: https://panchayat.gov.in/web/guest/reservation-of-women-in-pris, last accessed on 3 September 2020.

decision-making process. However, despite success stories, there are also instances where the elected representatives end up acting as proxies for male members of the family.

The majority of over 13.45 lakh elected women representatives in panchayati raj institutions, which constitutes 46.14 per cent of the total elected members,[1] often do not get to exercise their decisions effectively. India ranks 148th among 190 countries in Inter-Parliamentary Union's Women in Politics ranking,[2] with 64 women MPs in the Lok Sabha, 11 of whom have grass-roots political experience. This lack of female participation in the legislative process is also a contributing factor to the lack of gender parity in India.

Economic Disparity

The 0–6 years child sex ratio of 2011 Census at 914 females/1,000 males shows that right from childhood, females are at a disadvantage in India, which can be compounded with disparity in literacy rates between the sexes. In terms of employment in India, female labour force participation has declined from 34 per cent in 2006 to 24.8 per cent in 2020.[3] Most women are employed in the informal/unorganized sector, where they are paid poorly and have no job security, employment benefits or any sort of

---

[1]Dr Rajesh Kumar Sinha, 'Women in Panchayat.' Available at: https://www.pria.org/uploaded_files/panchayatexternal/1548842032_Women%20In%20Panchayat.pdf, last accessed on 3 September 2020.

[2]'Women in National Parliaments.' Available at: http://archive.ipu.org/wmn-e/classif.htm, last accessed on 3 September 2020.

[3]PTI, 'Female Labour-force Participation in India Declined from 34 pc in 2006 to 24.8 pc in 2020: Study,' *Business Standard*, 6 March 2020. Available at: https://www.business-standard.com/article/pti-stories/female-labour-force-participation-in-india-declined-from-34-pc-in-2006-to-24-8-pc-in-2020-study-120030601403_1.html, last accessed on 3 September 2020.

insurance. It goes without saying that progress and development of the country will be stymied if females, who make up half the population, are able to contribute a dismal 14 per cent to the workforce. It must be kept in mind that only increasing women's education is not enough to ensure equality; the focus must also be on ensuring that women have socio-economic independence and have a say in the timing of their marriage.

Social Discrimination

In India, discrimination and oppression exist amongst different castes, classes, creed, etc., but even in the same group, women often bear the brunt of being discriminated against by members of their own community. A patriarchal structure that mooches on one half of the population uses all possible means to keep the group under control. The discrimination manifests itself in not allowing women to gain an education, not allowing them the freedom to make their own choices and ensuring that they are not financially independent. Not just India, but even the most developed countries have large swathes of population that isn't comfortable with women leading the nation (in the public sphere) or taking charge of the household (in the private sphere) and everything in between. To ensure that women become equal members of society, we must come together to uproot biases and prejudices that we harbour against them.

Nanhi Chhaan: A Small Hope

Woman and nature, both are embodiments of selfless love and care. Just like Mother Nature, a woman gives birth to a new life and fulfils her commitment to nurture it. Protecting both these sources of life, in essence, implies protecting all life on earth.

However, unfortunately, no place is safe for a girl child, not even her mother's womb. She is often perceived as a burden and at times, even silenced to death before she is born. This shakes the very roots of humanity.

With a firm resolve to lead the charge against this, I launched this ambitious initiative called Nanhi Chhaan in the year 2008, in Punjab. The objective of the NGO is to 'Save the Girl Child, Save the Environment'. Nanhi Chhaan believes that protecting the girl child is a fundamental issue and women's empowerment is an important first step towards eradicating this menace of female foeticide.

The NGO has set up a wide network of sewing centres in villages and works for the capacity-building of women at the grass-roots level. Women from the economically weaker sections of society are imparted with vocational skills, such as tailoring and weaving, at the village level. Nanhi Chhaan provides the necessary handholding to these women and empowers them to earn their livelihood, thereby supporting them to become self-reliant. At the end of the skill training, women are presented with a sewing machine to 'weave' their own success story. Through this noble endeavour, Nanhi Chhaan is also working towards reviving the dying art of phulkari.

The organization has distributed more than 30 lakh of Boota Prasad (holy sapling)—a perfect embodiment of the philosophy that aims at preserving the environment—since 2008. Sapling, which is a symbol of life, grows to become a supporter and perpetuator of life, a role widely performed by women in our society. For the recipients, therefore, it becomes a blessing, not merely a sapling. It motivates them to nurture the tree, which ultimately becomes an insignia of the Nanhi Chhaan movement.

Prescriptive Policies

Gender mainstreaming in policymaking is crucial to address the elephant in the room and to ensure that the issues facing the second sex don't take a back seat. There are a slew of measures that the government can spearhead to ensure justice and equality for its female population, which accounts for almost 48.4 per cent of the total population. The key is to start early, as most of the cognitive development takes place at tender ages. Stances and prejudices are formed early, and society, caregivers, teachers and others are enablers of such developments.

The focus needs to shift to the primary development of gender imperative in kids. The motive should be to use holistic criteria via both education and art to impart it. There are numerous examples which could be emulated countrywide.

Scandinavian countries which perform the best in global rankings of women's status have been able to almost close the gender gap. Social awareness from a young age along with progressive legislation by the state have played a significant role in achieving parity between the genders. Children learn and emulate the behaviour that they see around them. They internalize whatever they encounter, especially when they are young and of an impressionable age. Scandinavian countries such as Norway and Finland have made Gender Education a compulsory subject. Introduced for children as young as five years old, it teaches them to undertake different tasks without assigning them 'masculine' or 'feminine' characteristics. This helps the new generation understand that women and men must be treated equally, and their actions have nothing to do with their gender.

Gender Education

The government should consider introducing Gender Education as a new compulsory subject to develop a sound political and social understanding of gender. This can serve as an official school curriculum for both boys and girls at post-primary level in all state and central education boards. This entails legitimacy and creates a robust impetus to talk about issues of gender neutrality and empowerment. The curriculum could be developed by both government institutions and stakeholders from NGOs working on the issue. Teachers are carriers of social change and awareness campaigns, and it's pertinent for them to imbibe a mindset of gender empowerment and communicate the same with the community and their pupils. This makes it inevitable to incorporate gender education in pre- and in-service teacher training programmes.

Female Workforce Participation

Female Labour Force Participation Rate (LFPR) is defined as the share of working-age women who report either being employed or being available for work. This share has a direct impact on the economy, with a greater availability of labour for productive activities and helping raise standards of living in families. India's female LFPR fell to a historic low of 23.3 per cent in 2017–18,[1] implying that three out of every four women are neither working nor seeking work. Now this is not to say that these women are not working at all—it's simply that domestic work is not included as part of the 'productive' work and is not added in the country's

---

[1]Rukmini S, 'India's Workforce is Masculinizing Rapidly,' Mint, 10 June 2019. Available at: https://www.livemint.com/news/india/india-s-workforce-is-masculinising-rapidly-1560150389726.html, last accessed on 3 September 2020.

gross domestic product (GDP).

One reason could also be that more women are pursuing education rather than participating in the workforce, but that is only a small share. There is a stark difference in urban–rural employment where rural women are engaged in agriculture while the most common jobs for urban women are in garment manufacturing and domestic help. High-skilled jobs, other than teaching, are rare for women.

India cannot reach its goal of becoming a US$5-trillion economy and a superpower if it continues to impede the path for over 48 per cent of its population towards becoming contributing members to its GDP. This demands not only a psychological change, but several legislative changes, too. Policies that help bring more women into the workforce such as paid maternity and paternity benefits (the latter would ensure that the entire burden of child-rearing doesn't fall on the mother alone), mandating quotas for a minimum number of female workers in a company, ensuring equal pay, etc., need to be introduced. Studies suggest that women also tend to be under-confident while applying for jobs and underestimate their skills, thus, creating a need for better soft-skills development and mentorship for female candidates.

Gender-neutral Employment

Certain professions such as nursing, caregiving, teaching young children, etc., have been feminized in our society. These are perceived as essentially female roles. One would find that a majority of people working in these sectors is women. This often results in significantly lower overall pay and fewer benefits in these areas, as compared to those in other employment sectors. Because of a combination of these factors, men tend not to take up these professions. This further worsens the problem. The need of the hour is to raise the pay and benefits for these feminized professions and ensure that there is a better balance of both genders across all professions. It will also enrich the field with a variety of viewpoints and experiences.

Women in Policymaking

Although Indian women got the right to vote at the same time as men (unlike many other democracies), there is still a dearth of women in policymaking and the executive branch. The seventy-third and seventy-fourth amendments guaranteed that 33 per cent seats at the local-level government structure are reserved for women, which has been expanded to 50 per cent in 20 states. A similar legislation was introduced in the Lok Sabha in 1996, but failed to pass even in successive sessions. In my decade-long career as an MP from a rural and backward constituency, I have personally witnessed the transformation that families and entire societies undergo when as much as one generation of girls is given the opportunity to learn and actively participate in panchayat settings. Enacting legislation for women's reservation will take immense willpower and support from all members of parliament (MPs), but it is a worthwhile exercise. Women will then not just be proxy players for their male relatives but will actually be able to administer effective policies. With greater female participation, policies will also have a gendered perspective and will be better equipped to handle the challenges that India will face 'tomorrow'.

Conclusion

As an MP from the oldest regional political party in the 'youngest country' in the world, I have witnessed great progress over the last few decades and am thus extremely hopeful about the future of gender parity/women empowerment. I firmly believe that our women are our greatest untapped resources and harnessing their fullest strength should be our primary endeavour. Women empowerment is by far the most effective tool for development. It is only with the help of the combined efforts of 1.3 billion Indians that we will be able to achieve this goal and propel our nation to superpower status in the coming decades.

Harsimrat Kaur Badal is associated with the Shiromani Akali Dal and was formerly Union cabinet minister of Food Processing in the Government of India.

21

THE NEW EDUCATION POLICY

SUPRIYA SULE

The then minister for human resource development, Ms Smriti Irani had announced in 2015 that the New Education Policy (NEP) would be formulated soon. The policy, however, has been declared on 29 July 2020. In the absence of a definite direction, the education system is in a state of chaos, as the decisions in the field of education are taken by the central and the state governments in an ad hoc manner, creating confusion in the minds of the parents, teachers and educational managements. Ultimately, the sufferers are the students. The need of the hour is to implement the NEP.

The implementation of the Right to Education (RTE) Act, 2009 completed 10 years on 1 April 2020. It would be appropriate to take a review of the implementation of the act at all levels, to check the success and/or failures of the same, and rectify where necessary. Extending the act to cover the age group of three to 18 years, and making other amendments, if any, need not wait for implementation of the NEP, but should be driven by the goal to make education universal to all age groups. A constant, comprehensive review of the act and the policy at regular intervals is a must, as education being dynamic in nature, would require that they stay in sync with changes taking place in the education sphere, to ensure success in delivery. The RTE and NEP should be on the priority list of the Government of India.

New Pattern of School Education

The NEP recommends the 5 + 3 + 3 + 4 pattern of school education, replacing the existing 5 + 3 + 2 + 2 pattern, thus extending school education from 12 to 15 years. Early childhood education of three years will now be an integral part of school education. This is a welcome change, but its implementation will be very challenging. Relocation of classes, adjustment of teachers and raising resources for new courses would involve an increase in administrative issues and the need for additional funds. In Maharashtra, a majority of schools still follow the 4 + 3 + 3 pattern up to Class 10. Higher-secondary classes are provided at both schools and colleges, as also in a few independent higher-secondary schools in Maharashtra. The NEP should take cognizance of such situations to address any financial losses incurred whilst switching to the new system.

Pre-primary education has been the most neglected sector in education. A recent research in Brain Science indicates that 85 per cent of a child's brain develops by the age of 5. Whilst there are pre-primary schools in urban areas, children in rural areas and those belonging to the weaker sections of society (living in urban areas) have to depend on anganwadis for their education. About 87 per cent of the children in the age group of three to five years in Maharashtra are enrolled in pre-primary schools or anganwadis. Though this percentage is satisfactory as compared to other states, educational inputs are far from satisfactory. While educational component is lacking in anganwadis, there is too much emphasis on writing in pre-primary schools, and negligible support for emotional and social development of the child. The NEP considers the need for an effective system of training of anganwadi workers in all sectors that are instrumental in a child's development in the formative years—emotional, social and education. Online training of six to 12 months, depending upon the qualification, is recommended. This applies as much to the parents of these children, a majority of whom in this age group spend most of their time with their mothers. Forming self-help groups (SHGs) for mothers and anganwadi workers, where guidance by experts is available, may be very useful. Anganwadis and primary schools are administered by two different departments at the state level, viz. the Women and Child Development Department and the School Education Department, respectively. Coordination between the two departments would be a prerequisite for effective implementation of the programme.

While there has been considerable improvement in enrolment and retention rates of children in elementary schools, quality at all levels of education is a cause of worry. The Annual Status of Education Report (ASER) has consistently pointed out that a large percentage of students in Class 5 cannot even read a paragraph expected from students of Class 2. The situation is not very different in higher education, wherein various reports show that only 7 per cent of graduates are employable. Reading is given prime importance in schools in all advanced countries. Once a child can read with comprehension and with satisfactory speed, he or she is much better equipped for learning any subject. The methods of self-directed learning and peer-directed learning can be effectively used for such children. This has been duly recognized in the NEP. For promoting the habit of reading, schools will have to organize various activities for children, and school libraries have to be well equipped with all kinds of books, both fiction and non-fiction. At the same time, adequate access to digital content, along with restriction on prohibitive content, must be made available in the libraries via the internet, as schools prepare for the digital world.

The NEP has put a lot of emphasis on ancient Indian knowledge, which has to be done with utmost care and based on reliable sources only, and no scope is given to hearsay or superstitions. Indian culture has a rich heritage and history, and it's only through education that the values learnt from history are passed on to the students to imbibe the same. This entails educating the student in understanding why in certain circumstances contrarian views are propagated under the guise of beliefs of ancient Indian culture, even though that may not necessarily be true.

Various techniques of e-learning are being used in schools on an increasing scale, which is a welcome sign. However, mere use of new techniques neglecting the educational objectives would be just eyewash. Due to lockdown caused by the COVID-19 pandemic, in-person modes of education are not possible. Hence, the alternative modes of online learning have been adopted by all schools. While mitigating with the downsides, it will be a need of the times to ensure that connectivity, devices, gadgets and infrastructure are made available to the students and that teachers are trained to conduct online classes effectively.

Internal evaluation in examinations has been a topic of debate. While unrealistic increase in the examination results is not a sign of a healthy education system, doing away with internal evaluation cannot be a solution. Marks of a student in written examinations do not indicate his or her real performance. It is necessary to undertake measures to make internal evaluation more objective, impartial and transparent. To track the progress and test the achievement of basic learning, the policy recommends examinations in the grades 3, 5 and 8 conducted by the appropriate authority. This may perhaps lead to additional stress on the students, in contrary to the recommendation of the policy to make grade and board exams easier and stress-free.

The NEP envisages doing away with hard partitions between different subjects, which is a welcome step. However, in order to ensure that schools in rural areas can also avail of this facility, it will be necessary to have relaxed norms for funding such schools. Revitalizing school complexes recommended in the Indian Education Commission (1964–66) is a good suggestion in the NEP. Mobilization of support from the youth, retired citizens, shopkeepers, industrialists, farmers and artisans would certainly help in inducing enthusiasm and motivation in the education system. However, this will have to be implemented in a mission mode, as was done in the National Literacy Mission three decades ago.

Optimum use of available resources is a good concept, but it should not serve as an excuse for curtailing government expenditure on education. Small schools in hilly and sparsely populated areas will have to be given special consideration. I would like to cite an example from Maharashtra. Two years ago, the education department of the Government of Maharashtra took a decision to close down 1,300 small primary schools. These schools were mostly in hilly areas. The state government took the decision with a view to providing better facilities to the students and better opportunities for their socialization. This justification was not at all convincing. Had these schools been closed down, the children would have to walk about 5–6 km daily to other schools. There was resentment and opposition from all segments of the society, including the parents, people's representatives and the media. This decision, which was hostile towards rural students, could not be implemented.

The Medium of Instruction

Any language policy in school education has always been a highly sensitive issue in India. Both the RTE and NEP underscore the importance of mother tongue as the medium of instruction, stating, '*Wherever possible,* mother tongue should be the medium of instruction.' The Constitutional bench of the Hon'ble Supreme Court in their decision on 6 May 2014 clearly stated that the medium of instruction is solely the choice of the parents and the state cannot intervene in it.

Like all other states in India, there is an increasing craze for English-medium schools in Maharashtra too and it's quite natural. The NEP admits that the 15 per cent persons who know English are better off than those who do not know it. Maharashtra is a highly urbanized and industrially developed state. Moreover, the mother tongue of 32 per cent of the population in Maharashtra is not Marathi, the state language, which is very high as compared to other states in India. These factors are favourable for choosing English as the medium of instruction in schools. Despite this, the percentage of students studying in English-medium schools in Maharashtra is much lower compared to the southern states such as Tamil Nadu, Andhra Pradesh, Telangana and Kerala. Percentage of students studying in English-medium schools in these states ranges from 45 per cent to 65 per cent, whereas in Maharashtra, it is only 27 per cent. This is mainly because of three reasons: a liberal language policy of Maharashtra; introduction of English as a subject in all non-English-medium schools over the last 20 years; and provision of bilingual education in schools where science and mathematics are taught in English, while all other subjects are taught in the medium of instruction of the school. The bilingual method is followed in Kendriya Vidyalayas also. In Maharashtra, the popular term used for the bilingual method is 'Semi-English', a system being implemented in no state other than Maharashtra. The

NEP has also suggested the bilingual method from Class 8 onwards.

The policy recommends creation of enabling mechanisms for providing quality education to 'Divyang' or children with special needs (CWSN) same as any other child. However, this can be achieved only when there is proper convergence between the different departments, such as Social Justice, School Education, Women and Child Welfare.

Teacher Education

Teachers play a pivotal role in the school system. Though new concepts such as constructivism, continuous and comprehensive education, self-directed learning, peer-directed learning, activity-based learning, project method and e-learning were introduced and are being implemented for the last 10 years, the general perception is that all teachers have not had access to these new concepts. Ineffective training of teachers is one of the most important reasons for this. Alvin Toffler, the famous author of the books *Future Shock* and *The Third Wave* says, 'The illiterate of the 21st century will not be those who cannot read and write, but those who cannot learn, unlearn, and relearn.' This applies to teachers and educators as to anyone else—in fact much more to them—as they are the ones who are instrumental in educating all the students entering schools from Class Nursery onwards.

There should be emphasis on self-directed learning and peer-directed learning; proper use of digital technology and various techniques of distance education in the basic teacher training programmes, and *adequate* funding provided to set up quality teacher training schools pan-India to train the teachers. The policy recommends a four-year BEd degree and 50 hours of training every year for continuous professional development. However, no teacher training programme should start without need assessment, and impact evaluation should follow every training programme.

Conclusion

However good the measures recommended in any policy, it cannot be better than its implementation. The task is challenging and it cannot be handled by government officials alone. Effective implementation is possible only if all the stakeholders of the education system, along with a large number of volunteers, come together and work wholeheartedly, ignoring ideological differences, if any. The focus should be on how to give quality education to students. This is possible. I am working as the chairperson of an apolitical organization known as Yashwantrao Chavan Pratishthan in Mumbai. We conduct various activities in different sectors of development, including school education. Persons interested in education voluntarily join us and help in organizing various activities such as conferences, seminars, forums, publication of books on various educational issues, operating WhatsApp groups and Facebook groups and many other programmes. We have been able to create a learning community having a few thousand members from all the districts of Maharashtra. Our publication, based on selected discussions on the WhatsApp group, was widely welcomed. Visible and speedy change is possible if we can achieve the goal of creating a learning society whose members work together. If a voluntary organization can do it on a moderate scale, it should be possible for the central and state governments to do it on a mass scale through a mission mode and in fact, they should do it.

◆

Supriya Sule is a Member of Parliament from Baramati in Maharashtra.

22

THE FUTURE OF JOBS IN INDIA'S US$5-TRILLION ECONOMY

ANURAG SINGH THAKUR

The Fourth Industrial Revolution is upon us. Its scale, speed and systemic disruption are far beyond our imagination and find no precedence in human history. It comes with the promise of raising global gross domestic product (GDP), and thereby incomes. It would also improve our healthcare, education and food production, and in turn, lift our quality of life to utopian levels in the decades to come.

Countries around the world will need to undertake swift systemic changes to take full advantage of its socio-economic and political impact. Policymaking will have to match the pace of technology, governance will have to become anticipatory rather than being reactive and industry will need to innovate to feed consumer demand or risk irrelevance in the face of 'technological disruption'.

For the average global citizen, the 'Future of Jobs' will be a matrix of physical, digital and biological worlds that collide and converge as time manifests. According to the World

Economic Forum's *Future of Jobs Report 2018*[1], there are seven emerging professional clusters: Data and Artificial Intelligence (AI); Engineering and Cloud Computing; People and Culture; Product Development; Sales, Marketing and Content; Care Economy; and lastly Green Economy. The report predicts that 'growth will be the largest among care roles and smallest among green professions'. If the current growth trends continue, 'these emerging professions will provide 1.7 million new jobs in 2020 and 2.4 million opportunities by 2022. The highest-growth jobs of tomorrow span all seven profession clusters', the report adds.

In the midst of this, the world has encountered a pandemic in the form of COVID-19, which has incapacitated almost all the countries around the world, both in terms of healthcare and economy. The pandemic has unsettled long-term plans of nations, unnerved the labour market, disrupted supply chains and forced local industries to the brink. Work from home (WFH) has redefined the traditional definition of jobs, many of which will become redundant, while new roles will emerge, as bureaucracy, corporates and citizens at large adapt and adopt digitalization in spheres that were unimaginable a few months ago.

Such an upheaval comes once in a century or generation, yet the scale, speed and implication of this global pandemic finds no precedent in history. Nations need to rethink individually and collectively on how to tackle this pandemic on an economic front. Within India, states must both cooperate and harbour a spirit of competition as 'Team India'. Our country must also become the preferred global investment destination and manufacturing hub for companies looking to shift base to a more reliable and cost-effective skilled labour force and a sizeable market to relocate their businesses, especially from China. How we deal with labour woes,

[1]http://www3.weforum.org/docs/WEF_Future_of_Jobs_2018.pdf, last accessed 8 September 2020.

supply chains and the interplay of technology will define whether India sinks or sails this storm. Amidst all this, while India was placed in a unique sweet spot till now, we will also have to align our direction into ensuring that we hit a soft landing and then recover from this shock in the best way possible.

India's three Ds—democracy, demand and demographic dividend—will define its trajectory towards the goal of achieving a US$5-trillion economy as the Fourth Industrial Revolution manifests. No other country in the world has these ingredients in the proportionality that is fuelling India's ambitious rise through the next decade of this century.

However, the question arises: what will be India's prescription to withstand this economic shock, whilst ensuring that we stay on track to becoming a US$5-trillion economy by 2024–25? The answer lies in our ability to innovate and continue with structural reforms and policies that will help in large-scale job creation. Further, our efforts towards tax and judicial reforms must continue. A hassle-free tax system, faceless assessment and swift refunds process will further assist the honest taxpayer and help widen the tax net. Revenue maximization will provide the government more funds for infrastructure spending and development.

Within months of becoming India's prime minister, Narendra Modi in his Independence Day address from the Red Fort on 15 August 2014 announced one of the biggest financial inclusion initiatives in the world—the Pradhan Mantri Jan Dhan Yojana (PMJDY). Five and a half years later, this scheme has 40 crore beneficiaries, with total deposits of over ₹1.20 lakh crore.[1] While

---

[1]Surabhi, '76 Per Cent of Jan Dhan Account Holders Have RuPay Debit Cards, Show Govt Data,' *The Hindu BusinessLine*, 27 February 2020, https://www.thehindubusinessline.com/money-and-banking/3-out-of-four-jan-dhan-account-holders-now-have-rupay-cards/article30928917.ece, last accessed on 14 October 2020.

many saw this as simply opening bank accounts for those 'unaccounted for' in the formal economy, it was a drive towards laying the foundations of a robust financial system for future generations. The scale and speed at which this was achieved was due to the efforts of hundreds of foot soldiers, 'bank mitras', employed in every village, where last-mile connectivity with the banking system was absent for the last 65 years.

It was on the shoulders of this Guinness World Records-breaking achievement that another major reform, the direct benefit transfer (DBT), was executed. While previous prime ministers lamented that only 15 paisa out of every rupee reached the poor, here was a prime minister who used the disruptive nature of technology to fix a broken system. Every rupee reached its intended beneficiary, timely and transparently. The same DBT was used to implement the Pradhan Mantri Garib Kalyan Package (PMGKP), wherein more than 42 crore poor people received financial assistance of ₹68,933 crore.

This was made possible by an aggressive push towards Digital India, wherein unlike the rest of the world, a generation leapfrogged from limited landline connections to affordable smartphones powered by low data prices. Such has been the rise of app-based payment gateways that the government's united payments interface, BHIM (Bharat Interface for Money), crossed over two billion monthly transactions. Digital India has not only brought about the financial inclusion revolution, but also created a plethora of app-based jobs and aims to connect 2,50,000 village clusters with high-speed broadband internet, thereby bringing the remaining 500 million Indians online. In India, the postman has not lost his job; he's picked up a handheld device and logged on, providing a bouquet of services where last-mile connectivity remains a challenge. It's important to point out here, that unlike the Western experience, the mere adoption of technology is not replacing humans at work in India; it is rather enhancing their output. From drone-based wedding photography to app-based delivery services, social media influencers to customer care bot programmers, big data analysts to digital election campaign strategists, Digital India is creating new avenues of employment and redefining the nature of 'jobs'. During the COVID-19 lockdown, not only did corporates truly switch to WFH, so did the government; what was perhaps unimaginable earlier became possible with ease. Circumstances brought a behavioural change that will altogether reshape the product cycle, skill set, movement of labour and work hours.

Moving on, once the un-banked had bank accounts, the MUDRA Yojana was announced. Self-employment and entrepreneurship gained emphasis under the Modi government and the easy availability of MUDRA loans helped provide credit without the need for collateral to entrepreneurs. Over 15 crore MUDRA loans, worth more than ₹7 lakh crore, were disbursed to small entrepreneurs. Under this Yojana, a total of ₹4,62,115.61 crore of loan amount has been provided to women entrepreneurs (November 2019) and it has been seen that each entrepreneur has created additional new jobs, particularly in tier 2 and tier 3 cities. A survey by the Confederation of Indian Industries (CII) revealed that the micro, small and medium enterprises (MSME) sector added about 1.49 crore jobs each year in the last four years. This means nearly 6 crore jobs were added during the Modi government's tenure in the MSME sector.

The role of the MUDRA Yojana is even more pertinent in the foreseeable future. The MSMEs, which form the backbone of the country by contributing heavily to the GDP and employment, will require credit to recover from the economic shock. Low-interest loans without any collateral will be extremely helpful for the MSMEs across the country.

The historic Insolvency and Bankruptcy Code, 2016 has helped the easy winding up for companies, thus enabling them to wind up operations within 90 days vis-à-vis 180 days for other companies. Post COVID-19, there might be a spurt in the filing of bankruptcy and there is a chance that the National Company Law Tribunal (NCLT) mechanism may be overwhelmed. It will be a challenge to ensure that the purpose of the Indian Banking Code (IBC) to maximize value along with resolving insolvency remains unaffected.

Globally, governments have focussed their efforts on boosting entrepreneurship, manufacturing and ease of doing business for the corporate sector as their economies transitioned from being agrarian towards manufacturing and service driven. To be on the right side of this transition, our government launched various schemes and initiatives such as Start Up India–Stand-Up India, Make in India, Digital India and Skill India, amongst others. There is a realization that the government's job is not to employ but rather create an ecosystem conducive to entrepreneurship; after all, entrepreneurs are the drivers of growth, employment and innovation in any emerging economy. They are the pioneers of change and their risk-taking spirit is a badge of honour when they triumph on the path to becoming billion-dollar unicorns. Realizing the immense potential of talent and opportunity for job-creation in the short and long term, a slew of measures are underway to make India the world's top entrepreneurial and innovations hub.

The Atal Innovation Mission (AIM) provides grant-in-aid of ₹20 lakh to each school to set up Atal Tinkering Labs. Additionally, in order to create women entrepreneurs in underserved regions through Swavalamban Silai Schools, Swavalamban Connect Kendras will try to set up 10,000 enterprises in 100 districts of five states within two years. Further, now the 2 per cent bill fund, a corporate social responsibility (CSR), can be spent on incubators funded by the central or state government or any agency engaged in conducting research in science, technology, engineering and medicine aimed at promoting Sustainable Development Goals. This would give speed to research and development initiatives across the country and encourage researchers and scientists.

As a result of these reforms and initiatives, India today has the third-largest start-up ecosystem and is amongst the world's top three innovation hubs. India's entrepreneurial spirit is bullish and the start-up ecosystem is growing. As on 26 November 2019, there were 25,115 recognized start-ups in India.

The future of jobs depends on the youth having a future. India's youth population needs the right skills to be 'job ready' and truly become a 'demographic dividend'. The expansion, construction and setting up of new higher-education institutions such as IITs, IIMs, AIIMS and other premier institutes has not only made higher education more accessible at affordable costs, but also made our workforce job ready. In fact, setting up these institutions has helped employ a larger labour force and allied employment opportunities around these centres of excellence. The local economy of these towns and cities has also witnessed a transformation, with new restaurants, local transport facilities, residential complexes and other services burgeoning.

Further, ₹99,300 crore is being pumped in for the education sector and ₹3,000 crore for skill development in 2020–21, apart from the New Education Policy (NEP) being recently announced. A National Police University and National Forensic Sciences University are also proposed for policing science, forensic science and cyber-forensics. Additionally, a degree-level, full-fledged online education programme is being launched by the top 100 institutions under the National Institutional Ranking Framework (NIRF) and a one-year internship to fresh engineers will be provided by urban local bodies to skill and make our workforce market ready.

Moving on, the recognition of yoga as a proven spiritual and physical path to well-being by the United Nations and its subsequent declaration of International Yoga Day (21 June), formalized the well-being sector into a flourishing industry, with centres opening up globally that have sourced talent from India. The tourism sector, too, has received a boost, with wellness tourism becoming a frontrunner. The opening up of decades-old travel restrictions with visa on arrival and e-visa facilities to dozens of nationalities has also helped this sector grow. The growth in air passenger traffic is credited with the UDAN scheme and the setting up of 100 smaller airports across India.

According to some estimates, India will leave behind New York's John F. Kennedy International Airport (JFK), London's Heathrow Airport and Singapore's Changi Airport in the total number of passenger traffic by the end of this decade. Our country is already a regional hub and the aviation sector, which is another huge employer, continues to boom. This is being further accelerated by nil goods and services tax (GST) on ₹1,000 hotel room tariffs and slashing the 28 per cent GST tariff to 12 per cent on ₹7,500 rooms. The prime minister's call to Indians to visit 15 domestic tourist sites has also propelled this sector. All these factors have resulted in millions of cyclical and formal jobs being created, which will only grow as India opens up to the world. According to a report by the Ministry of Tourism, the sector created 14.62 million job opportunities in the country in the last four years.

Real estate has traditionally been a large-scale employer. According to some estimates, the real estate sector in India is expected to reach a market size of US$1 trillion by 2030 from US$120 billion in 2017 and contribute 13 per cent of the country's GDP by 2025. The potential of the sector was plagued without a regulator till now. In a landmark move, the government announced the formation of the Real Estate (Regulation and Development) Act (RERA), 2016 and this was welcomed with open arms by the sector, particularly home buyers. A special fund (Alternative Investment Fund) of ₹25,000 crore was created to ensure last-mile funding for affordable and middle-income housing projects. This fund also aims to provide priority debt financing for the completion of stalled housing projects. Over 1,509 stalled housing projects comprising approximately 4.58 lakh housing units will benefit from this special fund. Not only this, the prime minister laid down the goal of 'Housing for All' and launched the Pradhan Mantri Awas Yojana (Urban). So far, 96.5 lakh houses have been sanctioned, out of which more than 56.37 lakh houses have already been taken up for construction and nearly 28.6 lakh houses have already been completed.

When we speak of the Ease of Doing Business rankings by the World Bank, India climbed up from the 142nd position to the 63rd position in 2019. The biggest gain was in the parameter of 'construction permit', where India climbed from the 52nd position to the 27th position. This sector has spearheaded multiple employment opportunities and service creation for the allied industry.

The Union Budget 2020 laid out the vision for this decade with the announcement of ₹103 lakh crore National Infrastructure Pipeline. Sectors such as energy, roads, urban development and railways amount to approximately 70 per cent of the projected capital expenditure in India. Investment in rural infrastructure, logistics, townships and manufacturing clusters has a multiplier effect and leads to job creation at multiple levels. Investment in rural infrastructure will require investment in rural highways, cold storage facilities, internet infrastructure, rural electrical grids, irrigation, etc. The funds allocated to the Mahatma Gandhi National Rural Employment Guarantee Act (MGNREGA) scheme can also be used for the labour component in these projects. Already these sectors alone have created millions of rural and semi-urban jobs and will be where the future of jobs lies.

In fact, the Union Budget 2020 has set the pace for the next 10 years, keeping macroeconomic fundamentals in mind. India has undertaken historic tax cuts for both corporates and the honest taxpayer, which will spurt consumption and investment in India. The foundation stone for the formalization and modernization of the economy and the 'future of jobs' has been laid. This is the result of a decisive decision-making process, a feedback-driven way of working and an action to outcome-driven approach. As a result, India today demands a greater voice on the strength of its growing economic clout. Economic heft has brought with it a greater strategic sway.

India has set a target, timeline and trajectory towards achieving a US$5-trillion economy. Intent, intensity and integrity are the three elements that define our government's vision for a global New India. The development of Aatmanirbhar Bharat will continue undergoing at a record pace, despite the pandemic. The future of jobs will also depend on our ability to transition towards an export-driven economy.

We are in the age of 'Howdy, Modi', 'Namaste, Trump', Brexit and China's global trust deficit. Amidst this is the declining era of multilateralism, world disorder, trade and data wars. A confident India is no longer dictated by the West, but looks the world in the eye, decides what is in her best national interest and is learning who her true friends really are.

The COVID-19 challenge has fractured the world in inconceivable ways and opened up fault lines. While the world reassesses its imbalance and rebalances with China, it is for

India and Indian enterprises to seize this moment and emerge as a dominant economic global power—one that fuels the world economy, one that the new world order trusts and respects. India means business, in a world where it's no longer business as usual!

◆

Anurag Singh Thakur serves as the Union Minister of State for Finance and Corporate Affairs in the present government. He represents the Hamirpur constituency (Himachal Pradesh) in the Lok Sabha as part of the Bharatiya Janata Party.

PART VI

OF TERROR, WAR AND JUSTICE

23

RELIGIOUS TERROR AND TOLERANCE

NISHKANT DUBEY

Historical religious conflicts have multiplied to such an extent that it becomes difficult to present a definition of religion. One can describe the historical religions as complex and composite, closely connected with and influenced by society and culture. They have emotional and ritualistic elements; they also have aesthetic, literary, artistic, as well as economic, judicial, institutional and political dimensions. They have individual and social components and their functions are encountered at all levels of society. This concept of religion has room for several main sects that are interrelated, but not all of which are equally developed. We may broadly identify them as a sector of religious practice, a component of metaphysical speculation, a component of religious socialization, and a component of religious institutions and organization.

Several criminologists have pointed out that theology, religion and philosophy have an important connection with terrorism. They point to the fact that about one in four of all terrorist groups and about one in every two of the most dangerous ones on earth are primarily motivated by religious factors. These outfits believe that their cause is sacred, that God demands their action, and if they fail to comply, then they are 'failing' their religion, their belief and their God. Religious terrorism is not about extremism or fanaticism, but it is about a militant interpretation of religious texts upon convincing believers or converts that a neglected duty exists in the fundamental part of the religion. Most religious traditions are filled with plenty of violence at their core, and destruction is a central part of the logic behind religion-based terrorism.

Religious fanaticism gives rise to terrorism. And most such outfits follow a similar trajectory: the emergence of a charismatic leader who places the blame on state functionaries and global/liberal values such as secularism, 'Westernization', modernity, etc., for the losses 'their' people have suffered—whether economic, political or otherwise. The strength of fundamentalism is its ability to guarantee a radical change without specifying exactly what it will look like.

Once the top leadership of the outfit can identify an 'enemy' from the 'others', the group assumes the idea of sovereignty over the population and sees itself as the only legitimate defender of the faith. In the minds of the leadership, it's their responsibility to restore *at any cost* the 'dignity' that the homeland has lost at the hands of the 'enemy'. There is a key theological transformation, that even though violence is despised, it is justified and is a form of worship that may help discover the true nature of God. And hence, terrorism is harboured. It must be maintained with all fairness that most religious groups with militant tendencies only adopt violence as a tactic of last resort.

Thus, religious doctrine becomes a tool of 'mobilization' or justification for terrorism rather than a direct cause. For instance, many radical Islamist groups were born due to discontent with the political and economic status quo of their context. It must be noted that religion itself is not a cause of political radicalism, but appeals to religion are only one way of representing the struggle of, and mobilizing those affected by injustices. As noted above, groups with similar goals also end up choosing varied methods of resistance and often disagree with each other over the means to reach that same end. Various factors contribute to any group choosing or resorting to terrorism as a means of resistance, including disillusionment over the possibility of change through peaceful efforts or violent means (such as guerrilla warfare) as well as conceptions of religious doctrine.

Religious justifications often combine with other overtly political goals such as self-determination or nationalism. In India, especially in Punjab, some Sikh elements belonging to different organizations took to terrorism to demand the creation of an independent state called Khalistan for the Sikhs. In Jammu and Kashimir (J&K), Muslims belonging to different organizations took to terrorism for conflicting objectives. Some, such as the Jammu and Kashmir Liberation Front (JKLF), want independence for the state, including all the territory that is presently part of India, Pakistan-occupied Kashmir (PoK) and lands donated to China.

Other outfits such as the Hizbul Mujahideen have explicitly defined goals wishing that J&K be merged with Pakistan. While those who want complete independence project their struggle as a separatist one, those who wish to merge with Pakistan adopt religion as the basis for their struggle and discontentment. Other states of India have also seen sporadic acts of religious terrorism, but have not had long-term effects. These are either due to feelings of anger amongst sections of the Muslim youth over illiteracy or due to Pakistan's attempts to cause religious polarization.

Terror acts in the name of religion have been the cause of the maximum number of human casualties and damage. The intensity of violence caused by non-religious terror groups can be rated as 'low or medium', but that of religious terror groups is classified as 'high or very high'. The latter have used sophisticated explosive devices and suicide bombers, among other ways, for the indiscriminate killing of millions of innocent civilians. These groups have also resorted to using methods such as hijacking, hostage-taking, blowing up aircrafts carrying civilians using improvised explosive devices (IEDs), etc.

There are several distinctions between the modus operandi and beliefs of terror outfits that have a religious basis as opposed to the others:

Suicide terrorism

i. Most often, non-religious terror groups in India do not believe in suicide terrorism, but the Liberation Tigers of Tamil Eelam (LTTE) does.

ii. Within the religious terror groups, the Sikh ones did not espouse the practice of suicide terrorism.

iii. Indigenous terror groups of the J&K Valley do not believe in suicide terrorism, but it is a unique characteristic of Pakistan's pan-Islamic Jihadi groups operating in the Valley and a few other parts of India.

iv. Interestingly, these groups did not believe in suicide terrorism before 1998; in fact, there were no such terrorist acts in J&K before 1999. They resorted to such tactics only after joining Osama bin Laden's International Islamic Front (IIF) in 1998. Ever since then, there have been 60 incidents of suicide terrorism, out of which 44 were carried out by bin Laden's Pakistani supporters who were part of these outfits.

Hijackings

i. Non-religious terror groups in India did not resort to hijacking and blowing up aircraft carrying civilian passengers.
ii. Within the religious terror groups, Sikh outfits were responsible for five hijackings.
iii. Both the indigenous group JKLF and the Pakistani Jihadi group, Harkat-ul-Mujahideen (a member of the IIF), undertook one hijacking each.
iv. A Sikh terrorist outfit, the Babbar Khalsa, blew up Air India's 182 Kanishka aircraft off the coast of Ireland on 23 June 1985, killing almost 200 passengers. On the same day, the group also made an unsuccessful attempt to blow up another Air India plane in Tokyo. The IED there exploded prematurely on the ground.
v. The Kashmiri and the Pakistani Jihadi groups of the Valley have not made attempts to blow up any passenger plane.
vi. The JKLF, however, did blow up an Indian Airlines aircraft, which it had hijacked to Lahore in 1971, after asking the passengers and crew to disembark.

Terror groups often have external and global links with other groups that share a similar ideology. For instance:

i. There exists a link between the militant Marxist groups in India, with similar groups of Nepal, Sri Lanka and Bangladesh.
ii. There exists a nexus between the indigenous militant organizations operating out of Kashmir with the fundamentalist organizations of Pakistan.
iii. Similarly, there is a link between a few student movements of India with Jihadi elements of Pakistan and Saudi Arabia and links between the Pakistani pan-Islamic Jihadi organizations operating in India with bin Laden's Al-Qaeda and the Taliban.

Ideology motivating the individual terrorist is rooted in religion or some other strong belief governing one's conduct. The terrorist might deem the law, as it is written and followed by states, as irrelevant. For example, Osama bin Laden, in his fatwa dated February 1998, claimed that according to Islam, it was acceptable for terrorists to target American civilians. Although this is against the law of the United States (US) and international law, the terrorists following fundamentalist Islam conduct their behaviour according to the fatwa and other religious guidance or interpretations not internationally recognized as law. To them, killing innocent civilians is a legitimate act. This idea of thinking that state/international law does not apply to the individual terrorist is commonly perpetuated from within terrorist organizations. Members pledge their allegiance to the organization and its ideology and often disregard the law.

Consequently, standard criminology does not apply when trying to combat the terrorist phenomenon as a whole because the notion of personal deterrence is largely irrelevant, warranting a different legal approach for terrorists compared to criminals.

In conclusion, terrorist attacks can exhibit several criminal characteristics. The fact that some of the specific actions involved in a terrorist attack are already classified as religious crimes and addressed within most nations' domestic law generates a positive correlation between terrorist acts and religious acts. However, attributes such as the underlying motivations of the terrorists and the organizational capability and impact of terrorist groups can greatly differ from what is usually observed in criminal cases.

An analysis of terrorism from the dimension of warfare will reveal that many aspects of terrorism are similar to acts of war. There exists a lack of proper understanding of tolerance as followed by Indian culture. Tolerance in Indian culture is often interpreted as a concept much narrower than that of religious liberty because traditional Hinduism does not proselytize, which means that a religion that doesn't proselytize cannot afford to be intolerant. However, there are countless examples of persecution even by those who follow different religions that did not proselytize. To give an example, Romans are known to have followed a traditional religion that did not proselytize and yet they persecuted Christians. Roman culture was that of aggressive expansionism and tolerance was only a small part of its culture. Rome could not afford to impose its religious belief on the populace of the captured areas and hence, there was some tolerance of Christian beliefs, which invaded roman territory regularly.

Roman religion could retain its separate existence only as long as its patron state was persecuting and the patronage was withdrawn. When Roman emperors started patronizing Christianity, the religion also became a persecuting religion along with a proselytizing one.

On the contrary, Hinduism did not wage a bold war against aggressive religious traditions like Christianity and Islam, even though the proselytizing activities of Islam were accompanied by a high level of violence towards Hindus. Hinduism endured the rule and violent persecution from the patrons of some of these religions for many centuries and that too, without enjoying the support of any powerful leaders or political power. Yet somehow, it survived from being wholly absorbed by any of the other more 'powerful' religions of the time. There exists a quality of persistence in the culture that even outside the patronage of political power, the religion persevered and thrived in the subcontinent. It is a sign of its strength that was lacking in other polytheistic religions that were absorbed by more powerful traditions. Hinduism has unparalleled quality of tolerance and it is not, therefore, a product of its weakness but an expression of its strength which can be understood in the following manner.

Firstly, various races that were originally called 'varnas' (colours) were absorbed and integrated into Indian culture. The Shaks, Huns, Greeks, Scythians and Assyrians were all such examples of continuous assimilation of smaller cultures into the ever-broadening structure of Indian culture.

Secondly, Indian culture in general and Hindu religion in particular have been essentially dynamic, experiential, reflective and valuational. The result was that they have permitted and often encouraged various ways of devotion and approaches to worship. There was an inherent belief that different approaches can together contribute to an understanding of the world and the reality. Syādvāda of Jainism, Chatushkoti of Nagarjuna, the doctrine of Maya and ineffability of Sankaracharya, and Integralism of Sri Aurobindo may be cited as illustrations of conciliating means for comprehensive nature of world and reality.

Indian culture gave birth to the concept of 'madhyam marg', which translates into 'middle path' or a balanced approach to life, like Syādvāda shows that judgement is conditional. From a logical point of view, negation and affirmation have provided for toleration of views and practices in our social, political and religious life.

Thirdly, Dharma as a concept emerged as an all-embracing way of life. According to ancient seers of Vedic times, at the summit of consciousness, there is a power of action that arranges forces and activities of the universe through a harmony of relationships and movements.

This automatic harmony is called 'Rita', which can be found in the true nature of reality and the universe (satyam), and its field of action is the totality, which is infinitely expansive (brihat). Since Rita originates from the vast consciousness of the truth, it is superior to any man-made laws and governing systems. Fundamentally, the idea of Rita also formed the basis of governing ideas of organizations by giving rise to the predominant tendency to place the law of truth as the sole law on which individual life and society depend.

In India, every individual and societal organization was given the freedom to develop by following the law of the truth. State law, too, had to conform to the law of the truth and righteousness; those who enforced the law also had to preserve truthfulness in their actions. I emphasized this thought to bring attention to the pertinent role played by the spirit of tolerance for the spiritual formation of our Indian culture. One needs to analyse various perspectives of tolerance to show that Indian culture was influenced by these various differing thoughts.

For us, the Bhagavad Gita is a wonderful message of hope, consolation, peace and above all, the divinity of man. The Gita holds within itself the answer to all the problems of life and is a source of great fearlessness for everyone who engages with it. It lifts individuals from the depth of penury and misery to the height of immortality and eternal contentment. There are, of course, issues of disharmony and conflicts at the surface level in India, but at its core, the country has a culture of unity and harmony amongst all its varied religions, sects and groups. Indians are peace-loving people, who understand that violence is not God's way. Amongst the nation's great men and women are several saints, sages and avatars who became the torchbearers of our culture.

All religious ideas of the world that have moulded the character of humankind, that have given shape to ethics and morality, that seek to raise humans to great heights of supreme perfection, all found their genesis in India. India's spiritual culture is that it is responsible for the survival of the great nation even during calamities and large-scale conflicts that have threatened its very existence. The Bhagavad Gita is the cream of the moral teachings of the culture while the Upanishads are the practical gospel of life. India, thus, serves a unique mixture of solidarity with all beings in the world.

Only through the path of religious tolerance towards all communities and the development of brotherhood amongst all sections can terrorism be eradicated. Religion teaches man lessons for every fight; terrorism is one of them. By following the ideas outlined in Hinduism and accepting all, the hatred of the heart will vanish and no such persecution will occur.

◆

Nishikant Dubey is a Bhartiya Janata Party politician and currently represents the Godda constituency (Jharkhand) in the Lok Sabha.

24

SECURITY ARCHITECTS TO PREPARE FOR UNRESTRICTED WARFARE

COLONEL RAJYAVARDHAN RATHORE

Those having a keen interest in defence and national security would be closely tracing the evolution of military technologies and the changing patterns of warfare in the last two decades. Whether it is an increased reliance on electronic warfare, with an emphasis on non-contact warfare or the focused discourse of getting artificial intelligence (AI) in warfare, the journey has not been bereft of sharp twists and turns—at times rapid and unpredictable, while slow and steady during others.

For many of us observers, the military and strategic thinking has shifted gears since the Kargil conflict of 1999. The change has been nothing short of drastic if one were to blink an eye, even as modernization of the Indian military had not exactly been able to match the pace with that. However, things have changed over the last one year. The deadly and highly contagious coronavirus struck the world and India, shattering all pre-decided paths and plans. In terms of finance or technology development, all focus shifted at once to COVID-19. And even as we were recovering from the pandemic, India and China got into a military and diplomatic stand-off at the Line of Actual Control (LAC) in eastern Ladakh, which peaked on the fateful 15 June 2020, when 20 Indian soldiers lost their lives fighting the Chinese at the Galwan Valley.[1] Now, each of the two instances, whether seen independently or together, changes our national security dimensions irreversibly.

The security architects of the past, who kept nations safe or prepared them for advancing dangers, are no longer valid. Though the old systems, which encompass the intelligence set-up, the armed forces and internal policing, are irreplaceable, the future requires a system that is geared to deal with unrestricted and often disguised warfare.

COVID-19 precisely brings up that challenge of gearing up for a probable weaponizing of the coronavirus or the threat of a bio-warfare by our adversary, solo or in a nexus. Interestingly, over the years, this very threat has been sitting in the corner of the room, but may not have elicited the maximum attention from any stakeholder. And this is what COVID-19 changes. Just before the beginning of this century, when internet or mobile phones were still not widespread, a Chinese military paper on the concept of 'unrestricted warfare' gave the world an idea of Beijing's thought process.[2] The paper spoke of how technology innovation is resulting in revolution of military tactics and that future wars will involve the technological and commercial might of nations, and not necessarily soldiers.

This unrestricted warfare requires an upgrade of traditional

---

[1]Although there is some ambiguity about the number of casualties on the Chinese side, the number has been considered over 40. Available at: https://eurasiantimes.com/how-many-chinese-soldiers-were-killed-in-the-india-china-border-clash/, last accessed on 19 November 2020.

[2]Qiao Liang and Wang Xiangsui, *Unrestricted Warfare*, PLA Literature and Arts Publishing House, Beijing, February 1999. Available at: https://www.c4i.org/unrestricted.pdf, last accessed on 13 October 2020.

structures. India has made the right start. The creation of a Chief of Defence Staff (CDS), expansion of the National Security Council Secretariat and reorganization of the armed forces into theatre commands[1] will forever change how India prepares for and fights a war. However, with the pandemic there also needs to be a relook at our current chemical, biological, radiological and nuclear (CBRN) defences in any possible eventuality of an attack by India's immediate adversaries. The pandemic may also prompt a change in the existing doctrines on CBRN and incorporate modern training, keeping in view the more recent threats.

The military, in their bases spread across far-flung areas of the country, eats, drinks, works and sleeps together. So, it will be increasingly crucial for the military leadership to plan their leaves and quarantines meticulously to avoid any spread among the troops and affect the operational preparedness. It would be increasingly important to ensure that there is an adequate amount of personal protective equipment (PPE) available for the defence forces, including masks and face shields to guarantee the highest amount of safety from the virus. The government would need to ensure adequate and timely flow of personal protective gear for the defence forces. Pharmaceutical R&D labs will need to allocate effort towards protection against emerging bio threats.

A few other things need to be kept in mind as India moves on to a new security structure. This also includes an improved coordination of all elements under the national security structure and also a better jointness and integration of the three defence services, a major part of which would be achieved by way of the theatre commands.

While there is no ambition to expand territory, the need of the day is global military partnerships, which requires India to have matching military capabilities. This influence is needed for

[1]A joint command (of the army, air force and navy) is called a theatre command.

an ever-competitive world, where commercial and trade interests often clash. The traditional powers of the world always had the ability to enforce discipline or protect interests wherever needed. The US has been doing this for decades with its phenomenal fleet of aircraft carriers that can travel the world with a dreaded complement of fighter aircraft. The erstwhile USSR did it by arming neighbours and sending military aid to allies. France and the UK retained island territories far away from the mainland that gave them the ability to extend the reach of their militaries.

China—the new big power—is going the three-pronged way to exert influence. It is building a capable navy; the domestic shipbuilding industry now has the ability to turn out destroyers and frigates in a matter of months and the aircraft carrier fleet is being expanded. Beijing is also investing heavily in creating infrastructure around the world that it can use for trade and to protect its interests if need be.

The One Belt One Road (OBOR) initiative and the creation of military bases in Djibouti and other nations are irreversible steps. Its third step was building a potent domestic arms manufacturing ecosystem that is now arming neighbouring nations, Africa and will soon be a major player in the Middle East as well.

Planners of the new Indian security architecture need to ensure that the system is built to counter or at least compete with the three-pronged approach. The immediate requirement is of reach; Indian armed forces should have the global ability to intervene if need be in the time of a grave crisis. This has been demonstrated in the recent past, with evacuations in the Middle East and Africa by Indian warships. A potent weapon for intervention is the aircraft carrier, which will enhance our blue water capabilities, enable strategic posturing and act as a latent threat without even engaging in combat. India's traditional values make it difficult for it to have overseas military bases and though it will be a question of resources, building up an aircraft carrier fleet would be a way to stay relevant in the changing times.

Similarly, while de-escalation talks between India and China are going on, India needs to continue to be on high alert, in the backdrop of the history of 1962. There is little doubt that if the situation with China escalates in the future again, the Indian Navy will play a huge role in the conflict. The Navy has the capability to squeeze the jugular veins of China if needed, especially the Malacca Strait, which is a vital line of communication for China's energy and trade resources. India's geography allows it to be a dominant player in the Indian Ocean region.

Our other capabilities should also be leveraged. We have a dedicated workforce and private industry that is slowly but surely taking on to defence manufacturing. Encouraging responsible military exports to friendly nations can be a good tool for exerting influence. A realignment of the line of credit policy to cover military sales in greater quantity could be undertaken. This would have the twin benefit of shoring up local industry as well.

India is in a unique position to emerge as a large-scale arms exporter. The fact that we are confident of selling our indigenous fighter, Light Combat Aircraft Tejas, is a prime example of that. India is the acceptable partner for natural competitors such as Russia, the US, Israel and the European Union. Companies from around the world are keen to partner with India and transfer technology to build joint production facilities. This goodwill needs to be leveraged.

Self-reliance in defence will also help India stand strong in a possible conflict scenario, where a delay in supplies from other countries could end up being a disadvantage for her highly professional military. The strongest arm of the future security architect, however, needs to be strategic partnerships based on trust, mutual respect and common values.

While the Chinese model of influence seems to be making nations dependent on it for the creation of infrastructure or exploration of natural resources, the traditional Indian way has been to become partners in growth, with mutually beneficial ties. Here, the expansion of the Quadrilateral initiative (also known as the Quad)—India, US, Japan and Australia—would be a good step ahead. The four nations hold common values, are all independent and democratic and have complementary strengths, including technology, a robust population and vast expanses of underdeveloped land.

The biggest strengths of this initiative are the common value and approach to smaller nations for a free, prosperous and open world. Being an equal member of the Quad would require shoring up naval resources, but this will pay long-term dividends, which cannot be quantified in terms of money.

Including other willing nations into the set-up (there are several in the region that have shown interest) could be one way ahead to counter what looks like an imminent proliferation of Chinese military bases around the world. India's huge military strength is its battle-hardened and professional army. Among the largest standing forces in the world, the Army has combat experience in a variety of terrain and against threats ranging from conventional war to guerrilla tactics and manpower to spare. The Army has proved its worth in UN missions across the world and is in much demand for training exercises by friendly nations.

The time is now ripe to think of a more global role for the Army. Taking lessons from the past, possible overseas deployment under a multilateral banner is one way of going forward. The current position of deploying troops abroad only under the United Nations mandate, needs a relook. If a friendly foreign nation desires, sending troops abroad should not be a closed option in the future. This is where the office of the CDS could play a defining role.

A political decision can be taken on the circumstances of a foreign deployment, but a blanket rule against sending troops abroad needs to change. The current reorganization of the armed forces to create lighter and more efficient integrated battle groups would go a long way in having options for intervention around the globe, if the need arises.

Among the new challenges going into this decade, information overflow will be one. Traditional ground-based intelligence gathering, though still relevant, is fast getting replaced by technology that can deliver faster and sometimes more accurate results. Here, India needs to leverage its great global advantage of mastery on software. No doubt, India will be the hub of AI, but most talent is still being lost to the West.

India also needs to strengthen its information warfare capabilities so that the right message, too, works as a potent tool to counter the adversary's psychological operations. A new approach on engaging this talent to work not just for material gain but for building a safe and secure future for the nation is the need of the hour.

Within the available defence budget, there is a need to prioritize the procurement of the latest and the most lethal weapons for the armed forces so that it continues to maintain its sharp edge.

The last great frontier is space and here, too, India has shown its ability to quickly close technology gaps in a much more efficient way. A strong component of the future security architect needs to be anchored on space technology.

The warming of space has already taken place and India needs to catch up. Building an offensive space capability, though unpalatable to some, is the next natural step. Let there be no fooling—space is being armed by India's neighbours. And the capacity to match that needs to be developed. While the model of a new security framework can look at catering to all foreseeable risks, it will not work without political will and a strong decision-making capability at all levels. This is where India has lagged in the past. Things changed drastically for the better with the change in government, as is evident from swift responses to Uri and Balakot. Even in the latest stand-off with China, the Army and the Air Force have stood strong and resilient in the cold heights of Ladakh. The Indian Air Force, too, has operationalized their Leh airbase for flying by night their MiG-29s, which is a huge strategic capability.

However, these swift actions are still driven solely by a strong and confident political leadership. For a secure India, this style of strong decision-making has to be encouraged at all levels of the security architecture.

◆

Colonel Rajyavardhan Rathore served as the MoS (I/C) for Information & Broadcasting and Sports and Youth Affairs in the Government of India till May 2019. He has won several accolades for the country as a professional shooter and secured a silver medal in the 2004 Olympics. He represents Jaipur rural constituency in the Lok Sabha as part of the Bharatiya Janata Party.

25

JUSTICE SYSTEM IN INDIA: A CENTENARY IN THE MAKING

MANICKAM B. TAGORE

An ideal society should be mobile, should be full of channels for conveying a change taking place in one part to other parts. In an ideal society, there should be many interests consciously communicated and shared.

—Dr Bhim Rao Ambedkar

The quote by the architect of post-modern India describes dutifully the evolving nature of the Indian Constitution and justice system—that it is a living document which is evolving as per the needs and demands of the society. The justice system in India is not a simple tool to segregate a right from a wrong or punish the guilty, but is the means to implement justice in a true social, economic and political sense in order to liberate people as was envisioned by the founding fathers and mothers of this great nation. The scope of justice was defined beyond the traditional terms of doing the right. It was a medium to achieve social liberation from the evils of caste system and class antagonism, to unite people under a scope of equality towards economic emancipation by bringing a country out of poverty and illiteracy, thus leading India to its 'just idea' of an egalitarian society, ensuring political power and dignity to all. To that vision of India, outlined in the Preamble of our Constitution, our justice system is a tool to achieve it.

Summarizing the evolution of the Indian judicial system in the past 70 years is a multifaceted task. Each landmark judgement of the Supreme Court, along with legislatures passed by parliament, is a stepping stone towards making ours a fully functional democracy, where the law evolves with the time and needs of the people. Some of the cases that can be regarded as the cornerstones of the evolving Indian judicial system are abolition of jury trial (*K.M. Nanavati vs State of Maharashtra*), supremacy of fundamental rights over parliamentary laws (*I.C. Golaknath & Ors vs State of Punjab and Anrs.*, and *Minerva Mills & Ors vs Union of Others & Ors*), basic structure doctrine (*Kesavananda Bharati vs State of Kerala & Ors*), environmental rights and public interest litigation (*MC Mehta vs Union of India*), validation of reservation (*Indra Sahawney vs Union of India*), restricted powers of President Rule (*S.R. Bommai vs Union of India*), defining of workplace rules to prevent sexual harassment of women (*Vishakha & Ors vs State of Rajasthan*), abolition of Section 377 (*Naz Foundation vs Government of NCT of Delhi and Ors*), generic medicine over patented medicinal rights (*Novartis vs Union of India and Ors*) and the Nirbhaya case (*Mukesh & Anr vs State For Nct Of Delhi & Ors*). In terms of the parliament's contribution to the evolution of our judicial system, the Consumer Protection Act 1986, the Environment Protection Act 1986, the Right to Information (RTI) Act 2005, MGNREGA 2005, the National Food Security Act 2013, the Criminal Law Amendment Act 2013 (Nirbhaya Act) and the Transgender Persons (Protection of Rights) Act 2019 are a few examples of benchmark legislation defining the course of Indian jurisprudence. Both the legislature and judiciary, after deliberate discussions and taking into consideration the countervailing opinions, have moved forward to lay the foundation for a progressive India into the twenty-first century.

As a Member of Parliament (MP) and a sworn representative of the people, it is our duty to not only be inspired by the historical achievements but also lay down the road map for future India. And in this context, it is our duty to envision a just, equitable, liberal India for all the individuals who could be proud of the legal tradition inspired by the works of Dr Bhim Rao Ambedkar and carry his work forward. To brainstorm ideas for Constitutional reforms, one needs to peruse through the recommendations made by the Venkatachaliah Commission Report of 2000. Though an exhaustive piece of report made by a joint committee of judges and parliamentarians, it never saw any concrete implementation. Certain ideas such as the fundamental right to a minimum guaranteed employment of 80 days every year (which later evolved within MGNREGA) along with laws of transparency in the functioning of the administration (seen in the RTI Act) along with compulsory education up to the age of 14 years (later incorporated in the Right to Education Act) were given statutory implementation through acts of Parliament. However, its incorporation within the fundamental rights sections would have given the tooth and arms to the judiciary to implement minimum basic rights to all citizens and make it the duty of the State to provide such facilities, not being implied, but being explicitly minimum guarantee. On several occasions, Prime Minister Shri Narendra Modi has emphasized the need to get rid of archaic provisions of the Indian Penal Code (IPC) and the Criminal Code of Procedure (CrPC). It is a positive move over the historical amnesia of the Macaulay era of the 1860s, but along with that, several other provisions of the Constitution as well as British-era laws need to be revisited. In this regard, a positive step would be striking down Section 124A of IPC (Sedition), which is the most controversial and misused law in present times. Only physical acts should be seen as a viable excuse for its enforcement—not mere speech—as on several occasions it has been used as a tool to suppress free speech. Ours is a developed, functioning democracy which cannot be threatened by the mere utterance of words. This law is as draconian as Section 377 of IPC, which was struck down by the Supreme Court.

Pendency of cases is another issue logjamming the efficiency of the judicial system in India. According to data collected from the National Judicial Data Grid, there are more than 3 crore cases pending in India. Of these, 65,000 cases are pending in the Supreme Court, 43 lakh cases in high courts while 2.7 crore cases are pending in the district and subordinate courts. Of these cases, 58 per cent are criminal cases and 42 per cent are civil litigation. This calls for an immediate rehaul of the procedure of the judicial system, mainly in the lower and subordinate courts which causes for the extensive delay in delivery of justice.

Another startling fact to consider is that 60 per cent of the pending cases are new (that is they are less than five years old). This high rate of pending cases is mainly because of an increase in commercial litigation owing to new laws such as the Insolvency and Bankruptcy Code, Commercial Courts Act, etc. It is also also due to the common man's growing awareness of his rights, indicating a socio-economic advancement, and more faith and courage in the courts of law for the delivery of justice. However, on the contrary, the main reason for inordinate delay is the lesser number of judges in our country. In India, we have a total of only 21,000 judges, which is equivalent to 10 judges for every 10 lakh of population. The Law Commission Report of 1987 recommended at least 50 judges for every 10 lakh people to ensure the smooth functioning of Indian courts. The population has increased by 25 crore since 1987 and this required ratio now has increased significantly. Also, India does not have enough courts. The budgetary allocation for the whole judiciary is at an abysmal low of 0.1 per cent to 0.4 per cent of the whole budget. This needs to be increased significantly for modernization of courts, including computerization and digitization of proceedings. The present focus of the government should be to overhaul its image as the largest litigant in India, where one department is suing another department of the Executive, leaving the decision-making duty upon the courts. The All India Judicial Service was a positive step in this regard where an immediate increase in the number of judges is required from current 21,000 to at least 50,000. Such a prestigious Group-A Service would also ensure that the judiciary attracts the best brains and talented individuals. Establishment of fast-track courts, Lok Adalats and Gram Nyayalayas would further assist the issue of tackling pending cases in an expedited manner.

In terms of future prospects of delivering justice in the area of commercial disputes, the alternative dispute resolution methods such as mediation and arbitration have proved to be effective. India enacted the Arbitration and Conciliation Act 1996 to align the procedural law of India in line with the UNCITRAL Model Law on International Arbitration, which was the turning point in the arbitration history of India. By providing timelines, transparency of arbitration process by mandating self-declaration by arbitrators with regard to the conflicts of interest (in line with IBA Rules on conflict of Arbitration), etc., the 2015 Amendment Act projected India as an arbitration-friendly country. However, by prohibiting various types of foreign nationals from sitting as arbitrators in India-seated International Arbitrations, the 2019 Amendments to the said 1996 Act has resulted in a big setback. Such negative actions would discourage foreign parties from choosing India as a seat for their arbitration. India envisions establishing itself as the future leading centre for arbitration, in line with New York, London, Paris, Singapore, etc. The solution lies in not only establishing the New Delhi International Arbitration Centre, but also aligning the law with global trends. India recognizes only 34 countries under the New York Convention on the Recognition and Enforcement of Foreign Awards, 1958, whereas progressive arbitration seats such as Singapore recognizes all the 183 signatories of the said convention. The Dubai International Finance Center (DIFC) and Qatar Finance Centre (QFC) are favourable arbitration seats because they are special economic zones where the national courts of those countries do not have jurisdiction and there are international courts established to handle commercial matters as per English law.

Moreover, post-arbitral award litigation such as the challenging of arbitration awards and enforcement of awards take a long time due to pendency of cases in courts. Hence, a special tribunal should be established to handle arbitration-related litigation.

International resolution of commercial disputes by mediation is on the rise. India also has signed the Singapore Convention on Mediation 2018, but we do not have a proper mediation law to make mediated settlements enforceable. Arbitration and mediation centres should be established in all important cities, such as Mumbai, Chennai, Bengaluru and Kolkata, to encourage resolution through arbitration. Also, the interference of jurisdictional courts should be very limited and arbitration-related litigation should not be treated as regular civil appeals; the court jurisdiction in such matters is only a supervisory jurisdiction and not appellate jurisdiction. Only then the method of arbitration will see success in India. As the methods of Alternate Dispute Resolution further develop, certain cases of civil nature (divorce and settlement, land acquisition, government contract, etc.) should be resolved through arbitration process only to reduce the burden on traditional courts.

Another important issue that needs to be tackled is the reforms in the Criminal Justice System in India. Archaic laws are a small part of the larger issue in concern. The real issues are botched-up investigation and repeated delays in investigation, which cause further delay in the procedures for dispensing justice. India has a conviction rate of just 21.2 per cent of the cognizable offences registered. Countries such as Japan and the US have a conviction rate of 98 per cent. This shows the dismal condition of investigating in India and also highlights the fact that a number of cases are false or mistrials, which should have been rejected in the initial investigation itself. This raises questions on the entire machinery responsible for its delivery including investigating agencies.

The Vohra Committee Report of 1993, the Malimath Committee Report of 2000 and the Madhav Menon Committee Report 2007 focused extensively on the issue of reformation of the Criminal Justice System. The Malimath Committee found that the current justice system weighed in favour of the accused and did not adequately focus on justice to the victims of the crimes. Hence, on multiple occasions, we have seen the civil society out on the streets showing their dismay at the outcome of certain courts of law which under due pressure revise their processes to take the right cause. However, such actions should be a simple reminder towards a much-needed bigger overhaul in the justice system. Instead of believing in the maxim of 'proof beyond a reasonable doubt' as the basis to convict an accused, the judiciary should focus on the rule 'if the court is convinced that it is true' as the basis for convicting a criminal. Along with punishing the guilty, victims must be given satisfactory compensation as well. A Victim

Compensation Fund on the lines of the Compensation Scheme for sexual assault and acid attack victims should be constituted. Overcrowding of our prisons is another issue, with 67.2 per cent of the total prison population consisting of under-trail prisoners alone. In cases of non-heinous crimes and non-repeat offenders, bail should be made obligatory along with provisions of house arrest (monitored through geo-tagging). Community service and rehabilitation should be made part of the reform system to decongest prisons.

Digitization of courts in India is another target that needs to be achieved in the coming years. The E-Courts Project, which was conceptualized on the basis of the National Policy and Action Plan for Implementation of Information and Communication Technology (ICT) in the Indian judiciary by the e-Committee of the Supreme Court, has a vision to transform the Indian judiciary by ICT enablement of courts, thereby drastically enhancing common citizens' access to courts. Paperless courts and electronic filing service help courts to reduce paper trials, while a National Data Grid could help to hold all information pending on a subject matter in a common database accessible from the lowest court to the highest authorities under the same umbrella, thus simplifying court procedures and saving time. This would bring in further transparency and ease of access to citizens. Courts should start accepting electronic disposition of witness testimonies to save time and ensure witness safety. Along with that, artificial intelligence (AI) can be used to educate citizens about their legal rights in languages they can comprehend and technology can be harnessed to empower the poor and unprivileged.

Thus, the Indian justice system and Indian jurisprudence have evolved gradually over the years, transgressing through the contours of time and patiently addressing the demands of society. We have a long way ahead and multiple targets are yet to be achieved. However, the justice system has shed its colonial underpinnings to a great extent, getting a pan-India outlook, which is studied and appreciated by legal scholars around the world. We have come a long way. We had certain detours and diversions in the middle; yet in the end, we were realigned to the actual cause, which was to have a justice system that guarantees social, economic and political emancipation to all. And that shall be the true testament to the story of this great nation when it completes its centenary, holding up the Gandhian-Nehruvian and Ambedkarian ideals into the latter half of twenty-first century.

Manickam B. Tagore is currently a Member of Parliament in the Lok Sabha, representing Virudhunagar, Tamil Nadu from the Indian National Congress.

PART VII

BEYOND THE PANDEMIC'S SHADOW

26

HEALTHCARE IN POST-COVID INDIA

SANJAY JAISWAL

I write this as our nation confronts a crisis of unprecedented proportions. The COVID-19 pandemic has completely altered people's lives, the rhythm of our economy and has undoubtedly emerged as an existential threat to the collective humanity. 'Those who cannot remember the past are condemned to repeat it,' said writer and philosopher George Santayana. If smallpox, Spanish flu and cholera epidemics seem too far in history for us to recall, we should have never forgotten the lessons from HIV, SARS, MERS, Zika and Ebola. Yet, the global response to COVID-19 shows that we failed to learn from these crises. There has undoubtedly been an increased clamour over the past few months for bolstering our health systems. However, this increased attention to public health during new outbreaks quickly wanes as the epidemic subsides, and other priorities take over.

Most countries have been scrambling to take measures in the hope of bringing a semblance of order. While we as a nation have fared better than many in crafting a coordinated and sensible response, we can no longer afford to work with a business-as-usual approach. This is the time for us to reorient our public-health strategies to plan for the future and these strategies will invariably determine the economic growth and development of the entire nation.

Over the years, India has made significant gains in healthcare: from reducing maternal and child mortality to ensuring universal healthcare for all (through Ayushman Bharat). However, a few challenges such as the lack of health infrastructure and shortage of human resources, persist. There is an 82 per cent shortage of specialists across Community Health Centres (CHCs) in India. Although India fares favourably when compared to other countries in terms of the number of physicians, 74 per cent of our doctors are located in the lucrative urban areas, leaving rural areas starved of quality health services. Additionally, there is inadequacy of physical infrastructure. Buildings, beds, ventilators, testing kits, equipment and ambulances are essential for doctors to react effectively to a pandemic such as COVID.

According to World Health Organization (WHO) statistics, while China has 18 doctors per 10,000 people, India has only eight. To take another statistic, India has just about 40,000 functional ventilators as of October 2020. Seeing that availability of ventilators was crucial for India's battle against the COVID-19 pandemic, according to reports, the government has already ordered for the procurement of about 60,000 ventilators, a good number of which has already been supplied to hospitals and facilities. The PM CARES Fund Trust recently allocated ₹2,000 crore for supply of 50,000 'Made-in-India' ventilators to government-run COVID hospitals across the country.

The current procurement systems are very ad hoc and not backed by sound forecasting. Multiple parallel supply chains exist—RMNCH (reproductive, maternal, newborn and child health), family planning, immunization, etc., all have their own physical/digital systems, leading to highly inefficient planning. A proactive approach to healthcare is clearly lacking and this must change.

India's public financing for health remains at around 1 per cent of the gross domestic product (GDP), which is lower than that of many of its neighbours and much below the global average of around 6 per cent. Low public spending ultimately leads to high out-of-pocket expenditure, which hurts the poor the most. While the Centre is committed to raising this figure to 2.5 per cent by 2025, the states, too, need to ramp up healthcare spending. This figure should gradually move up to 5 per cent of GDP by 2035 and, within the investments we make, primary health must get greater priority. Health and Wellness Centres (HWCs) under the Ayushman Bharat programme should be equipped with the latest technologies for diagnostics and availability of essential drugs that can prevent disease, save lives, relieve suffering and improve health outcomes. A well-functioning procurement system and effective linkages with Central Diagnostic Units (CDUs) are key to the effectiveness of such services at the Primary Health Care (PHC) level.

The government's aim to expand Jan Aushadhi Kendras across the entire country by 2024 should be fast-tracked.

What is also needed is an integrated approach to health, considering its linkages with agriculture, WASH (Water Sanitation and Hygiene), environment, etc. In recent years, programmes such as the Poshan Abhiyaan and Swachh Bharat Mission, which focus on such linkages, have been launched. However, more is needed for comprehensively addressing the sociocultural and environmental determinants of health.

COVID-19 has also opened a window of opportunity. With limited resources available to treat an increasing number of COVID cases, the healthcare system is being forced to prioritize who receives care, while transitioning entire practices to virtual methods for the first time. In response to this overwhelming volume, the healthcare system is witnessing fast-tracked innovations in digital health and telemedicine, leading to a new landscape built on streamlining efficiencies, reducing costs and delivering care with new technological models.

The government leveraged several innovations in our pandemic-management efforts. While applications such as Aarogya Setu and ITIHAS facilitated rapid contact tracing and surveillance, COVID India Portal enabled real-time tracking and monitoring and portals such as Integrated Government Online Training (iGOT) provided a platform for training our front-line health workers. The healthcare sector can leverage technology to improve critical processes that today pose a big challenge in the delivery of quality healthcare. Setting the goal of constructing a digital system for healthcare is key in today's time and is doable. This will also allow reliable healthcare information to all. It will also make the management of any future epidemic more streamlined and push India into the digital age. Access to large amounts of real-time data will serve as the foundation for artificial intelligence (AI) and machine learning to create solutions for the sector.

There is also a need for concurrent investments in building robust health information systems. The existing models of disease surveillance under the Integrated Disease Surveillance Programme (IDSP) suffer from various shortcomings. A very low-budget (a few hundred crores across all states), poorly skilled human resources, especially field-level staff, and a low number of public labs are some of the limitations ailing the existing disease surveillance models. Another major bottleneck is the lack of a modern data collection system, an absence which not only reduces the credibility of the data, but also limits the use value of the data. In this context, the success of countries such as Taiwan, South Korea and Singapore is in part attributed to the use of modern methods for data collection and prediction. A decentralized data collection framework supported by a strong digital backbone is the need of the hour.

The pandemic has also brought forth the need to invest in strong secondary and tertiary care systems. This year's budget proposed a viability gap funding for establishing hospitals in tier 2 and tier 3 cities under the public-private partnership (PPP) model. It is indeed a welcome step that alongside our party's vision of having one medical college per district can be helpful in filling critical gaps in healthcare access, especially for the poor and vulnerable. If these moves can be supported by donors and governments by offering partial occupancy/offtake guarantees to operators, then, as has happened historically in the vaccine industry, this could further augment the risk-bearing capacity of those interested in this national agenda.

Converting district hospitals to medical college in PPP mode is another welcome step. What we now need is to not only continue on this path, but at a stronger momentum than before. A strong primary care network should, however, continue to be the anchor of our health regime. The health workforce must be expanded at all levels of care—the dismal doctor-to-population and nurse-to-population ratios have been the subject of discussions for long.

Our government took a decisive step to substantially increase the number of seats at medical colleges and usher in transparency in admissions. The incentives for front-line workers were enhanced and they have been brought under the ambit of insurance nets. Alongside, we must also build a dedicated cadre of epidemiologists, and social and behavioural scientists within our health cadre. Support from state governments will be crucial here.

Another issue that needs urgent attention is import substitution of bulk drugs (API). This has implications not only for health but for national security as well. According to the Government of India's own estimates, India accounts for about 10 per cent of the world's production by volume and 1.5 per cent by value.[1] This

[1]'Pharma Industry Promotion', Department of Pharmaceutical. Available at:

points to the high demand of Indian products in the global market. India's role as the 'pharmacy of the world' is well acknowledged by experts. However, ironically, it imported nearly 2.5 billion dollars' worth of bulk drugs from China in 2018–19. Faced with the rise of competition from China in the production of bulk drugs, the sector has been urging the government to back domestic industry by creating industry clusters. This is yet to take off despite the issue being on the government's scope for very long. Likewise, the Indian medical devices market has been dominated by imported products, which comprise around 70 per cent of the total sales.

It is against this backdrop that the government has decided to give a push to domestic manufacturing of medical devices to reduce India's dependence on imports. The government's move to approve a stimulus package of approximately ₹3,800 crore to promote medical devices manufacturing in India is a step in the right direction. India's need to produce its own bulk drugs and medical devices can perfectly align with its ambition of becoming an exporter to markets such as Africa. Given this context, India should consider embracing economies of scale and increasing the production to aggressively compete with the Chinese and other foreign players.

A policy shift is necessary to make a meaningful impact. This also brings me to another area of attention: vaccine stockpiling. Although India is a leading supplier of vaccines (one out of every six children over the world receives vaccines manufactured in India), we don't have a stockpiling policy of vaccines for our own population (if they are available) and in cases where vaccines are not available, there is almost no focus on investing in research and development (R&D). The government needs to focus on these issues as emergency stockpiles can play an essential role

---

https://pharmaceuticals.gov.in/pharma-industry-promotion, last accessed on 21 October 2020.

both as part of a comprehensive disease-control strategy and in maintaining global health security.

A related issue is the complex drug regulatory regime in the country, which adds to the coordination burden. Major economies across the world have just one agency/ministry in the effort. It is counterintuitive to have both the Ministry of Health and Family Welfare (MoHFW) and the Ministry of Chemicals and Fertilizers being involved here. There is a strong case to integrate all these functions within the MoHFW itself, a point that has been made several times in the past by many experts.

Conclusion

The vulnerability of urban and rural centres to pandemics points to the need for strong public–private coordination involving organizations beyond the traditional healthcare sector. Better preparedness to tackle future pandemics requires investing now in both strengthening public health systems and prevention efforts, as well as in new and flexible financing instruments.

The ability to mobilize a response from sectors as diverse as food production, telecommunications and corporate supply chains will determine how epidemics are fought in the future. Local, national and cross-border government agencies need to build bridges with all stakeholders and learn from what worked in the past to shape systems with the capacity to respond to pandemics and build the resilience to bounce back afterwards.

The current pandemic is an opportune time for us to reflect on these issues, shift gears and take measures to ensure that we are able to provide affordable, accessible and quality healthcare to all.

◆

Dr Sanjay Jaiswal represents the Paschim Champaran (Lok Sabha constituency) of Bihar since 2009 as a Bharatiya Janata Party member. He also holds MBBS and MD degrees and is a member of the governing body of the All India Institute of Medical Sciences Patna.

27

NEW INDIA, NEW ECONOMY: AATMANIRBHAR BHARAT

RAJEEV CHANDRASEKHAR

The Indian economy, like every other major economy around the world, is today faced with the shock effects of the COVID-19 pandemic. This shock comes at a time when the Indian economy was in the midst of a major transformation from a crony economy to a high-quality, efficient and globally competitive economy, offering opportunities to all investors—ranging from start-ups and farmers at one end of the spectrum, to big Indian and multinational corporates at the other. The coronavirus shock has put a temporary brake on this process. However, a lot of what has been done in these last five to six years of transformation is helping as the nation deals with this shock, and so it's worth understanding the last six years of change.

The last six years have seen both a clean-up of the economy and financial sector and at the same time, economic expansion of over 7 per cent. The Indian economy was poised to be a global economy, with growth rates higher than traditional growth giants such as China. Our economy had become the fifth largest in the world (current US$) and third largest measured in terms of Purchasing Power Parity.

India, pre-COVID, was almost a US$3-trillion economy. It took us nearly 60 years to reach the US$1-trillion mark, seven years (2007–14) to reach the US$2-trillion mark and only five years (2014–19) to move from US$2 trillion to US$3 trillion. (See Graph 1.) The next goal was to achieve the US$5-trillion mark by 2024–25, but the pandemic disrupted the world and India.

Graph 1: GDP (USD trillion)

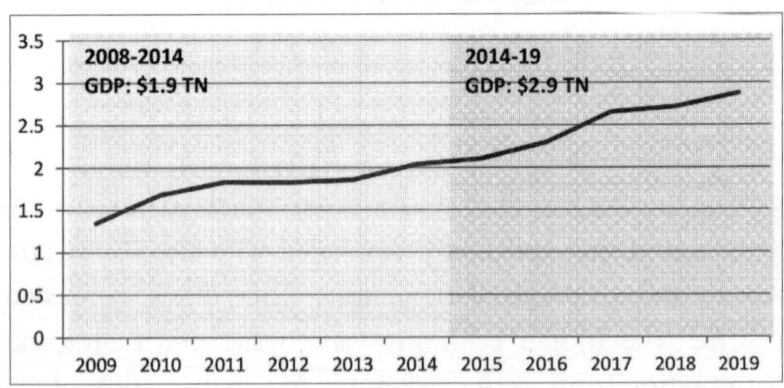

Source: National Statistical Office (NSO), 2019

The impact of the pandemic on the global economy will be deep and disruptive. The outlook for the coming years is unclear and deep structural changes on world economy and indeed the Indian economy will be forced on us. China's role in this crisis and its future place in the global economy will be in focus in the coming months. The global manufacturing supply chain that had China as its epicentre will see deep and lasting transformation.

Pre-COVID: Clean-up and Consolidation of the Economy

Economy Had Been Rebuilt from 2014 Lows

The Indian growth story is based on its strong fundamentals (growth with stability). The economy experienced oscillations since 2008 and went into complete doldrums between 2011 and 2013. In 2014, it was on the brink of a collapse. The average inflation was 10 per cent, fiscal deficit was 5.3 per cent and current account deficit (CAD) was at 4.7 per cent of gross domestic product (GDP).

In the last five years, the Indian economy had undergone a clean-up and structural changes and reforms such as fiscal consolidation, goods and services tax (GST), Insolvency and Bankruptcy Code (IBC), Expansion of Direct Tax-GDP, formalization, etc. The Indian economy had grown as a result of this as well as a determined and fiscally responsible governance. The economy had finally come out of the doldrums and was moving out of the negative legacies of the past, devastated financial sector and weak macroeconomic stability. India had regained its position from an economy with a combination of low growth and high inflation to the fastest-growing major economy of the world.

On the macroeconomic front, there was unprecedented stability; the consumer price inflation, fiscal deficit and external-sector deficits were best in the past two decades. The twin deficits—current account and fiscal deficit—had significantly declined from their peak of 4.7 per cent and 5.7 per cent respectively in 2012 (see Graph 2.) CAD was at a historic low of 1.5 per cent in the first half of 2019–20 (see Graph 3). Foreign exchange reserves reached an all-time high of US$460 billion and cumulative foreign direct investment (FDI) inflows stood at US$62 billion. India had improved its ranking significantly in the World Bank's Ease of Doing Business Index from above 150 in 2014 to 63 in 2019.

Graph 2: Gross Fiscal Deficit % of GDP

Source: Reserve Bank of India (RBI)

Graph 3: Current Account Deficit as % of GDP

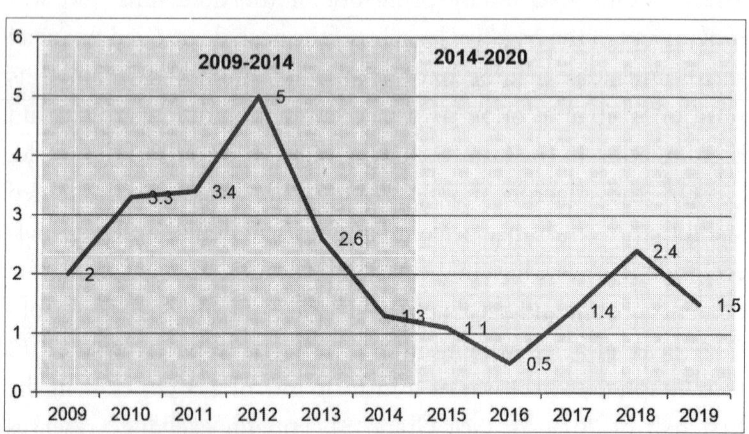

Source: Reserve Bank of India (RBI)

Pre-COVID, the present government's biggest achievements were rebuilding the crippled financial sector by tackling non-performing assets (NPAs), recapitalization and bank governance. The Indian economy had been challenged with the legacy problems of weak public-sector banks' balance sheets and bad loan portfolios/NPAs. The prime reason for NPAs was a combination of a weak regulatory framework of government and a combination of incompetent risk management/crooked governance and lending practices in public-sector banks. The cost to the taxpayers and exchequer from the NPA-related problems in the public sector was real and expensive. It has cost the taxpayers almost ₹3.8 lakh crore—an amount recapitalized in public-sector banks.

The Narendra Modi government had taken up the task of rebuilding the financial sector head-on. Through its policies of recognition, resolution, recapitalization and reforms, it has first made the banking sector recognize concealed NPAs and later through recapitalization and IBC resolved them. NPAs had peaked in the year 2018, reaching 11.5 and since then declined to 9 per cent in 2019 (see Graph 4).

Graph 4: Gross NPAs of Schedule Commercial Banks

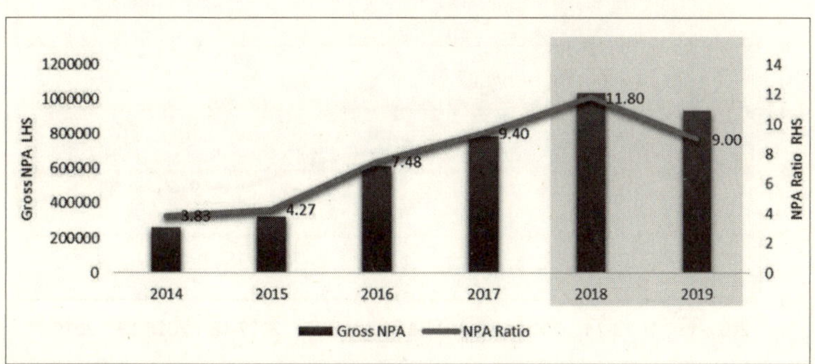

Source: Reserve Bank of India (RBI)

Second, inflation used to be the biggest problem for policymakers. It is a heavy burden on the poor and middle class. It erodes the purchasing power of the poor and middle class, causes economic hardships and creates economic crisis. Renowned economist and Central Bank Governor Y.V. Reddy once said, 'In India, fighting inflation is higher priority than growth, because spiralling prices hurt the poor immediately, whilst economic expansion takes time to trickle down to the poor.' All this has now changed; from double digits, inflation has been brought down to 4 per cent. Consumer price inflation declined from a peak of 10 per cent in 2012–13 to 3.3 per cent in H1 2019–20 (see Graph 5).

With the internal and external macro stability, India's exchange rate has been relatively stable, and it has become an important investment destination among its peer emerging economies (see Graph 6 and 7.)

Graph 5: Consumer Price Index (CPI)

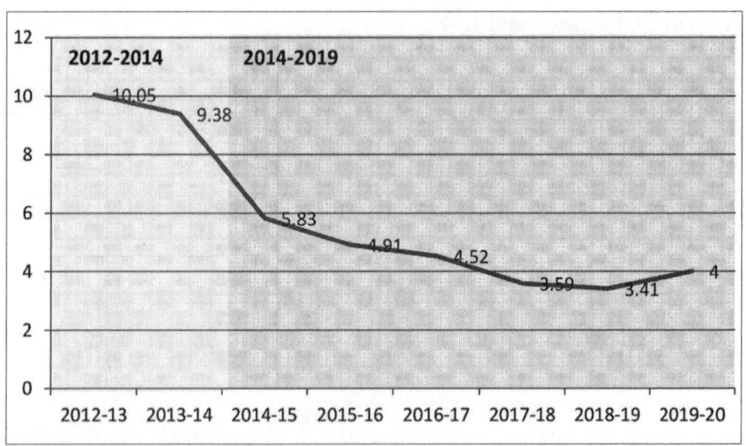

Source: Reserve Bank of India (RBI)

Graph 6: Snapshot of Indian Economy

GDP Growth Rate %
GDP USD Trillion
PCY Growth Rate
Fiscal Deficit % GDO
Consumer Price Inflation
Bank Credit Growth Rate
Tax Receipts Growth Rate
Revenue Expenditure % of GDP
NPAs %
CAD % of GDP
0 2 4 6 8 10 12 14 16 18
2009-14
2014-19

Source: Reserve Bank of India (RBI), National Statistical Office (NSO), Centre for Monitoring Indian Economy (CMIE)

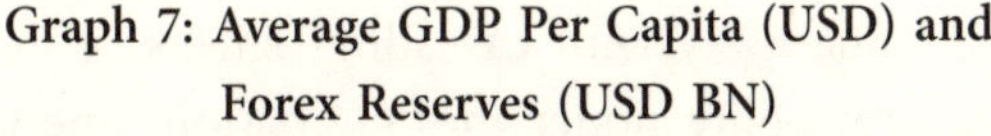

Graph 7: Average GDP Per Capita (USD) and Forex Reserves (USD BN)

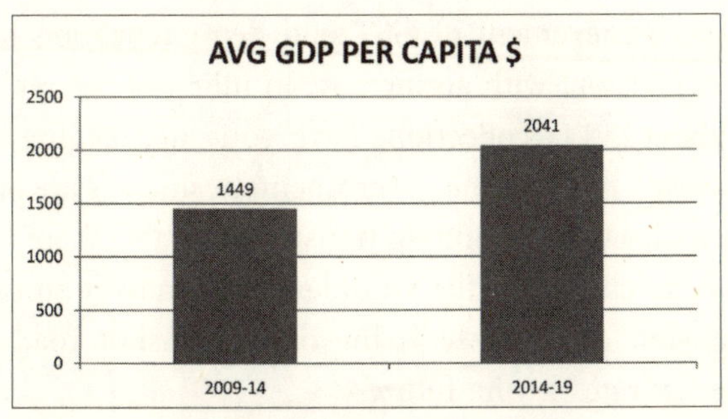

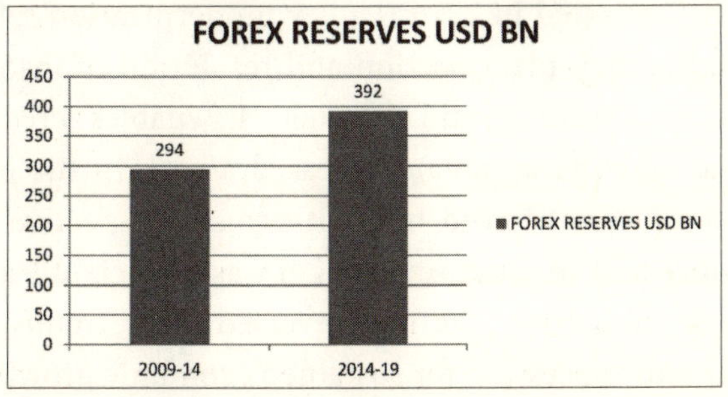

Source: Reserve Bank of India (RBI) and CMIE Database

Pre-COVID: Modernization and Structural Reforms

In the last six years, the government has delivered on growth and expansion by embarking on modernizing our economy. As part of the modernizing focus, it delivered on structural economic reforms such as GST, IBC, the Real Estate (Regulation and Development) Act 2016, demonetization, Monetary Policy Committee, recapitalization and governance reforms of public-sector banks.

The informal nature of the Indian economy is the biggest challenge. It hampers growth and employment generation. Demonetization, GST and digitization were reforms to modernize and formalize the Indian economy. Businesses that were earlier taking place outside of the formal economy are now being brought into the formal economy.

GST has done away with cascading effects of taxation and brought a federal polity under the one nation, one tax regime. The biggest achievement of GST and demonetization has been tax base expansion, with an increase in filling of tax returns and tax compliance. Tax collections have gone up, leading to more resources available with the government; businesses are operating under formal set-ups, bringing transparency, and there has been a behavioural change in the attitudes of businesses and citizens. The expansion of tax base is the only sure-shot road map to moderate tax rates in the future.

The IBC enacted in 2016 is a key modernization reform for the strengthening, identification and resolution of insolvencies in India in a time-bound manner. It enables creditors to obtain the maximum value of stressed assets. In the erstwhile system, the promoters did not exit firms, irrespective of their performance and conduct, and capital was inefficiently allocated to unviable industries. The IBC reversed these trends and the financial sector necessary for sustained economic growth is now working much better.

These fundamental structural reforms are transforming and modernizing the economy and will push India towards a long-term sustainable growth trajectory to create a New India's new economic model.

Pre-COVID: Equitable Opportunity and Growth with Behavioural Change Reforms

The 'New Economy' paradigm adopted by India post 2014 is a clear sign of the benefits of a stable political government. The political stability has changed the traditional politics of short-term fiscally expensive populism and built governance on long-term multi-year schemes that can bring behavioural change in the lives of citizens. It adopts an inclusive economic model, enabling citizens to enhance their ease of living.

This aspect of New India as highlighted by Prime Minister Narendra Modi is that: 'Economic prosperity can only be achieved through a Jan Aandolan where every Indian is empowered to recognize her role and also experience the tangible benefits accruing to her in the form of better ease of living'.

Schemes such as direct benefit transfers, Ayushman Bharat (free access to healthcare), Swachh Bharat (Clean India Mission), Ujjwala Yojana (for LPG connections to women of Below Poverty Line families), Saubhagya Yojana (to provide electricity to households), MUDRA Yojana (to extend affordable credit to micro and small enterprises) and Jan Dhan Yojana (financial inclusion) are part of the New Economy, ensuring that every Indian has an opportunity to realize her aspirations.

The JAM (short for Jan Dhan-Aadhaar-Mobile) trinity is probably the best thought-through example of New Economy. JAM tackled head-on decades of scourge of leakages and corruption in government subsidies meant for the poor. The JAM-powered direct benefit transfers have brought about efficiency, effectiveness, transparency and accountability in the government system. As on January 2020, ₹9.35 trillion has been transferred through direct benefit transfers and 379 million have availed benefits of the Jan Dhan Yojana, which has connected beneficiaries to the government directly—a powerful sign of democracy and responsible governance. It is this Jan Dhan Yojana architecture that the Modi government used to directly fund the poor and farmers during the pandemic. Several millions of vulnerable Indians, more so during lockdown, were able to receive direct money transfers from the government in addition to the food as a solid social security net.

India has achieved 100 per cent village electrification in 2019 through the Deen Dayal Upadhyaya Gram Jyoti Yojana. The number of affordable houses completed under the Pradhan Mantri Awas Yojana (Urban) are 1,84,00,000.

The Pradhan Mantri MUDRA Yojana was launched to provide access to institutional finance to unfunded micro/small business units by extending loans. Under the PMMY, ₹23.5 crore loan accounts totalling an amount of ₹10.24 lakh crore have been sanctioned up to 1 February 2020. The government launched the Ujjwala Yojana to provide clean cooking fuel through LPG connections to all the uncovered households in the country. A total of 8.03 crore LPG connections have been handed over to poor households as on 1 February 2020.

These achievements are big, but there's more to be done to further meet the rising aspirations of our population. India needs to achieve and get back to high rates of GDP growth in this new post-COVID world.

Post-COVID Softlanding, Rebooting and Building a Global and Self-sufficient Economy

The COVID pandemic represents an unprecedented crisis, both in terms of healthcare and economically. The healthcare emergency and required lockdown effects are amplifying fast into the real economy. The supply, consumption and income disruptions could cause real damage to businesses and jobs. The challenge to governments everywhere is to softland their economies and minimize business failures and job losses. (see Graph 8). The four pillars of foreign investment, services sector growth, manufacturing and consumption holding the Indian economy have all been adversely impacted and so has been India's economic march.

Graph 8: Coronavirus: Ways to Recover

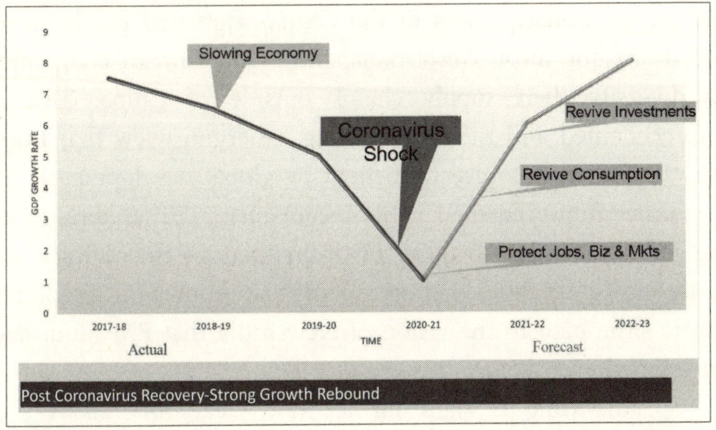

Undoubtedly, there are challenges and costs to softlanding during the pandemic and rebooting the economy in the post-COVID world, where the healthcare challenges remain alive as long as a cure or vaccine isn't available. It is in this new COVID reality that India has to relaunch and rebuild its growth trajectory (see Graph 9).

Graph 9: Growth after Coronavirus

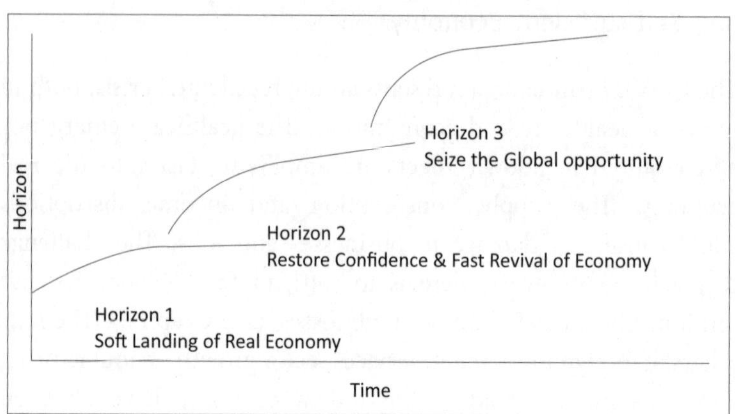

However, it is also clear that crisis resolution also calls for examination of opportunities within and outside India. One of the biggest consequences of the China-originated pandemic is the desire for most Western, Japanese and Korean companies to diversify their supply chains outside of China. This is unprecedented and there is a strong, emerging view that India has the potential to greatly benefit by global developments—in a manner unprecedented in its recent history. Therefore, India has an opportunity to move on from theories that arrested us to the past to realities that are opening up opportunities for the future—the path to the vision of New India that PM Modi had envisioned even before this crisis.

So, the time is right for a 'New Deal' for Bharat (i.e. Aatmanirbhar Bharat) to realize the dream of a New India over the next decade.

- 2020–21 >> Coronavirus Shock
- 2021–31 >> Decade of New India

This Aatmanirbhar Bharat can be principled on the following principles:

i. India will invest to protect and grow its economy
ii. India will reform and modernize its government and economy
iii. India will achieve its 'New Deal' for Bharat using the spirit of its people and finance it through enormous natural resources and wealth

Ten Potential Missions of the Aatmanirbhar Bharat Abhiyan

Modernize, Expand and be a Globally Competitive Self-sufficient Economy

i. Services sector (IT, healthcare/medical, etc.)
ii. Public asset monetization
iii. Repurposing/redesigning of the government; Formalizing the informal sector and social security
iv. Expansion of the financial sector (credit and equity), liquidity and interest rates
v. Manufacturing
vi. Food and farmer welfare
vii. Digital India 2.0
viii. Third-tier reforms and urbanization (in the new post-COVID world)
ix. Good healthcare for all
x. Volunteering for Bharat

Mission: US$3-Trillion Services Sector

Currently, services account for US$1.5 trillion of the GDP and should be targeted to be at US$3 trillion in the next five years. That would be the easiest way to boost exports and domestic consumption, and for that, we should tap into the global demand for services. The world needs more technology services, healthcare, clinical R&D and education, among other things. We need to focus on remote delivery of services, for which Digital India 2.0 is critical as well.

Mission: Manufacturing Sector

The expansion of the manufacturing sector is vital and needs to be seen through two perspectives.

i. First, opportunity arising out of the global trade changes vis-à-vis China and the scope to pick up opportunities of multinational companies' supply chain diversification out of China. The recent coronavirus pandemic has further exposed the risks of having a China-based supply chain to multinationals.
ii. Second, it is imperative to manufacture for India as Indian consumption grows in the future into a substantial consumption demand. It would be critical to plan for the future.

For example, meeting domestic demand growth will require a significant increase in manufacturing capacity. The sector will be an important driver of growth of the housing sector. It is estimated that an additional 15 million houses will be constructed in the near future, implying an addition of US$100 billion to the manufacturing sector including steel, cement, etc. The domestic infrastructure-related manufacturing sector is expected to add another US$150 billion. Fast moving consumer goods such as groceries, apparel and electronic appliances are expected to add another US$100 billion along with the automobile sector, which is expected to add another US$40 billion in demand. The exports sector is expected to add US$300 billion (see Graph 10).

Graph 10: Strategic Road Map for Manufacturing

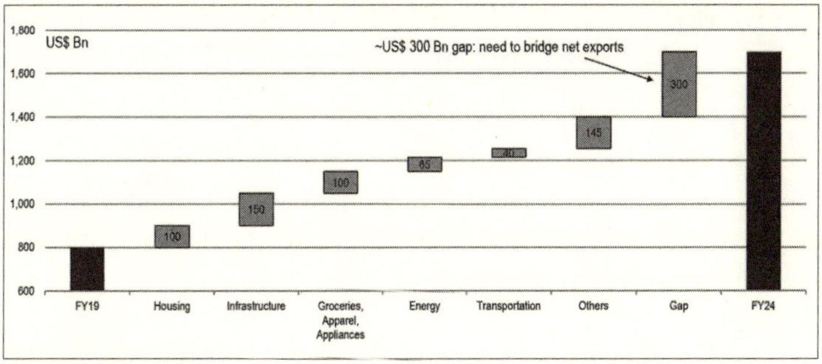

Source: Credit Suisse

Road Map for Manufacturing: How to Get There?

Labour Market: Replace 50 million Chinese workers with Indian workers

The Chinese labour force is shrinking due to ageing and its one-child policy (see Graph 11). There is a significant increase in the real wages in China, making it unattractive for global MNCs. The current coronavirus pandemic has exposed the vulnerability and risks of a China-based supply chain to the world. The space vacated by China is increasingly been tapped by countries such as Bangladesh, Vietnam, Indonesia, the Philippines and Thailand. However, given the smaller size of these economies, in the next decade, India is the only reasonable alternative with demographic dividend.

In order to become a viable alternative for global MNCs, India needs to reform its labour laws. The jurisdiction of labour laws is complicated with most of them in the Concurrent List of Schedule VII of the Constitution and some in Union and state lists.

The Union government tried some rationalization by bringing labour code bill in parliament. However, that was restricted to only labour laws administered by the Labour ministry. The Union

Graph 11: China Labour Supply

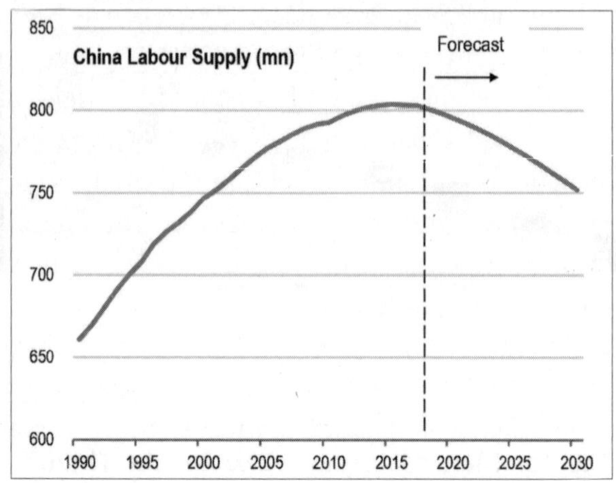

Source: Credit Suisse

government has codified around 40 labour laws under four codes of safety, social security, wages and industrial relations. However, these have taken statutes as they stand, without examining them from first principles. This is not enough as silos remain between industry and services, between unorganized and organized sectors. What is required is to draft a single code as template, which can be adopted by states under Article 254(2) of the Constitution. Other steps such as revamping and reforming the logistics sector, power sector reforms to reduce industrial tariffs, creating mega industrial townships, tax and GST reforms, etc. are needed as well.

Mission: Financial Sector Expansion

The biggest challenges to India's economic growth target are liquidity, limits and capacity of the financial sector. The financial sector has been battling with the syndrome of twin balance sheet and mounting NPAs. Since 2008–12, Indian banks' lending expanded significantly. However, this had increasingly been driven by a select few corporate groups and select sectors such as steel and power. Total debt of these groups has jumped five times between 2008 and 2012 and equated to 13 per cent of bank loans and 98 per cent of the banking system's net worth. These bank loans have largely become NPAs post 2015. Most of the NPAs in the last cycle were with public-sector banks. One of the biggest achievements of the Modi government was the clean-up and recapitalizing of the Indian banking system. From a bankrupt, corrupt sector, it is today a sector that has over ₹7 lakh crore of liquidity. However, challenges remain; for instance, the retreat and then risk aversion of public-sector banks have caused a significant gap in credit to the economy, thus impacting both consumption and investment, and in turn affecting taxes and jobs. Legacy NPA issues had made the banking system risk averse. (See Graphs 12 and 13.)

Graph 12: Credit Growth

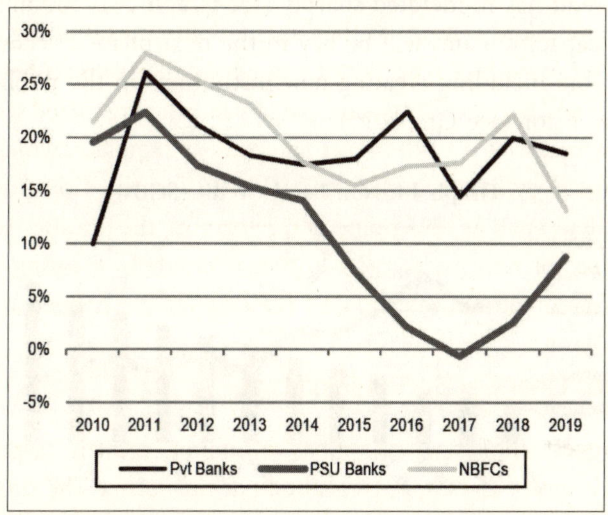

Source: Credit Suisse

Graph 13: Non Performing Assets

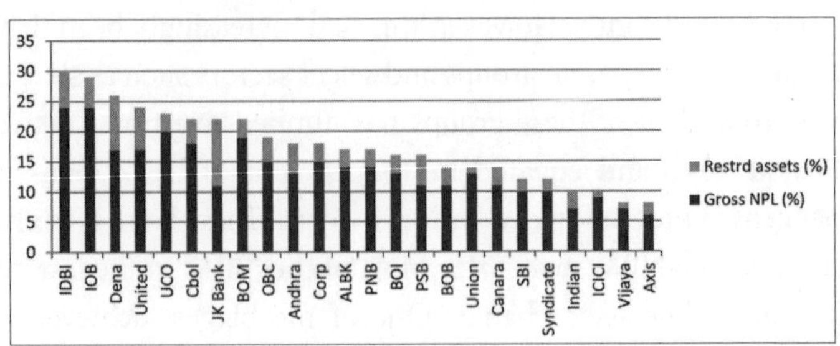

Source: Credit Suisse

Non-banking financial companies (NBFCs)/housing finance companies/bonds stepped in and contributed 30–60 per cent of the incremental credit for FY2016–18. However, the IL&FS and DHFL defaults have created a funding problem for NBFCs, too. Because of two issues of risk aversion of public-sector banks and the NBFC crisis, the annual credit growth has declined from 21 per cent in 2011 to 7 per cent in 2019 and growth in non-food credit has moderated sharply (see Graph 14). The financial sector capacity issues will be key in the next phase of economic expansion, including creating new institutions in the public and private sector (see Graph 15).

Graph 14: Non Food Credit (SCBs)

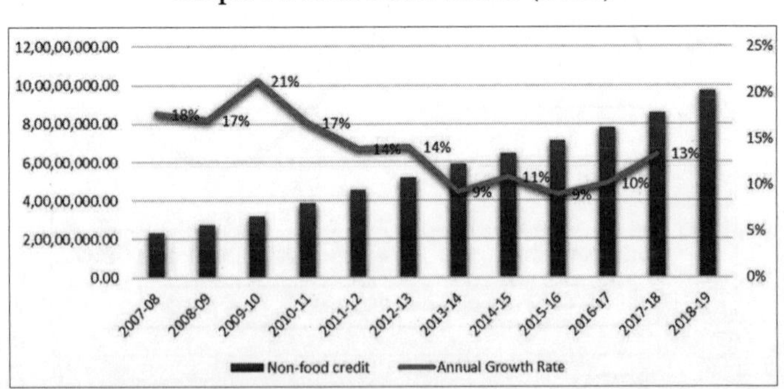

Source: Reserve Bank of India (RBI)

Graph 15: GDP Growth Rate

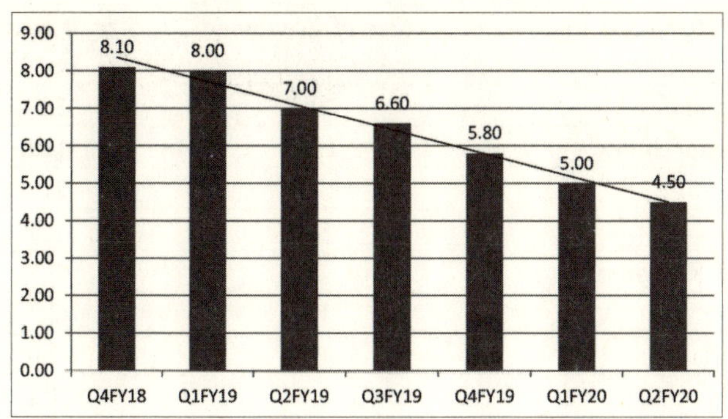

Source: National Statistical Office (NSO)

Ending Financial Sector Woes: Long-term Actions

Significant Increase in Financial Capacity

For India's reboot and growth aspirations, we need a much larger and efficient financial system. Even if we do not adopt the over-financialized models of China and the US, the current system will not be enough to help us reboot and grow (see Graph 16).

Graph 16: Financial Systems around the World

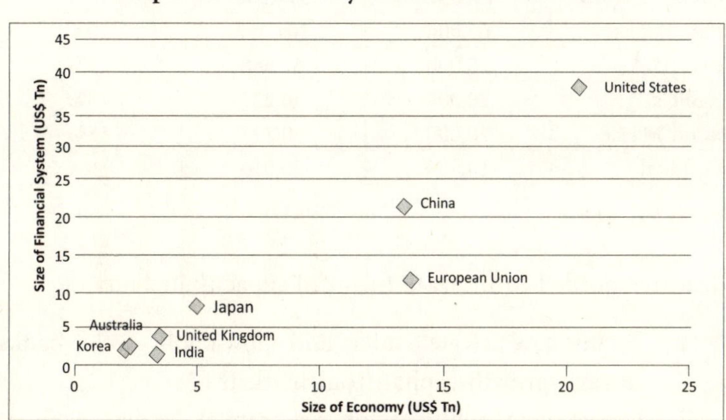

(Contd.)

2018, US$ Tn	*Size of Economy*	*Size of Financial System*
United States	20.5	38.1
European Union	13.7	11.8
China	13.4	21.6
Japan	5.0	8.4
United Kingdom	2.8	3.8
Korea	1.6	2.4
Australia	1.4	2.0
India	2.7	1.4

Source: Credit Suisse

Most of the new GDP will come from the formal sector. Demand for formal credit is expected to rise faster than nominal GDP (1.2–1.5 times nominal GDP). The private sector is still too small and cannot grow beyond twice the GDP. Even if NBFCs and bonds grow at 15 per cent, not enough capacity is available (see Table 1).

Table 1: India's CAGR for 2019 and 2024: A Comparison

India	**2019**	**2024**	**CAGR**
Credit, US$ bn	1,955	4,500	18%
Credit, INR bn	138,829	319,500	18%
PSU Banks	63,000	101,462	10%
Pvt. Banks	25,000	67,568	22%
NBFCs	20,000	40,227	15%
Bond Market	20,000	40,227	15%
Residual	10,829	70,016	45%

Source: VIF-CES

Measures needed to increase financial capacity include:

i. Permit new private lenders and allow public-sector banks to raise growth capital from markets
ii. Create new public-sector risk capital lenders such as

development finance institutions (DFIs)

iii. Address NBFC logjam, so that fresh capital/liquidity continues to enter the sector

iv. Encourage and boost private sector confidence

v. Allow the National Investment and Infrastructure Fund (NIIF) to raise US$100 billion in capital

vi. Aggressively attract FDI

vii. Monetize public assets to create substantial investible equity with government

viii. Bring in reorganization/reforms in the RBI and Finance Ministry

Mission: Resource Mobilization from Public Assets

India is not a poor country; it is rich in assets and resources. This can be used for raising money to build a New India for its people. Monetization of public assets can be a catalyst for New India—the 'rocket fuel' to propel the Indian economy. A credible multi-year public asset monetization programme of this size will significantly reduce any fiscal downside risk in our economy and give investors the much-needed confidence in the medium- and long-term strength of the economy, with consequent impacts on currency, long-term capital costs, etc.

The surplus public assets of India are estimated to be over ₹1,500 lakh crore. Public assets that can be monetized include equity investments in various companies including public-sector undertakings (PSUs) and public-private partnerships (PPPs) (estimated at ₹34 lakh crore). This public wealth includes land, minerals, hydrocarbons and other assets under the control of the government. Estimate of mineral wealth alone is more than ₹5,000 lakh crore. This includes hydrocarbons, mines and minerals. This estimate does not include the value of spectrum, movable surplus assets, intellectual property held by the government, etc. The surest way to accelerate the government's mission to deliver opportunity and prosperity and do that in a fiscally responsible way is to include monetization of public assets in its set of resource options.

Different structures that can be tapped into include bond and equity (NRI, foreign and domestic) issuances from:

i. Government equities holding company
ii. Government mineral resources holding company
iii. Government land assets holding company

Asset monetization for the next three to five years, without political resistance and/or using NRI and domestic investors in unlisted government companies, is another measure that can be adopted.

Mission: Smarter Government Expenditure

Mission: Maximum Governance 2.0

i. Repurpose government expenditure
ii. Reform governance and expand digital government (mygovnet.gov.in)
iii. Introduce reforms in the Department of Industrial Policy & Promotion (DIPP), and commerce and finance ministries
iv. Attract experts/talent into the government (in education, health, etc.) after proper vetting
v. Introduce speedier litigation resolutions as well as judicial reforms and capacity
vi. Modernize the police and law and order
vii. Formalize the informal sector (social security)

Mission: Formalizing the Informal Sector

i. The informal sector was the most impacted by the coronavirus pandemic.

ii. The PM's vision and reforms on Jan Dhan Yojana and DBT were the most important social security nets during this difficult time. This needs to be built on urgently.
iii. Over 80 per cent employment in the informal sector must be brought steadily into the formal identified sector so that they can avail healthcare and other benefits that the government will roll out from time to time.
iv. A comprehensive social security architecture of work/stipend/credit (funded by Social Security Cess) to be developed (including MGNREGA and Urban Eqvt), which covers every Indian (rural and urban poor) in the next five years.

Conclusion

India has suffered a setback in its economic transformation process, which aimed to create a modern global economy six years ago, due to the unprecedented coronavirus shock and its impact on the economy. However, India, with its strong political leadership, is poised to reboot its economy post the coronavirus shock. This is also a historical opportunity for India, unprecedented in its recent history. The seeds of this had been sown with the New India vision by PM Modi.

While 2020–21 will be severely impacted by COVID-19, the following decade can be one that sees the full economic potential of India present itself for the benefit of all Indians and indeed the world community. The path that India chooses and the choices that it makes in the coming months are crucial, and if made right, can put India on a path to a globally competitive and self-sufficient economy, an 'aatmanirbhar' economy—the New India.

◆

Rajeev Chandrasekhar is a technology entrepreneur-turned-BJP MP, representing Bengaluru, Karnataka in the Rajya Sabha. He is the national spokesperson for the BJP.

ACKNOWLEDGEMENTS

This book owes its existence primarily to my publisher's belief that not only should I be writing but also be a catalyst to get more of my peers to do so, and thus contribute to an ongoing national discourse on governance and policy. The encouragement and support of Rupa Publications are much appreciated. I am grateful to the authors of these insightful chapters, all of whom are active, prominent and influential politicians of this era, who readily agreed to contribute to this forward-looking book. I know most of them well, having served alongside in parliament or interacted on various forums, and some have become good friends as well.

I must also thank my own policy team and staff, whose support was crucial to all the behind-the-scenes work that went into gathering and editing the content. Sanya Dhillon, Deepak Panda and Simran Pachar made crucial contributions, while Durga Madhab Achari and, especially, Shabina Sheikh were critical to the logistics involved.

INDEX